The Service of the Heart

A Guide to the
Jewish Prayer Book

by

EVELYN GARFIEL

The *Siddur,* or Jewish Prayer Book, projects ideas about Judaism and the characteristic Jewish conceptions of God that often elude modern men and women although they may read their prayers in an English translation. Even a good translation of the Prayer Book does not succeed in conveying all of its meaning correctly. This is due to the great antiquity of most of the prayers and to the fact that rabbinic or Talmudic Judaism, which produced the Prayer Book, is today operative only in fragments for many Jews. Most modern Jews therefore need not only a translation of the Prayer Book but also a commentary that describes the history and structure of the prayers and explains the major religious concepts of each prayer in terms that are readily comprehensible.

The Service of the Heart is a basic guide to an understanding of the Jewish Prayer Book. Simply and lucidly, in an interpretation acceptable to all Jewish groups—Orthodox, Conservative, and Reform—it reveals the significance of the various prayers, defines the moral and ethical concepts that lie at the core of Judaism, and gives the historical background of the material contained in the Prayer Book. As a result, the Prayer Book is made more meaningful in contemporary terms, and the reader is enabled to gain a deeper appreciation of the heritage that has sustained the Jewish people through many dark centuries.

Because Judaism is not essentially an "other-worldly" religion, the Jewish Prayer Book reflects every facet of human life—study, logic, ethics, the physical and mental well-being of the individual, the political well-being of community and state. These—together with the dominating emphasis on God's love, mercy, and compassion to all men—are some of the themes that appear in the *Siddur.* In Dr. Garfiel's brilliant, readable exposition, these themes are welded into a structural unity that conveys the magnificence and eternal value of the authentic Jewish tradition. For the individual eager to grasp the essence of Judaism, for parents and children seeking a greater bond within their faith, for all religious study groups, *The Service of the Heart* is an informative, richly rewarding, and inspiring guide.

About the Author

Evelyn Garfiel is a graduate of Barnard College and holds a Ph.D. in psychology from Columbia University. In addition to lecturing widely on religion and psychology, she has taught at the University of Chicago, at the College of Jewish Studies in Chicago, and in the Department of Neurology at the University of Wisconsin Medical School. She is now on the teaching staff of the Women's Institute of the Jewish Theological Seminary of America.

THE SERVICE
OF THE HEART

A GUIDE TO THE JEWISH PRAYER BOOK

by

Evelyn Garfiel
Foreword by Rabbi Hillel E. Silverman

Published by
Melvin Powers
WILSHIRE BOOK COMPANY
12015 Sherman Road
No. Hollywood, California 91605
Telephone: (213) 875-1711 / (818) 983-1105

Library of Congress Catalogue Card Number: 57-6900

Printed by

HAL LEIGHTON PRINTING COMPANY
P.O. Box 3952
North Hollywood, California 91605
Telephone: (213) 983-1105

Printed in the United States of America
ISBN 0-87980-140-9

TO

MY MOTHER

"WHAT IS THE SERVICE OF THE HEART? . . . . IT IS PRAYER."

Taanit, 2a

FOREWORD

Nothing is more crucial for the survival of the Jewish Religion than a wholesome and relevant *prayer* experience.

And yet, *prayer* today is a lost art for millions of our people and the *Prayer Book,* aside from the Bible, the best known of the Jewish classics, is a forgotten and little used text.

If the truth be told, we have metamorphosed into "Jews Without Prayer." Identification with our religious civilization assumes the form of Zionist, philanthropic, humanitarian, communal, cultural and social activities galore but the pews of our synagogues are all but empty on Sabbath morning.

Why?

The answer, in all simplicity, has to do with the fact that the new generation has lost its faith in a Supernatural God who "listens" and on occasion even "answers" human supplications.

One may advance a plethora of sophisticated reasons for the lack of participation in traditional Jewish prayer on the part of our young people. One may expound numerous hypotheses predicated upon philosophical, psychological, sociological and emotional considerations.

But the primary cause is that Prayer no longer "turns us on." It is not fashionable to pray. Pure and simple, when one cannot believe in a Supreme Being, it is impossible to engage in formalistic and meaningless mumbo-jumbo. For so many of us today, prayer is no longer dialogue with God but monologue in which the Jew is merely talking to himself.

Open up a conversation about this topic with young

people. Listen to their inevitable reaction: "Prayer is tedious . . it's meaningless . . it's irrelevant . . it's a bore . . who needs repetitious doxologies couched in medieval poetic anachronisms that make even less sense in the English translation than do their Talmudic and Midrashic allusions in the Hebrew original."

It is my contention that prayer is crucial and essential for a Jew today *even if no One is listening or answering.*

I would define prayer as *"communication with those powers in the Universe that we call divine."* Notice, purposefully I avoid the phrase *conversation.* Conceivably, a prayer experience might be achieved through pure thought and contemplation, by participation in music, dance or the creative arts, a visit to a museum or a walk in the stillness of the forest.

Prayer can have little intellectual relevance unless first we come to a definition of the God to whom we address our prayers. Fortuitously, Judaism allows a wide gamut of definition, if definition of God is even remotely possible. God may be personal and supernatural, transcendent or imminent, a Power, Force, Spirit, Ground of Being, Process, Becoming, the Sum Total Of All Those Forces Making For Good and much more.

But, even if there is no God who is actually "listening," prayer still has tremendous relevance for four basic reasons.

1. *Philosophically,* when we pray we appeal to the very best *within ourselves. Prayer is the process of the reintegration and the existential recovery of self,* living as we do in a depersonalized, dehumanized and mechanistic society in which the self counts for very little. *Prayer is the experience of the mystery and the transcendental* in the world about us, the channel for the articulation of the awe and wonder of the ineffable in our day-to-day encounter with the Universe and with our fellow man. *Prayer is the recovery of the sense of life as poetry,* for all human articulation and expression of

the divine is metaphor and symbol at best. *Prayer is the moral re-assessment and recommitment of the individual,* if you will "spiritual monologue" at its very highest.

2. *Sociologically and psychologically,* when a Jew prays he identifies himself with the Jewish people, past, present and future. He perpetuates the transmission of an ancient liturgy which molded the Jew together as he marched on to his historic destiny. The emotional gratification of togetherness with hundreds of our fellow Jews at a Sabbath or a Holiday service singing and responding in unison, is *raison d'être* sufficient for formal and organized prayer.

3. *Educationally,* prayer is part of the study process in which we are provided an opportunity to consider and mull over the religious values of Judaism. A goodly portion of the Siddur consists of study passages from the Bible and rabbinic literature. Even the affirmation of our faith, the *Sh'ma Yisrael,* is not a prayer but a study text from Deuteronomy. We designate it the "Kriyat Sh'ma", the "reading" not the prayer of the Sh'ma. In many of our prayers we discover the most relevant expression of those religious and ethical values which for the Jew constitute his noblest religious experience.

4. *Aesthetically,* in still another dimension, there is for many of us the joy and pleasure of "dovening," the moving experience of listening to a good Chazan and melodious Choir, shedding tears at a Hineni or Sh'ma Kolenu, being stirred by an Untaneh Tokef or a Kol Nidre.

Please note, none of these four basic reasons need necessarily postulate a supernatural God who listens to prayer.

In the Bible, the Hebrew word for prayer is *"Hitpallel,"* meaning literally, to *judge oneself.* When man addressed God, even in the times of the Bible, he was judging himself, taking stock of his moral and ethical inventory. When he prayed, in reality he was addressing the *God within himself,* namely, the conscience, which in truth is the divine spark within man. When we pray we speak to that higher self within us which we call the conscience.

For example, when we say thrice daily in the Siddur: "Oh God, keep my tongue from evil and my lips from speaking guile," in effect we are disciplining ourselves to avoid the slanderous use of the tongue. When we pray, "Help me to be a brother to my fellow-man," we are not so much asking God to produce a miraculous transformation in our character, as we are *pleading with ourselves* to be more tolerant and understanding of our neighbors. When we ask God to deliver us from evil, the words themselves tend to serve as a self-imposed discipline which caution the worshipper to avoid temptation and evil. When, on a sick bed, we pray to God for healing, in reality we are appealing to the courage, fortitude and patience of our own being to face the crisis of surgery and convalescence ahead.

Prayer is the most powerful form of moral persuasion that exists, far more effective as a guide to righteous conduct than all the law enforcement agencies combined.

But prayer is more than a guide to individual conduct. It is also a powerful communal and social force. While it is perfectly acceptable and proper in any faith to pray alone and away from everyone else, most of us choose to engage in prayer together with other human beings. That is why we establish synagogues. When we see others about us engaged in divine worship, we become strengthened in our own resolves. A bond of unity springs up among us. The knowledge that others are pursuing the same lofty goals to which we aspire makes that ideal more possible of attainment. Our fellow Jews kindle the spark within us and we do the same for them. Furthermore, the fact that we are together with other people makes of communal prayer an expression of true social idealism, for prayer at its best is a device for bringing us together into a common brotherhood and fellowship.

Prayer will not produce miracles, if by miracle we mean the supernatural suspension and violation of the laws of nature. Prayer will not produce rain in drought, safety in disaster, victory in defeat nor the winning number in a lottery. But prayer can and does produce miracles in the sense that it impels men *to produce miracles within themselves.* To the sick, prayer can inspire the courage and will to become well again. To the lame and afflicted, prayer can create the determination to overcome a handicap. To the faint of heart, prayer can provide new hope and self-confidence. The more we pray for peace, the more we will be goaded into doing away with those evils that produce war; the more we pray for the end of a dread ailment, the more we are impelled to carry on the research that will produce a cure or elimination of disease.

There is so much more about prayer that we might discuss in an ancillary vein using these comments merely as a springboard. Hebrew or prayer in the vernacular, public or private devotion, the need for original supplementary prayer, the balance of the traditional framework with relevant original supplementary additions are just a few of the many areas that merit serious discussion.

In my own congregation numbering many thousands, when it comes to the introduction of original prayers, I always ask myself three questions: Is the prayer Jewish in spirit? Is the prayer intellectually and morally relevant? Can members of a congregation truly participate in the recitation of the prayer?

No doubt, in the last analysis participation by the congregants is crucial for a meaningful prayer experience. Writes Rabbi Jack Riemer: "We must fight against the increasing clergification of Judaism, against the monopolization of the service by rabbis and cantors which has become the pattern of services in our time. The rabbi has become the master of ceremonies, the cantor has become the soloist, and the congregation has become the audience.

"I sometimes tell my congregation that a service is very much like a drama, with one difference. They think that I mean that the rabbi and the cantor are the performers, the prayer book is the prompter, and that the congregation is the audience. They are wrong. I mean that the members of the congregation are the performers, the rabbi and the cantor are the prompters and God is the audience. If you accept this concept of prayer, the whole perspective changes. Then the roles of the rabbi, the cantor and choir become subsidiary and the test of the service becomes how much the congregation participates and how much spirit is in their hearts. If you accept this point of view, prayer is not a performance to be watched and judged but a summons to which each person present must respond."

If we are indeed serious about making prayer relevant for this generation, I can think of no better beginning than a careful consideration of this most remarkable book, THE SERVICE OF THE HEART by Dr. Evelyn Garfiel.

Before we can proceed to an intellectually satisfying approach to meaningful communication with that which we define as God, it is incumbent upon us to understand the historical and spiritual development of the great Jewish classic, the *Siddur*.

This we can accomplish by a reflective study of this informative book. Written in lucid terms, THE SERVICE OF THE HEART includes a description of the history and function of the Siddur and contains a plethora of historical material and spiritual insight. This text helps make the Siddur more meaningful in contemporary terms and enables the reader to gain a deeper appreciation of the rich heritage of Judaic thought which draws upon many centuries of religious experience. Dr. Garfiel shows how the Siddur reflects every facet of human life — study, logic, ethics, the physical and mental well-being of the individual, the political well-being of community and state. These themes are all welded together by the author into a structural unity that conveys the magnificence and eternal value of the authentic Jewish tradition.

Dr. Garfiel's work encompasses the Sabbath and daily services and deals with selected special occasions. Her fascinating history of the prayer book is material alone for much thought and reflection. She examines in great detail the format of the daily and Sabbath prayers, suggesting theological answers to individual prayers that oftentimes trouble the communicant. In addition, she considers the prayers for the marriage ceremony and the grace after meal. Interspersed in her chapters is incredible insight into authentic Jewish theology.

In the words of the author, "The difficulty most modern Jews find in acquiring a sympathetic understanding of their prayer book stems from the fact that they are no longer familiar with its religious outlook. For rabbinic or Talmudic Judaism which produced the prayer book is today, unfortunately, operative only in fragments for many Jews. That is why their reaction to the prayer book, the great source book of Judaism, is often confused by the intrusion of alien ideas of religion.

For all these reasons, modern Jews require not only a translation of the prayer book but a commentary as well. Such a commentary must describe the history and structure of the prayers, of course, but its most important function is to present an explanation of the major religious concepts of each prayer in terms that a modern man can understand."

This fascinating and carefully researched book can well serve as a worthy text for adult and teenage study groups.

Dr. Hillel E. Silverman

Rabbi, Sinai Temple
Los Angeles, California

Preface

Even a good translation of the *Prayer Book* does not succeed in conveying all of its meaning correctly. In part, this is due to the great antiquity of most of the prayers; we are so far away from the life and times from which they have sprung. In part, it is due to the fact that we are no longer aware of the particular historical circumstances which dictated the inclusion of one or another of the prayers, and therefore its real intent escapes us.

But chiefly, the difficulty most modern Jews find in acquiring a sympathetic understanding of their *Prayer Book* stems from the fact that they are no longer familiar with its religious outlook. For rabbinic or Talmudic Judaism which produced the *Prayer Book* is today, unfortunately, operative only in fragments for many Jews. That is why their reaction to the *Prayer Book*, the great source book of Judaism, is often confused by the intrusion of alien ideas of religion.

For all these reasons modern Jews require not only a translation of the *Prayer Book* but a commentary as well. Such a commentary must describe the history and structure of the prayers, of course, but its most important function is to present an explanation of the major religious concepts of each prayer in terms that a modern man can understand.

An appreciation of the unique character of Talmudic Judaism, a recognition of the mode of operation of the rabbinic mind and of its inner organization, has become available with the appearance of three books by Max Kadushin: *The Theology of Seder Eliahu, Organic Thinking,* and *The Rabbinic Mind.* In these books he subjects certain representative rabbinic sources to a painstaking analysis.

Every idea he found expressed there is permitted to tell its own story, and the pattern of relationships among them determines the organization of rabbinic thought, as Kadushin describes it. Through these and other methods, he has succeeded in revealing the native qualities of the Jewish religion in the rabbinic era—that is, in the creative period from about 200 before the Common Era to about 500 of the Common Era. On this analysis of the rabbinic mind I have drawn heavily. In fact, Kadushin's approach and materials have often entered into the interpretation of passages even where no specific acknowledgment has been made in a footnote.

I am greatly indebted to Mr. Theodore C. Garfiel and to Rabbi Phineas Kadushin for their careful reading of large sections of the manuscript. Many of their suggestions have been incorporated into the final text of this book.

To my friend, Mrs. Anne Waterston, I am especially grateful. She has read the whole manuscript with meticulous care and has contributed in no small measure to the clearer exposition of ideas not always easy to convey.

To understand the *Prayer Book*, one must penetrate as deeply as possible into the minds and the hearts of the men who created it. Approached in this spirit, the study of the Jewish *Prayer Book* can be profoundly rewarding—can be in itself a "Service of the Heart."

E. G.

Tishri, 5718
October, 1957
New York

Contents

1

The Function of the
Prayer Book

POPULAR MISCONCEPTIONS ABOUT JUDAISM

Everyone has at one time or another heard a sophomore, just returned from college full of the wisdom of the world, pronounce the shattering judgment that the God of Israel is a stern, harsh Judge, and that in Judaism love and forgiveness and mercy are not qualities of God.

Unfortunately, that youngster is not alone in his misapprehension about Judaism. Too many of his elders have accepted this evaluation of their religion, never troubling to discover the truth from genuine Jewish sources.

If, however, we look into the *Prayer Book,* we find that God's tender mercy, His long-suffering kindness, His care and love for all His creatures are the themes of prayer after prayer.

Every morning a Jew recites this prayer: "Blessed art Thou, Lord our God, King of the universe, Who in mercy gives light to the earth and to all them that dwell thereon, and Who, in His goodness, renews creation every day." A Jew never eats a morsel of bread nor sips a drink of water without feeling God's Providence, and the blessing he recites each time expresses his gratitude for God's loving-kindness in providing the food and the drink man requires.

Every day we plead humbly, but in confidence, for God's

mercy: "Our Father in heaven, deal lovingly with us for Thy
great Name's sake . . . Lead us not into the power of sin or of
transgression or of temptation or of scorn. . . ." In every event
of life, in every joy or sorrow, and in all the simple, every-day
experiences of life, a Jew turns to a tender and loving Father
in gratitude or for help, mercy, and forgiveness.

The whole gamut of human experience is reflected in the
Prayer Book because, to the Jew, every function of man, indeed,
all of life creates opportunities for the worship of God. Getting
up in the morning, eating, the healthy functioning of his body,
study of Torah—each in turn becomes an occasion for thanking
God for His endless kindnesses.

All these facets of the Jewish religion find expression in the
Prayer Book, and so it comes about that even a slightly closer
acquaintance with it can open our eyes to qualities in Judaism
we never suspected were there.

THE Siddur—A LIVING BOOK

Unfortunately, many of the Jewish classics have become
just so many impressive tomes on a library shelf. The Prayer
Book is almost the only one among the great source books of
the Jewish religion that still remains functional. For as solid
Jewish learning becomes rarer, and as personal piety comes to
seem more and more an oddity, as even basic home observances
of the religious tradition dwindle away, the synagogue service
becomes increasingly the only mode of religious experience
for many Jews. And in the synagogue it is the Prayer Book,
however modified or abridged, which every Jew actually holds
in his hand, perhaps reads or hears recited. This Prayer Book,
the Siddur, is the one ancient text still in common use by Jews

all over the world. The Hebrew name for the *Prayer Book,* *Siddur,* means literally "order" or "arrangement." It is, in fact, an abbreviation for the full phrase, *Seder Tefillot,* Order of Prayers.

No matter how far from home a Jew may wander, no matter how strange to him the language and the customs of the people among whom he finds himself, he need only enter a synagogue and open the Hebrew *Prayer Book* he finds there to feel himself in familiar surroundings, perfectly able to share and communicate his experience with brother Jews.

THE BEST "TEXTBOOK" OF JUDAISM

The *Siddur* not only continues to function today; it is in addition the only authentic, original source book of the Jewish religion still comprehensible to Jews.

The Bible, of course, is the foundation of Judaism, the greatest book in all the world. But the Jewish religion is not any longer, and has not been for more than two thousand years, limited to the religion of the Bible. Only the Karaites, a Jewish sect now nearly extinct, tried to live by the Bible alone and rejected the foliation of Judaism into its more advanced religious form, rabbinic or Talmudic Judaism. That development occurred during the six or seven centuries from about 200 before the Common Era to about 500 after.[1]

Most people are amazed to learn how much of Judaism is not Biblical at all. *Hanukkah* celebrates an event that occurred after the text of the Bible had been finally decided upon and closed. Observances connected with *Purim,* the *Seder* at Passover, the lighting of candles on the eve of Sabbath and the Festivals and the accompanying blessings, most of the dietary laws, our prayers in large measure—all these are only a part of the practices of Judaism which originate in the rabbinic period.

Even more important, many of the religious *ideas* of Judaism are products of that same great creative age. It is in the huge folio volumes of the Talmud and in the Midrash that this second level of authentic Judaism is found.

Since we have occasion to use the names of the three divisions of rabbinic literature rather frequently, we had best make clear now just what each of these terms means.

They are *Mishnah, Gemara* or *Talmud,* and *Midrash. Mishnah* is the body of Jewish law and tradition developed after the Bible and transmitted as an oral tradition until it was committed to final form in writing about 200 C.E. *Gemara* or *Talmud,* used interchangeably, is the further development of that law and tradition after the *Mishnah.* The *Gemara* was crystallized into its final form in writing about 500 C.E. The word *Talmud* is also used, however, to designate the combined literature of *Mishnah* and *Gemara;* it is indeed, in this larger, more general sense that it is ordinarily used.

Midrash is a literature parallel to and contemporary with the *Talmud* (in its larger sense). *Midrash* contains nonlegal rabbinic material: sermons, parables, tales, commentary on the Bible. It constitutes the major source for the ethical and religious ideas of the Rabbis.

This rabbinic literature, written in Hebrew (the Mishnah) and in Aramaic (the Gemara), in a peculiarly cryptic style, requires years of intensive study for its mastery. Not many Jews can expect to study, let alone master, it in our time. But they need not resign themselves to being always dependent upon second- or third-hand accounts of their own religion—not if they know the *Prayer Book.*

For the *Siddur* is also a product of this same Talmudic period and, in a sense, of these same Rabbis. In the Talmud a whole tractate, *Berakhot,* is devoted to the subject of prayer. The time, proper place, and various occasions for prayer are there discussed. In this tractate, the Rabbis develop the form and the contents of most of the prayers still in use today. Out of that rich store of materials in the Talmud and from that rabbinic tradition, the Rabbis of the later, post-Talmudic period (about 500 to 900 C.E.) crystallized the service and the *Siddur* substantially as we have received it.

Now, these rabbinic prayers were meant to be said and understood not merely by an elite group of scholars, but by every single Jew. That is why even now, more than a thousand years later, any Jew, with a little effort and some guidance, can himself delve into this original source of Judaism and can learn to know his religion from an authentic source—the *Siddur.*

THE FUNCTION OF FORMAL PRAYERS

Not infrequently today, people are heard to say that religion should "come from the heart," be freely expressed in our own words, and that one should pray only when the spirit moves him. For such people the *Prayer Book*—by the very fact that it is a book of prayers written down for us by others and meant to be recited at prescribed times—is necessarily unsatisfactory. But is it not possible that this plea for spontaneity may sometimes be a cloak for sentimentality, perhaps even an excuse for not praying at all?

In Judaism, prayer is an institution as well as the natural, occasional, purely individual expression of a fleeting mood or a cry for help; self-centered preoccupation with the state of one's own soul is not encouraged in the Jewish religion. Today, when the habit of prayer is rare, when the mood of prayer is so difficult to achieve, today more than ever, most of us need the stimulus of inspiring atmosphere if we are to pray at all. We depend upon a community—that is, a synagogue—to induce in us the frame of mind receptive to prayer. We certainly are in need of beautiful forms of expression in which to couch our prayers, since the appropriate words and even the proper thoughts no longer come readily to our minds. Great prayers, created by great souls in a religious age, focus for us the vague yearnings and aspirations that would otherwise remain confused, inchoate—or not felt at all. And these recorded prayers of Judaism remind us of the needs, hopes, and sufferings of other human beings. "He who fails to include his fellow-man in his prayers is a sinner," say the Rabbis.[2]

Literary prayers perform another function we do not often recognize. For it is only when we pray that we can take the time to mull over the religious values of Judaism. And it is in the prayers that we find the most moving expression of those religious values which for the Jew constitute his normal religious experience. The prayers serve as occasions for "exercising" the values of *Malkhut Shama'yim,* the Kingship of God; *Kiddush Hashem,* Sanctification of God's Name; *Teshuvah,* Repentance; *Tzedakah,* Charity or Love; *Mitzvah,* Religious Commandment or Good Deed; *Torah,* and many more. These are the themes the Rabbis have expressed in their prayers, for their religion is a living, nondogmatic pattern of many such values, focused on the problems all men have to deal with at some time in their lives. But this matter will become clearer as we study the actual text of the prayers in some detail.

We must remember, however, that prescribed prayers, although they constitute the framework of Jewish worship, are certainly not the whole of it. The very Rabbis who fixed the times for prayer and established the prayers to be recited also said: "Do not make your prayer a fixed thing." [3] The individual is encouraged to put his own fresh meanings into the received text, to formulate his own prayers too, and to allow for a period of preparation for prayer in order to come to it in a receptive mood.

Certainly there is no insistence on traditional forms as the only acceptable service in this passage from the Midrash: "God says to Israel, 'I bade thee read thy prayers unto Me in thy synagogues, but if thou canst not, pray in thy house; and if thou art unable to do this, pray when thou art in thy field; and if this be inconvenient to thee, pray on thy bed; and if thou canst not do even this, think of Me in thy heart'." [4]

Form, but not just form, is what the Rabbis strive to achieve in their prescription for prayer. Surely, getting the required prayers said hastily and perfunctorily is not true prayer in their view. And this attitude has been characteristic of Jewish religious teachers down through the ages. In the twelfth century, Maimonides, the great codifier of Jewish law and interpreter of the Jewish religion, put it this way: "Prayer without devotion is not prayer. . . . He whose thoughts are wandering or occupied with other things ought not to pray. . . . The worshipper ought to bring himself into a devotional frame of mind, and then he must pray quietly and with feeling, not like one who carries a load, unloads it and departs." [5]

Only men who felt the need of regular, frequent periods of prayer could have produced that extraordinary literary prayer book, the *Siddur*. The more one studies it, the more one comes to understand and respond to the wide range, the delicacy and nobility of its various prayers.

2

Before There Was a *Siddur*

Like every product of a living people, the *Prayer Book* has a long history. It was not composed by one man, nor even by a single authoritative synod. It took centuries to complete. The *Shema Yisrael* (Hear, O Israel, the Lord our God, the Lord is one) and the Ten Commandments are, of course, very ancient. The earliest Psalms go back to David's time, about 1000 B.C.E., whereas *Lekhah Dodi,* a hymn of welcome to the Sabbath, was composed as recently as the sixteenth century—the whole *Siddur* covering a span of close to three thousand years! Naturally its form and its contents reflect and represent the long religious history of its people.

Prayer is probably as old as man. But early worship all over the world, certainly formal worship, consisted chiefly of sacrifices. This obtained in Judaism as late as the days of the Second Temple,[1] and very much later among other peoples. Sacrifice-services were necessarily conducted by members of a priest-class especially trained in the intricate ceremonies established by tradition. But among the Jews, the people, too, had some share in these services. They brought their sacrifices to the Temple, the fine meal and the appropriate animals; they recited a simple formula of confession, and they responded to the songs and praises of the Levites with "Amen," "Selah," or "Halleluyah." The evidence seems clear that even in the days

24

of the First Temple, prayers as well as sacrifices were part of the regular Temple service. The Levites sang and probably composed many of the Psalms. The most famous prayer of all, the *Shema Yisrael,* and the Ten Commandments were also recited daily. Now so many generations later, all of these are still found in the *Prayer Book.*

Side by side with the Temple prayers, the Bible itself records many ardent personal prayers from the earliest days of Israel's history. Who can forget that touching picture of Hannah at prayer in the Sanctuary at Shiloh? Long before the days of King David, this childless woman came alone to pour out her heart before the Lord, pleading for a son.

There are, of course, other examples of individual prayers in the Bible, but of all the personal prayers recorded the most important are the Psalms, many of which are of very early origin. No description can convey the variety and magnificence of these hymns. Their match has never been found in all the literatures of the world. They run the whole gamut of human experience from triumphant joy to utter despair, from abject acknowledgment of sin to paeans of praise and thanksgiving to God for His wondrous world, and from an almost cowering awareness of God's justice and power to a quiet confidence in His mercy and goodness to man. It is no accident that the Psalter constitutes the backbone of the *Book of Common Prayer* of the Episcopal Church and of the prayer books and hymnals of every Protestant Christian sect. Naturally, the Book of Psalms—and "saying Psalms"—has been the greatest resource of comfort and courage for Jews throughout the long terrors of their history and in every personal sorrow and emergency.

THE SYNAGOGUE—A NEW HUMAN INSTITUTION

It is difficult for us to imagine how radical a mere prayer service must have seemed to men in ancient times when everyone *knew* that to worship God adequately one had to go to a temple or an altar and there offer up a proper sacrifice. At that time the very notion that a service of prayer and Torah might be real worship was daringly new. Yet it was this revolutionary idea that the Jews embodied in an institution when they created the synagogue. About five hundred years later the Christians, and then the Moslems, modeled their religious institutions—the church and the mosque—after the synagogue. Thus arose the primary social form of worship known to modern man.

Exactly when the change from sacrifices to a service of speech alone first occurred, no one knows. There are two main theories, each supported by some facts and each apparently reasonable.

The first theory supposes that while the Jews were in exile in Babylon, with no Temple of their own and therefore no place in which to offer sacrifices, they must have gathered for some kind of religious expression or they would have perished as Jews. But they did not perish. This was, in fact, the first instance in history of a people's surviving exile and maintaining its identity in a foreign land. What held them together was their religious tradition, for their teachers and prophets did not allow them to forget their God and His promise that they would surely return to their land to rebuild God's Temple in Jerusalem. It seems natural therefore to assume that they must have come together occasionally, or regularly at least on the Sabbath, to hear the Torah read, to recite some Psalms—in short, to worship.

The other theory tells this story. After the return to Palestine, in Ezra's time, when the Temple had already been rebuilt—that is, in the fifth century B.C.E.—representatives of each hamlet and village in a district would gather in a central town to choose from among their number one man to go up to Jerusalem to represent Israel at large at the offering of the *Tamid* sacrifice, offered up daily in the Temple in the name of the people of Israel. While they awaited the return of their representative and his report that he had satisfactorily completed his mission, they would meet to read Torah, recite Psalms, perhaps some other prayers, and from this nucleus the service developed. That may be the correct account of the origin of the synagogue, or perhaps both theories are right. Not enough facts are known for anyone to be absolutely sure.

In any case, the development of either or both of these embryo institutions into the synagogue we know occurred largely during the days of the Second Temple. Thus, by the time the Temple was destroyed again in 70 C.E., the habit of meeting for prayer and for the reading of Torah had already become an established custom upon which the Jews could draw when the need for a service without sacrifices became urgent. The ancient pattern, probably well established before the Second Temple was destroyed, has determined the unique character of the Jewish service to this day—the interweaving of prayer and study into a unit of worship.

DEMOCRACY ENTERS RELIGION

The synagogue from its earliest beginnings represents a democratization of religion. Strangely enough, the pivotal requirement for a synagogue is not a consecrated spot on which a synagogue building is erected nor even the building itself. Services can properly be conducted in a tent or in a moving picture theater or in someone's back yard, if need be. Of course, this does not mean that the synagogue building, once it does exist, is of no importance. On the contrary, it possesses a certain limited degree of holiness in Jewish law, associated with the holiness of the Scroll of the Torah which it houses. Yet the synagogue itself is essentially not a place at all; it is people, the worshippers. A *Minyan*, ten Jews anywhere, constitutes a synagogue and can conduct a full service. The house of worship, when there is one, is called the *Bet Hakenesset*—literally, the House of Assembly. *Synagogue*, therefore, is an exceptionally happy translation of the name *Bet Hakenesset*, for it is derived from a Greek word meaning "bringing together, assembly."

Perhaps this emphasis on the people instead of on the building accounts in large measure for the absence of a specific pattern of synagogue architecture. Its form has always varied with the local and contemporary styles of architecture current in the country in which it was built. Some synagogues in the Far East look like pagodas, those in Arab lands, like mosques; the famous Capernaum Synagogue in Israel, built in Roman times, resembles a Greek Temple with its lovely Corinthian columns. In many of the synagogues built in America during the past ten years, one perceives a groping after "Jewish" forms, but since traditionally there are none, the results are synagogue buildings of more uniform, undifferentiated, modern architecture than their builders may have intended. For there is no characteristic form that distinguishes a building as a synagogue.

Because the synagogue is essentially a *Minyan*, not a building, a new synagogue building is never properly "consecrated." The Hebrew term for the formal inauguration of any new building is *Ḥanukkat Haba'yit*, the dedication of the building. It is from this term, by the way, that the name of the Festival of *Hanukkah* is derived, for the Temple in Jerusalem was re-dedicated after its pollution by the Syrian king, Antiochus.

In the light of its history, therefore, it is rather startling to find a modern Jewish place of worship called a Temple. The very word *Temple* is derived from the Latin *Templum*, meaning a "space marked out, a sanctuary." But we know that the only holy spot of land for Jews is the site of their ancient Temple on the hill in Jerusalem where the Mosque of Omar now stands, on Mount Zion, called in Jewish writings the *Har Haba'yit*—literally, the Mount of the House (of the Lord). Now, however, no specifically marked out space is any longer necessary for a Jewish service, nor, for most Jews, is any present house of worship to be equated with the ancient Sanctuary in Jerusalem.

Yet the use of the term Temple to designate a synagogue has become almost universal among non-Orthodox American Jews. This usage in our times derives from early German Reform Judaism. By the name Temple they intended to indicate that for them every Jewish House of Worship in whatever land was to be considered the Temple of the Jews, replacing the ancient Temple in Jerusalem whose reestablishment they no longer desired or prayed for or expected. By now, much of this theological background has been forgotten. Yet the term Temple persists as if it implied a more modern, somehow a more Western house of worship than the old synagogue. How strange, since it is the Temple which represents a very ancient, almost primitive form of worship now long outgrown by the Jews, and it is the Synagogue which is the newer, more modern institution.

Only when a service is completely freed of the complex ritual of sacrifices can a layman take over its direction, and only then is the shift in emphasis from priest to layman complete. This shift constitutes another element in the democratization of the Synagogue. In a synagogue, the service may be read or chanted by a layman. If he knows the traditional chants, the *Nussah,* that is all to the good. But whether he is a trained cantor (singer) or not, he is called the *Sheliah Tzibur,* the representative of the community. In no sense is he a priest, possessor of a mysterious craft known only by the chosen few. Nor, in fact, is the rabbi a priest, for he has neither hidden knowledge nor special powers of any sort. He cannot forgive sin nor is he God's vicar on earth. He cannot act as an intermediary between a Jew and his God, and until rather recently he was not a professional at all. Rabbi means "my master," or, as we would say, "my teacher." Indeed, every functionary of a synagogue is basically a layman.

Freedom from dependence on the specialized knowledge of a priest was not the only condition which contributed to the democratic spirit of the synagogue. The wide diffusion of knowledge of their religious culture among the Jews made it possible for the synagogue to function as it did. Torah and *Talmud Torah* (Study of Torah) together were the keys to the process of democratization not only in the synagogue, but in the religious life as a whole. Certainly by the Mishnaic period, around the second century of the Common Era, most Jews knew and understood the *Humash* (Pentateuch) and, from oral instruction, much of rabbinic lore as well. They certainly knew the basic prayers which then made up the synagogue service. It was on the basis of this educated laity that the synagogue was able to become the first genuinely democratic religious institution in the world.

No people with so long a continuous history as the Jews' can fail to carry along with them some vestiges of their past. The role of the *Kohanim* in the service of the synagogue is an interesting example of this. *Kohanim* are Priests, and the familiar name *Kohen* is only the singular form of the word *Kohanim.*

The *Kohanim* had special duties in the Temple directly associated with sacrifices. Yet they were not merely members of a guild; they were a blood-related family of the tribe of Levi, descendants of Aaron, the first High Priest. Because Jewish families have always carefully marked their descent from a *Kohen*, they have established a line of relatively pure heredity, probably unique in the human race. The tribe to which the *Kohanim* belong, the tribe of Levi, was given no land of its own when the territory of Canaan was divided up after its conquest. Instead, they were assigned to various duties in the service of the Temple and were supported by tithes from the rest of the people.

Two reminders of those ancient days remain in the service of the synagogue. One is the blessing of the people by the *Kohanim* on the Festivals and the Holy Days. Another related matter is the order in which men are called up to the reading of the Torah in the synagogue. The fixed order or precedence is: first, a *Kohen;* second, a *Levi;* then any Jew—in Hebrew, a *Yisrael.* In a traditional synagogue, it would never occur to anyone to suggest that, when a *Kohen* is present at the service, any but a *Kohen* be called first to the reading, or any but a *Levi* be called second. On the other hand, since the third man called, *Shelishi,* is the first in the order permitted by tradition to a *Yisrael,* it is *Shelishi* which has become the coveted position, the one reserved for the Rabbi, for the learned, for any man the congregation wishes to honor.

Some synagogues have recently eliminated the blessing of the people by the Priests and a few congregations also ignore the traditional order of precedence in calling men up to the Torah in order to achieve what they feel to be a more perfect democratization of the service.

3

The History of the *Siddur*

It would be easy enough to tell the story of the *Siddur* from the very beginning if only we had all the facts. But unequivocal records of the early stages of any human institution are very rarely to be found. So little is known with any degree of certainty about the stages in the development of the synagogue service that one must be careful not to state as historic facts what are only probabilities.

Let us try, then, to summarize the available material on the history of the service until about the middle of the ninth century of the Common Era when the first *Prayer Book* was compiled. It is reasonably certain that by the early days of the Second Temple, about 400 B.C.E., some form of group prayer service existed among the Jews. That service included recitation of Psalms, the *Shema*, possibly some other prayers, and readings from the Torah. At the Temple in Jerusalem during this same period, almost the same prayers—without the readings from the Torah—were recited daily in addition to the sacrifice service.

The prayer service grew in importance during the next two or three hundred years until it became, in addition to the Temple service, an established mode of worship—the synagogue. Its prayers increased in number; two benedictions were added before the *Shema* and one after it. The benedictions of

the *Shemoneh Esray* (the "Eighteen Benedictions") were composed by various Rabbis, probably in large part during these
years, and they became an essential element of every service.
For some mysterious reason, not much is actually known about
the religious development or, for that matter, about any of the
events of this period in Jewish history. But it must have been
a time of active spiritual ferment, for the rabbinic tradition
and its literature, including a large part of the prayers, were in
process of creation during those "silent centuries." By the generation after the destruction of the Temple in 70 c.e., the synagogue service was fairly well established, though there was as
yet no written *Prayer Book* recording in one place all the
prayers then already in use, nor any single written record of
the order of the various services.

As we approach the Middle Ages, about the year 800, we find
that differences in the service from place to place have increased—quite naturally, in the circumstances. For Jewish communities were scattered over most of the then known world
from Babylon to the far western reaches of the Roman Empire.
Communication over any distance was difficult and dangerous.
Each community, therefore, had in large measure to go its own
way. Its contacts with the main stream of the living Jewish
tradition were necessarily infrequent and sporadic. The only
connecting link was the tenuous one of whatever advice and
legal opinion might come to them from the faraway Academies
in Babylon and Palestine. In such circumstances, the possession
and regular use of a written prayer book in common was
imperative.

It is true that these various communities of Jews were not
entirely dependent upon their shared oral tradition. They had,
of course, the Scrolls of the Torah, some manuscript copies of
parts of the Talmud, and some *Midrashim* as well, but their
existence as one great religious community was endangered;

sectarianism was sure to develop unless they could share a common *Prayer Book*. Because they were aware of this danger, the Jewish scholars in Spain appealed to Rav Amram, the Gaon of the Sura Academy in Babylon, to supply them with a guide to the correct order of the prayers. They turned to him because, as President of the Academy in Sura, the Gaon (literally, the great or illustrious one) was in effect the spiritual head of the Jews of the world. It was in response to the request for a definitive text of the prayer services that Rav Amram produced the first complete written *Prayer Book*.

He compiled it from oral tradition, from the service as he knew it in practice, and from numerous Talmudic sources. Since he was preparing his *Siddur* for the benefit of scholars and Rabbis, he accompanied the text with a brief running commentary from the Talmud. It has been said that Amram's *Siddur* appeared in 865 C.E., but that is no more than a "historical guess." It is not known just when Amram was born, but it is fairly certain that he died in 875 and there is reason to believe that he completed his *Siddur* about ten years before his death. Of course, his original manuscript no longer exists. Perhaps, as that great scholar, Louis Ginzberg, once suggested, it was "used until it was used up." Of the manuscript copies found, even the earliest have been added to and changed so much that we cannot entirely reconstruct the text of the original. But amended and much revised copies of this very ancient book do exist. And just about one thousand years after it was completed, Amram's *Siddur* was published for the first time—in 1865, in Warsaw. In spite of periodic, forced wanderings in all the far corners of the earth, Jews have carefully guarded and preserved their treasured books.

An even more famous Gaon of the Academy in Sura was Saadia, who was born in 882. He was a brilliant and stormy personality. Like many men of genius, he had unbounded energy and versatility. The range of his communal activities and his studies was tremendous. From philosophy to elucidation of the Bible, from translations to writing original religious poetry, from studies in *Halakhah* (Jewish law) to the compilation of the first really complete and well organized *Prayer Book*—in every field he touched, he made original contributions.

Amram's earlier *Siddur* had been prepared for scholars. Saadia's aim was quite different. In the preface to his *Siddur*, he tells how and why he came to write it. On his travels through many different Jewish communities in many different lands, he says, he found so many changes in their religious services that in a very short time a common liturgy might cease to exist among Jews and the traditional order of prayers be confused and forgotten. He decided therefore "to collect and arrange the established prayers, praises and benedictions so that the original form should be restored." [1] He wrote not for scholars, but for the people everywhere, because he wanted "to see his [established] order of prayers used everywhere and by everyone." [2] He included not only the traditional prayers but many new liturgical poems by leading poets of his time, and here and there even allowed one of his own to creep in, for which he modestly apologizes by saying, "it is the shortest." Some of his prose prayers, simple, pure in style, profoundly moving in content, are far superior to his prayer-poems, at least to the modern ear. Two of his famous Supplications (*Bakashot*) are to this day part of the Penitential Prayers (*Selihot*). Not long ago, a very old manuscript copy of Saadia's original *Siddur* was discovered, far from his home in Babylon—in Fayyum, the city in Egypt in which he was born.

These two Prayer Books—of Amram and Saadia Gaon—have given to the traditional *Prayer Book* we know today its basic structure. Customs may differ in minor details from place to place. Some divergence exists between the Sephardic *Siddur* and the Ashkenazic [3] text used by Western Jewry; different *Piyyutim* (poems) by this or that medieval liturgist have been included by some synagogues, rejected by others, but essentially the Jewish *Prayer Book* is one from China to Peru. Only in very recent times have such radical revisions in the traditional *Siddur* been made by certain Jewish groups that their followers do not find themselves altogether at home in every synagogue, everywhere in the world.

A "PERFECT TEXT"

Amram's and Saadia's Prayer Books were hand-copied over and over again. That is why minor changes, local variations, and sheer errors crept in to confuse the original text. So great was the demand for copies of the *Siddur* that it was only about thirty years after the invention of printing that the first printed *Prayer Book* appeared—on April 7th, 1486. In those days, printers set type by hand; and so, from generation to generation, errors multiplied, changes were admitted through the whim of this printer or that, until the very meaning and original intent of some of the prayers were quite obscured.

But men accustomed to the careful scrutiny of every word in a document of religious importance were not likely long to overlook these incongruities in the text of the *Siddur*. By the eighteenth century, Jewish scholars began to take note of the accumulating errors. They recognized, very simply, that not every word in the printed *Siddur* was holy, original and unalterable; and they began to apply themselves to the problem of discovering and correcting the errors that had crept into the different texts of the prayers. They found that some incorrect readings marred the simple beauty of the original and that others, more radical in their effect, entirely distorted the basic religious ideas the prayers were meant to convey. Long before modern critical studies of the ancient classics had shocked the Western world by questioning the accuracy of our versions of Homer or the Bible, the Gaon of Wilna (in the eighteenth century) and other Jewish scholars of unquestioned piety were critically comparing various readings of the prayers and correcting the text of the *Siddur* in the light of their vast knowledge of the original rabbinic sources of the prayers.

In 1868, Seligman Baer, a German Jewish scholar, published a definitive text of the *Siddur*. He had carefully compared all the manuscript versions available and had traced all the prayers back to their original sources in the Talmud and elsewhere. Baer's corrected text of the *Siddur* is used in all recently published traditional Prayer Books.

TRANSLATIONS BECOME NECESSARY

Until the nineteenth century, Jews had been concerned with having as full and as correct a version of their *Prayer Book* as could possibly be had. Besides, they kept adding to the prayers. They wanted to spend more time in prayer, make more adequate preparation for approaching God properly. And so we find the *Prayer Book* growing longer and longer during the Middle Ages. New supplications, new penitential prayers, new poems on a variety of religious themes—some very prosey and intricate and involved in form, others that are really great poetry—all these were added from time to time.

But it was not only the desire to pray that stimulated the expansion of the *Siddur*. It was the fact that Jews could read.

Jews are a literate people; their religion encourages literacy, for it requires them to be able to study Torah. That is why, at a time when most men in Europe could not even sign their own names, literacy was so high among Jews that even some of their women could read. We know this, oddly enough, because, in the sixteenth century a translation of the *Siddur* was made especially for women, by one Elijah Levita. He translated the *Prayer Book* into Judeo-German, a very early form of Yiddish. He explains in his introduction that his translation is intended for women "that they too may understand the prayers." This indicates not only a high degree of literacy among Jewish women of that time, but it also points to the serious concern of the learned men for women's special spiritual needs.

And yet, there must have been some Jews in the sixteenth century whose knowledge of the Hebrew language was not all that it should have been, for the very first translation of the *Siddur* antedated its "feminine" counterpart by about twenty-five years. The language was Italian but the book was printed in Hebrew characters. Like so many people today, they seem to have mastered "mechanical reading" of Hebrew without understanding what they read.

The first translation of the *Siddur* into English was made about two hundred years later. But the Elders and Rabbis of the Jewish community of London frowned upon it, and the translator was obliged to hide his identity under a pseudonym. When, in 1766, another adventurous person tried to get a new English translation published, permission was withheld and no publisher in England would take the book. Nothing daunted, the author turned to printers in the English colonies across the sea, in America. That is how it happened that the first translation of the *Prayer Book* to be printed in the New World appeared in New York ten years before the Declaration of Independence.

Since that time, the number and variety of translations has increased—perhaps with the decrease in the knowledge of Hebrew—until now the *Siddur* is available in a large number of the languages known to the civilized world: Italian, Spanish, Yiddish, French, German, English, Dutch, Hungarian, Danish, Polish, Bohemian, Russian, Rumanian, Croatian, Flemish, Arabic, Ethiopic, Maharati, and others.

REFORM AND REVISION OF THE OLD *Prayer Book*

For generations after its basic form had been established, the *Prayer Book* continued to grow by accretion. People, just ordinary people, prayed often and at length. Poets were moved to write new prayers; many of these found their way into manuscript copies of the *Siddur* and later into the new printed editions. There are *Piyyutim*, religious poems, on a large variety of themes—personal, historical and even legal. Some *Piyyutim* were added to the Sabbath service, many more have been included in the Festival and High Holy Day services. Dirges on the destruction of Jerusalem and on their own frequent persecutions were added too. Collections were made of the dirges chanted on Fast Days, the *Kinot*, and these grew in number as the trials and expulsions from land after land stimulated their creation.

No rabbinical synod met to vote on which new prayers to accept for inclusion in the *Prayer Book* and which to reject. But, by a process of sifting, the people themselves put their stamp of approval on more and more of these expressions of religious devotion. So informal was the procedure for adding to the *Siddur* that even a printer might include in his edition a favorite formulation of theological beliefs or some religious

song that appealed to him, and there it would remain in sub-
sequent printings because others felt as he did or because they
hesitated to remove what was already in the *Siddur*. Revision,
in other words, had always meant addition. The people so
loved to pray that they were hospitable to all manner of new
prayers and many were accorded a place in their Hall of Fame,
the *Siddur*.

Soon the *Siddur* grew so long as to be unwieldy. In a *Prayer
Book* of the sixteenth century, the publisher apologizes thus:
"Observing that the material in this book is constantly increasing . . . and has become too cumbersome to be carried to the
synagogue, the present publisher, with a pure heart, decided
to print the *Siddur* in two volumes. . . ." [4]

In the nineteenth century, however, the prevailing intellectual climate became distinctly inhospitable to religion. Jews
took to the new knowledge of the day with enthusiasm. Their
generally high level of education and their intellectual interests undoubtedly helped to sweep them into the stream of the
new thought just as it had involved them in Aristotelian philosophy during the Middle Ages. On the political front, they first
won civil emancipation from Napoleon—but at a high price. In
a formal Representative Assembly, they had publicly to con-
sent to abjure some of their basic religious ideals in order to
gain acceptance as citizens of France. These new intellectual
and political forces broke up communities which had for centuries been self-contained. Too suddenly, within one generation, the jump between the two civilizations had to be made by
the individual Jew. Jews found themselves no longer at home
in the old Jewish tradition, but not yet rooted in any other.

Many of them revolted against everything in their past. A
prime target for their criticism was their religion and the
Siddur which embodied it. Those who were not willing to sever
all ties with tradition tried to correct the faults they found in

the *Siddur*. In the effort to make it conform more nearly to the accepted beliefs and patterns of worship of the day, one revision after another was undertaken. In almost every instance, change now meant not the addition of new prayers but the elimination of what had become for them untenable, as if by radical pruning they hoped to exclude the vestiges of their ancient past and at the same time to reveal a still acceptable core with which to recapture some of their former devotion.

The first published Reform *Prayer Book* appeared in Germany in 1818. It contained both a Hebrew text and its German translation. The book opened from the left, thus underscoring the primacy of the German. References to the ancient Temple service, to sacrifices, to the Messiah, and to the restoration of Israel to Zion were eliminated. There were other omissions as well, and the result was a much slimmer *Prayer Book* and a much briefer service.

Right after the Holy days in October of that year, the Hamburg Rabbinate denounced the new *Prayer Book* in all the synagogues under its jurisdiction, but no *Herem* (excommunication) was issued. Needless to say, their denunciation, like all denunciations, had little effect on the movement to modernize the *Prayer Book*. Many revisions continued to be made. They differed somewhat in the amount of Hebrew retained. Some countenanced a little more deviation from the old text than others, but in general, they were all rather closely patterned after the first Hamburg edition.

In America, a flood of new versions of the *Siddur* followed each other rapidly after 1850. Similar principles determined the changes made here, but, characteristically, they were far more daring on this side of the ocean. In 1888 a Reform *Service Ritual* was published in Philadelphia. It was so popular that a second edition was required only four years later. Very little of the old *Siddur* remained. Most of this manual consists of

readings and choral chants; in fact, the author claims to have
preserved only the "spirit" of the prayers.

Fashions in social reform, almost like fashions in women's
dress, seem to swing like a pendulum from one extreme to the
other. When the effort to contract and rewrite the *Prayer
Book* had finally worn itself out, the movement to recover and
reinstate some of the valid richness of the traditional *Siddur*
began to gain momentum. Until 1895, all revisions had been
made by individuals or small, self-constituted groups. In 1895,
however, *The Union Prayer Book for Jewish Worship* was
edited and published by the Central Conference of American
Rabbis, the official organization of the Reform Rabbinate of
America. The first *Union Prayer Book* reveals that a halt had
already been called to the process of paring down the classical
Siddur. It restores some of the Hebrew original which had been
removed in earlier revisions. Silent Devotion, omitted from the
Hamburg Edition, is here made much of and considerable
emphasis is given to the *Kaddish* for Mourners.

The first *Union Prayer Book* underwent several minor revisions in the next fifty years, but in 1940 a group of Reform
Rabbis initiated a movement for a new, far more thoroughgoing
revision. They wanted more Hebrew in the service, adequate
recognition of the role of Zion in the Jewish religion, the restoration of some of the old rituals to their place in the religious
life, and, wherever possible, a reorganization of the service to
conform more closely to the historical structure of the *Siddur*.
Out of the lively discussions of the Revision Conference came the
new *Union Prayer Book*.

It might be interesting to make a crude statistical comparison
of the first *Union Prayer Book* (of 1895) with its 1940 revision.
A trend toward tradition is clearly revealed by these figures.
Though the same in type and format as its predecessor, the new
Prayer Book is a hundred pages longer, indicating that many

additional prayers have been included. Instead of 15 per cent of the text being in Hebrew as it was in 1895, the new edition allots 25 per cent of its space to Hebrew. The Daily Services show the most extreme change, having been enlarged from fourteen to eighty pages. The ceremony of candle-lighting on Sabbath Eve and the *Kiddush* at home have been restored, and, in fact, there is appended a new section entitled, "Services in the Home." English is still the language of many of the prayers and the translation is therefore of paramount importance. Every translation is necessarily also an interpretation, and this translation naturally reflects the theological views of Reform Judaism.

The new *Union Prayer Book* is, however, a far cry from early nineteenth-century attempts at revision of the *Siddur*. It represents a marked return to tradition.

THE RECONSTRUCTIONIST *Siddur*

A fresh start at revising the traditional *Siddur* has been made by the Reconstructionists. Some of their criteria for the unacceptable are quite different from those of Reform. They are Zionists, warmly devoted to the people and the Land of Israel. They do not denigrate the Hebrew language; on the contrary, they consider it an essential element in the "religious civilization of Judaism." (This phrase was originated by Mordecai M. Kaplan, the founder of the Reconstructionist movement, to describe his view of the nature of Judaism.) On what grounds, then, have the Reconstructionists found it necessary to revise the *Siddur?* They object to the *Siddur* on two grounds. One is the relatively minor matter of the length of the traditional service. To remedy this, they have shortened all their services considerably by reducing repetition to a minimum, contracting some prayers, and eliminating others.

More important have been their objections on theological grounds. Many of the ideas, whether definitely stated or, according to Reconstructionism, implied in the prayers, are for them simply not true. They have therefore systematically expurgated all mention of them from their *Siddur*. Like Reform, the Reconstructionist *Prayer Book* "omits all references to an individual Messiah," [5] to sacrifices, to the *Kohanim* and the Levites, to reward and punishment as described in the *Shema,* to "those Biblical episodes which relate of miracle and supernatural events," [5] and to "the doctrine of corporeal resurrection." [5] In addition, prayers which they feel imply Israel's "superiority over other peoples" have been excised or changed. Most notable among the latter is the blessing said by a person who is called to the reading of the Torah at a service. The Reconstructionist *Prayer Book* has substituted its own formula for the traditional *Berakhah* (blessing). Interestingly enough, in the Reform *Prayer Book* Service for Torah Reading, no change has been made in this blessing.

The *Prayer Book* "must also create new prayers . . . reflective of our age. . . ." [5] To this end, the Reconstructionists have added numerous prayers and readings to their *Siddur*. Some were borrowed from the *Prayer Book* of the Liberal Synagogue of London, some are adaptations from essays on Israel by modern Hebrew writers, some were composed by the editors themselves; other material is taken from sources as varied as Ibn Gabirol (a medieval Jewish poet whose *Piyyutim* appear in the traditional *Siddur*) and Rabindinrath Tagore's *Gitanjali*.

In spite of these and other striking departures from the old *Siddur*, the Reconstructionist *Prayer Book* avers that it is "traditional in spirit." In many ways it might be said to represent a further step in the return through revolt back to the Jewish tradition.

THE CONSERVATIVE *Siddur*

New translations of great classics appear from time to time. The need for them implies no criticism of their predecessors, for language is continually changing. Words and phrases that a hundred years ago seemed natural today sound stilted, archaic. The classic itself is ageless; its translation gets out of date every so often. That is one reason why the Conservative Rabbis felt the need for a new translation of the *Prayer Book* a few years ago. Morover, "the conviction grew that the time was ripe for . . . a *Prayer Book* that would express the view-point of Conservative Judaism. . . ." [6] A commission of Rabbis was therefore appointed to prepare such a *Prayer Book,* and it appeared in 1946.

In the Foreword, they set forth their guiding principles. "First is . . . continuity with tradition." [6] They approach all changes in the Hebrew text with great diffidence and they admit that our age "cannot pretend to a genius for religious expression." [6] Their own contributions within the text are there-fore kept to a minimum. Supplementary Readings are placed in an appendix, leaving the familiar structure of the *Siddur* undisturbed. These readings are chiefly from the Bible, though rabbinic and modern Jewish sources are also represented.

But, they say, no matter how much additional new material the *Siddur* may contain, it will still fall short of satisfying "the ideals of our time" if it also contains passages to which we can-not give intellectual assent. Yet the *Siddur,* they remind us, is not prose. It is religious poetry and it must be read as poetry—

not as a bald statement of fact—if it is to be understood at all.

In some cases, only a too literal translation is at fault, for the problem of translation is, of course, a fundamental one. Often, they say, the intent of a prayer is misunderstood because one is not aware of the fact that conjunctives in Hebrew may have their own peculiar shades of meaning. What looks at first like a simple *and* may have several other connotations as well. For example, in spite of the construction so often placed upon certain references to Israel in the *Prayer Book*, it is not true that Israel is there described as a people with "inherent superiority." The apparent ascription of special status to Israel in some prayers is, in fact, a statement of their gratitude for the Torah which Israel is so fortunate as to possess, or for the *Mitzvot* they feel privileged to perform.

We may point out here that no matter what one's Jewish orientation may be, the problems involved in trying to translate a religious text from the Hebrew are, for everyone, equally insurmountable. Reform, Reconstructionist, Conservative and the most traditional groups alike, as soon as they undertake a translation of the *Siddur*, are faced with questions of interpretation. In fact, at almost every word one must ask: will deviation from a literal translation better convey or will it distort the true meaning, the real intent of the original?

This difficulty arises because the crucial vocabulary of the *Prayer Book* is so largely made up of native Jewish value-words.[7] Such words have no simple definition; each one of them may suggest several ideas at the same time or at different times, depending upon the other value-words with which it is used. How is one to break into a circle of this kind in which all the words have to be understood in terms of each other? And yet, people who "speak the language," who are familiar with the whole interrelated pattern of ideas, understand exactly what such a word means in any given context, though it might require a whole paragraph to explain it to someone who does not habitually think in those terms.

The word *Torah* is an excellent example. For years it was translated into English as *Law,* until it became apparent that *Law* is far too limited in meaning to represent all that *Torah* connotes. For *Torah* may mean the Scroll from which we read in the synagogue, the Five Books of Moses, the Mishnah alone or the whole Talmud, the religious texts and laws and homilies as a whole, or a single verse from any of them, or one law; it sometimes means instruction in Torah or the practice of the laws and commandments—any one or all of these, and others are suggested by the word *Torah.*[8] Torah is an integral part of the Jewish religion and *only* of the Jewish religion. That is why there is no equivalent for the word *Torah* in English or in any other language.

It is therefore no small matter to try to transpose both the exact meaning and the spirit of the *Siddur* into English, and no one has ever succeeded in making a perfectly satisfactory translation.

The third guiding principle of the Conservative Commission is "intellectual integrity." There are passages, they say, which "cannot be made to serve our modern outlook" either through interpretation or in any other way. The most compelling instance is found in the *Musaf* Service. Instead of omitting it entirely because it contains "passages dealing concretely with animal sacrifices," they have changed the tense of two verbs both in the Hebrew and in the English of those passages and have made "a few other minor modifications." The prayer as they have it now reads, "*They* [our forefathers] *brought* . . . the offerings in place of "*We will bring.* . . ."

For the same reason, they have made another change in the text. Among the Preliminary Blessings in the Morning Service are three to which many had long taken exception. Each of

these benedictions names a class of persons which is *not* required to perform certain *Mitzvot*,—namely, Gentiles, slaves
and women—but each, we may add, is exempted for different
reasons. To the Jew, this was a serious abridgment of privilege, and, for that reason, he happily and rather naïvely
thanked God every morning that he was not a Gentile, a slave,
or a woman. Since there is clear warrant in tradition, however,
for stating each of these benedictions in the positive, the Conservative Commission adopted the variant texts which read,
"Blessed art Thou, O Lord our God, . . . Who has made me
in Thine own image" (instead of "not a Gentile"); ". . . Who
has made me free" (instead of "not a slave"); and ". . . Who
has made me an Israelite" (instead of "not a woman").

The violence of revolt against tradition has abated and the
virtues of the classical *Siddur* have come to be more warmly
appreciated in our time. In this renaissance, much will probably be rediscovered concerning the *Siddur* which has been
lost to us in the course of its long history.

THE OLD *Siddur* ENDURES

The *Siddur* expresses in language at once poetic and very
simple a rich variety of human needs and aspirations. It allows
even an untutored person to rise to expression in prayer beyond his capacities for articulation, perhaps for feeling. But
its selections from the Bible and rabbinic literature, its suggested nuances of meaning, its numerous references to the experiences and events of Israel's long and painful history, and
its noble literary form make it an inspiring book of prayer for
the most cultured and sophisticated of any generation.

4

The Order of the Service

THE STRUCTURE OF THE SERVICE

No matter at what point in the long morning service they
arrived, Jews of a generation ago seemed always able to
"find the place" in their Prayer Books at once, though no one
thought of announcing the pages to them. It was not because
all Jews were so very learned, that they could accomplish this
feat; there is another explanation.

First, of course, everyone recited the prayers often. Men
prayed three times daily, and women at least once a week on
the Sabbath. Naturally, they were all familiar with the liturgy.
But habit and repetition are not the whole answer. The second
reason lies not in the people but in the book itself. For the
Siddur is not a series of hymns, psalms, and meditations strung
together by chance or by the whim of some ancient priest. The
Prayer Book has structure, form that developed out of its history, as we have seen; and that form was carefully guarded by
religious law (*Halakhah*). There is a good reason—valid within
its own framework—for the location of each prayer in the liturgy.
The architecture of the service as a whole is a steadfast pattern common to all the services—morning, afternoon and evening, daily, Sabbath and Festival. Neither minor variations nor
the major additions for certain special occasions nor the prayers added by later generations can blur that pattern for those
who understand the essential structure of the service.

Two basic prayers dominate this common pattern. One is the *Shema* and the other is the *Amidah* (Standing or Silent Prayer). ". . . and thou shalt speak of them [words of Torah] . . . when thou liest down [at night] and when thou risest up [in the morning] . . . ," says the *Shema* (Deuteronomy 6, 7). The Rabbis understood this as a direct command to recite these verses evening and morning. Therefore they made the *Shema* the core of the evening and the morning services every day. Tradition—already old in their day—supported them in this, for the *Shema* had for generations been recited in the Temple every day, long before there was a synagogue.

The *Amidah,* the second basic prayer, is called by the Rabbis *Hatefillah, the* Prayer. It consists of nineteen separate benedictions, to be said in silence by each person alone, three times a day—morning, afternoon, and night. All the other Psalms and prayers in the *Siddur* are woven into and around this unchanging framework, as introduction, explanation, or conclusion.

On Sabbaths and Festivals there are two major additions to the morning service: the Torah is read, and there is a series of benedictions known as *Musaf* (Addition) which follows the reading of the Torah. The *Musaf* is a substitute for and a reminder of the additional sacrifice offered in the Temple on Sabbaths and Festivals. On Sabbaths and on Fast Days, the Torah is read at the afternoon service as well.

In spite of all these additions, the configuration of the service is not destroyed. The variety gives the service added latitude and interest. Complexity and unity are the qualities that distinguish every work of art. We find them both in the *Siddur* if we known how to look for them. A sonnet has no greater perfection of form than this, the ancient Jewish service of prayer.

THE ANCIENT OUTLINE OF ALL THE SERVICES

I. *Shaharit* (Morning Service)
  1. Preliminary blessings and Psalms
  2. The *Shema* (including two blessings before and one after)
  3. The *Amidah* (Standing or Silent Prayer)
  4. Reading of the Torah (on Monday, Thursday, Sabbath, and Festivals)
  5. *Musaf* (on Sabbath and Festivals only)
  6. *Alaynu* (God's Kingship)
  7. Mourners' *Kaddish*
  8. Closing Hymn

II. *Minhah* (Afternoon Service)
  1. *Ashray*, a Psalm
  2. "A redeemer shall come to Zion" (on Sabbath and Festivals)
  3. The *Amidah*
  4. Reading of the Torah (on Sabbath and Fast Days)
  5. *Alaynu*
  6. Mourners' *Kaddish*

III. *Ma'ariv* (Evening Service)
  1. Short Reading from Psalms
  2. The *Shema* (including two blessings before and two, after)
  3. The *Amidah*
  4. *Alaynu*
  5. Mourners' *Kaddish*

5

The Morning Service—*Shaḥarit*

ARISTOTELIAN PHILOSOPHY IN THE MORNING SERVICE

Shaḥarit, the Hebrew name for the morning service, comes from the word *Shaḥar,* morning dawn, early morning. It opens with a long section of what is sometimes called "Preliminary Prayers." They are preliminary to the core of the public or synagogue service which begins, appropriately enough, with a "Call to Prayer." But this long introduction, as a matter of fact, was not meant to be an introduction at all. It consists of prayers originally said by each individual at home, before attending the synagogue. It includes blessings that accompany getting up, getting dressed, and generally preparing for the new day. There is also a stint of study from Bible and Mishnah—for a Jew could not imagine beginning his day without a little study of Torah. In the course of time, however, all these and more were integrated into the morning service.

The first part of the introductory service is known as *Birkot Hashaḥar,* Morning Blessings. The opening hymn is *Yigdal.* *Adon Olam,* a hymn sung in some synagogues right after *Yigdal,* is in other places sung only in the evening for it was in origin probably a night hymn. *Yigdal* (May He be magnified) was written in the fourteenth century by an Italian Jew, Daniel of Rome. In poetic form, it recites the *Thirteen Creeds* of Maimonides, the *Ani Ma'amin* (I believe) made familiar to this generation by the "Song of the Warsaw Ghetto." It must be stated categorically that this "Confession of Faith," as it has sometimes been called, has no legal, doctrinal standing in Judaism; that it is not, in any case, *the* Jewish creed. It was written (in his Commentary to the Mishnah) by Maimonides when he was twenty-three years old, and he never referred to it again in all the rest of his writings.

The need to formulate the Jewish religion in a clearly stated creed had apparently not been felt in the previous two millennia of its existence. It was only in the late Middle Ages, when Aristotelian philosophy dominated the whole intellectual world, that Maimonides was impelled to try to set down the basic axioms of Judaism as he understood them, and in the light of the philosophy current in his day. When Moslem and Christian thinkers vied with each other in the attempt to prove the "truth" of their religions by showing how perfectly Mohammedanism and Christianity conformed to Aristotle's conception of the origin and nature of the universe, the Jews too, produced philosophic "proofs" of the validity of Judaism. As a corollary to this new theology, they began to devise logically derived, clear-cut summaries of Jewish religious beliefs. Maimonides was not the only Jewish philosopher who tried his hand at this kind of dogmatic formulation of Judaism. All during the fourteenth and fifteenth centuries, a number of fundamental Jewish Creeds were proposed by various Jewish thinkers. Naturally, none of them agreed on the nature or number of the necessary beliefs, since Judaism does not readily lend itself to doctrinaire oversimplification.

During his lifetime and for many years afterward, Maimonides was bitterly opposed by many Rabbis. They felt that something extraneous to the genuine Jewish tradition was being injected into it by this precipitation of Aristotelian philosophy and by these strange formulations of belief. They went so far as to have his *Guide for the Perplexed* burned, in typical medieval fashion. Thus far, the Rabbis. But even some philosophers took exception to the Creeds. Crescas, in some ways the most subtle and brilliant of the Jewish philosophers, Nachmanides (the Ramban), Abarbanel, and others all registered strong opposition to Maimonides' Creeds. Abarbanel's view is that ". . . it is a mistake to formulate the dogmas of Judaism. . . . It was only by following the example of the non-Jewish scholars that Maimonides and others were induced to lay down dogmas." [1]

The *Shulḥan Arukh*, the code of Jewish law and practice written by Joseph Caro in the sixteenth century and since then generally accepted by Jewry as its standard guide in every detail of Jewish life, does not even mention the *Thirteen Creeds*. Someone—perhaps a printer, but no one knows exactly who—included the Creeds in an edition of the *Prayer Book* sometime after 1400. Only in certain Sephardic synagogues are they recited as part of the daily service. But at that, they are said after the *Tallit* and *Tefillin* have been removed—on the way out, so to speak.

A prospective convert to Judaism is not asked to accept these thirteen, or any other, creeds as a condition to conversion. In fact, as Israel Abrahams puts it in his *Companion to the Daily Prayer Book*,[2] ". . . no Jewish authority has ever practically employed these thirteen articles as a *test* of Judaism. . . ."

THE WHOLENESS OF MAN

The order and range of the *Berakhot* (plural of *Berakhah*, benediction) of the morning reflect the normal actions of a man as he rises to begin a new day. There is a benediction to be said when he opens his eyes, rises, dresses and so on. These blessings were obviously meant to be recited at home. Nevertheless, as we have said, many of them were, in time, integrated into the formal service.

The very first *Berakhah* in the *Prayer Book* concerns the "washing of hands." This washing is a ritual act, reminiscent of the priests' ablutions before they performed their functions in the Temple, and it precedes one of the strangest and most startling prayers in the *Siddur:* "Blessed art Thou, O Lord our God, King of the universe, Who has formed man in wisdom and created in him several apertures and pipes. It is clearly known before the Throne of Thy Glory that if one of these be opened or one of them be sealed [contrary to its nature], it would be impossible to exist and to stand before Thee."

In the morning a man goes to the bathroom, then washes his hands and thanks God for the normal performance of the most elemental of his natural functions. To the Western-trained mind, such a prayer is almost shocking. Yet it is thoroughly characteristic of the simplicity, purity, and wholeness of outlook of the Jewish religion. For that dichotomy between body and soul which in other religions has come to be accepted as fundamental is foreign to Judaism.

This fact is reflected in the Hebrew terms—or lack of them—for *body* and *soul*. In the Bible, the word *Nefesh*—so often incorrectly translated *soul*—means a living creature, man or animal. It may mean also mind, emotion, or life itself, but the very same word, *Nefesh*, is used for *body* as well. *Nefesh Mayt*, for example, means a *dead body*. Infrequently the Bible uses another word, *Neshamah*, sometimes taken to mean *soul*. Like *Nefesh*, it comes from a root that means *to blow* or *to breathe*, and it too, always implies breath—breath of anger, breath of life, or mind. There is only one instance in the Bible—in Proverbs 20, 27—where *Neshamah* may be construed to mean *soul*, *spirit*. But, on the other hand, there is no word for the living *body* apart from the whole person. The word nearest to that notion is *Gufah,* and it also means a *corpse.* Certainly these words give no indication of a fundamental distinction between body and soul.

In rabbinic times, the old meanings of these words persist, but there is a word now for *body,* as we understand it today. That word is *Guf* or *Gufa.* As soon as we find a word meaning just *body,* the living body, we are likely to find another, meaning *soul.* And we do. For now *Neshamah* begins to acquire more of the connotation of *soul.* But the meanings of both *Guf* and *Neshamah* are varied and sometimes overlap. The contrast between them is far less clear and clean-cut than we can here indicate.

In the *Siddur,* a rabbinic document, there is a prayer which reads, "The *Neshamah* which Thou didst give me is pure," but nowhere does it say that the body is impure. On the contrary, the body which God gave us is also untainted and none of its functions, when properly disciplined, are necessary sources of evil. Eating is not sinful; good food is an element in the proper celebration of the Sabbath and the Festivals. Wine is used for *Kiddush,* and then drunk; indeed, four cups are prescribed for the *Seder* on Passover. Sex is not considered inherently evil either. All men are expected to marry. To have children is a *Mitzvah* expressly commanded in the Torah. Celibacy is not only *not* regarded as a holy state, it is definitely frowned upon for anyone. One Rabbi goes so far as to call a celibate a murderer! The English word *carnal,* with all its connotations of the wickedness of the flesh, has no equivalent in the Hebrew language.

Now, this does not mean that there is no recognition in Judaism of the evil in man. There are words in Hebrew for "the good impulse" and "the evil impulse," but Judaism does not lay all the blame on the *body* for the evil a man may do. One

Midrash expresses the opinion that it is possible for a man to worship God with both his impulses. At any rate, the Jewish religion is not preoccupied with sin as a function of the body. There is, instead, the reverence aroused by the intricacy and perfection of the human body, which God so wonderfully made.

The blessing on the proper functioning of the body ends with this closing *Berakhah,* "Blessed art Thou, O Lord, Healer of all flesh and Maker of wonderful [things]."

SWEET ARE THE WORDS OF THE TORAH

It was the custom in the days of the Rabbis, to study some Torah every day before dawn, before the time for morning prayer. That is why we find here, preceding the beginning of the service, several *Berakhot* on the study of Torah. There are three *Berakhot* merely because the Talmud records the versions preferred by different Rabbis, and a later compiler of this section was apparently unwilling to choose among them.

The second of these benedictions, "Make the words of Thy Torah sweet in our mouths . . . ," overflows with the sheer pleasure Jews felt in the study of Torah. The *Berakhah* continues: "May we and our children, and our children's children . . . may all of us of the House of Israel know Thy Name and study Thy Torah." The enjoyment of the study of Torah is not reserved for an elite class—priest or intellectual—it is extended to the whole people of Israel.

Having said the blessings on the Torah, one must proceed at once to carry out the act (*Mitzvah*) which the blessing describes. The *Prayer Book* therefore supplies sample passages from the Bible, the Mishnah, and the Talmud, so that every man can study at least a little Torah every day. From the very beginning, as we pointed out above, the pattern of a Jewish service is the interweaving of prayer and study.

The selection from the Bible is very short; it is the priestly blessing from Numbers 6, 24-26. The section chosen from the Mishnah for daily study enumerates five deeds for which no maximum is prescribed in Jewish law (the more you do of them, or the more often, the better): the corner of the field (to be left ungarnered for the poor), the first fruits brought to the Temple, appearance at the Temple on the Festivals, deeds of loving-kindness, and the study of Torah. Three of these are ritual, two are ethical acts, but the distinction is ours, not the Rabbis'.

The passage then continues with additional material from the Talmud on the same topic. It cites "things, the fruits of which a man eats in this world while the stock remains for him for the World to Come: honoring father and mother, deeds of loving-kindness, promptness at morning and evening service, hospitality, visiting the sick, dowering a bride, attending the dead to the grave, devotion in prayer, making peace between a man and his fellowman and the study of Torah which outweighs them all." Now these ten (including Torah which here is said to "outweigh them all") are as essential, but not more so, than other deeds or ideals named in other lists of five or three or ten as the "most important" in Judaism. The "Ethics of the Fathers," also part of the Mishnah, records several different summaries—for example: "Upon three things does the world rest—upon Torah, upon divine service and upon deeds of loving-kindness" (Chapter 1, 2). However, in the same chapter but in another Mishnah [3] (number 18), we read, "Upon three things is the world established—upon Truth, upon Justice and upon Peace."

We cannot and we need not determine which list is the most

authentic, which of these ideals the Rabbis intend us to take as fundamental in Judaism. We cannot and we need not, for each summary emphasizes different, but equally valid and equally important ideas or value-concepts [4] of Judaism. In the Bible, and especially in rabbinic literature, we find the ideas which give its unique character to the Jewish religion. The Rabbis interpret their experience in terms of these ideas. They apply them again and again to different concrete situations and thus make clear their range of meaning. But there is no attempt to agree upon an authoritative, limited list of "the most important" value-ideas of Judaism. Some of these religious values are given in our daily portion of Mishnah, some in the daily quota of Talmud. Each idea is precious, fruitful and important but there are others, not in these lists, that loom just as large in any total picture of the Jewish religious mind.

AN EARLIER BEGINNING OF THE SERVICE

The day of prayer really begins for a Jew the moment he opens his eyes. A man awakens in the morning to full consciousness. He discovers with delight that he is alive again, and he at once thanks God for having restored him to life after the deathlike sleep of the night. "Blessed art Thou, O Lord, Who returns the breath of life [*Neshamah*] to the dead" [literally, dead bodies].

The *Neshamah* You gave me, God (says the prayer), is pure. You guard it and You will take it away from me at the appointed time, only to return it in the Future (World) to Come. But as long as the *Neshamah* is within me, I will acknowledge You, O God, and God of my fathers, Master and Lord of all.

Several other beginnings are preserved in the *Siddur* and some of them are found in the benedictions that follow.

THE FIFTEEN BENEDICTIONS

We have already discussed several of the morning benedictions. Before us now is a long list of them. One is a reaction to the mystery of cock-crow at dawn; another, to the miracle of sight restored with the return of daylight; another is to God's goodness in giving us strength to stand up on our own feet as we rise from bed, and in providing us clothes to wear as we dress. There is a benediction on the solid earth revealed afresh in the new day, on Israel strong and beautiful; one in gratitude for energy renewed after the weariness of yesterday, and more.

These very brief prayers, each occasioned by a different, specific situation, have one striking thing in common—the formula in which the emotion is expressed: the *Berakhah*. "Blessed art Thou, O Lord our God, King of the universe, Who has . . ." done this or that . These are the words a Jew is supposed to find occasion to say a hundred times a day. They are the characteristic form of Jewish prayer and they compress within themselves—if any formula can—the distinctive nature of the religious experience in Judaism.[5]

"*Barukh* art Thou, O Lord," says the Jew, again and again. Is he, then, praising God, thanking Him? He is both praising and thanking Him, but more, he is invoking the "sense, more than physical, of God's nearness." The mystical experience of God in the Jewish religion is the sense of God's Presence, close and real, yet entirely free of abnormal visions and locutions. That is why the distinctive nature of the religious experience in Judaism is best described as "normal mysticism."[6] Without images of any kind to help him or visual aids of any sort, manmade or present on earth or in the heavens, it was no small matter for a Jew to achieve awareness of God's continuous nearness to him. Yet this intimate experience of God could be his every time he recited a *Berakhah*. No phenomenon was too ordinary or too exceptional to elicit a blessing. When he experienced a frightening or wonderful occurrence in nature, when he performed a ritual act or said his prescribed prayers, and most often in response to his own simple, daily acts and experiences, the Jew reacted by reciting an appropriate *Berakhah*. Each time he addressed God intimately, directly, saying: "Blessed art *Thou*, O Lord, our God. . . ," he became conscious again of God's near Presence. Psalm 16, verse 2 reads, "I have set the Lord before me." The Rabbis made this verse the basis for the *Berakhah* and add, "He that prays ought always to regard himself as though *Shekhinah* [God] were in front of him."

Close and direct as is the relationship to God expressed in the first clause of the *Berakhah*, that relationship is not completely represented by the words, "Blessed art *Thou*. . . ." For the second half of the *Berakhah*, with complete disregard for the rules of grammar, slips directly into the third person when it relates what God has done. This arresting switch from direct address to the third person in one sentence is ordinarily masked in translation, for the English usually reads, "Blessed art *Thou*, . . . Who *hast* sanctified us by *Thy* commandments. . . ." But the Hebrew really says, "Blessed art *Thou*, . . . Who *has* sanctified us by *His* commandments . . . ," or "Blessed art *Thou*, O Lord, Who at *His* word *brings* on the evening. . . ."

Addressing God directly is all very well, but there is no simple I-Thou relationship between man and God in Judaism. God is not a Person or a King, even a very great King, that man should expect to converse with Him. He is God, and there is nothing else in the whole universe like Him. The *Shekhinah* (God) is near, say the Rabbis, but notice, they say it is *"as though Shekhinah* were in front of him" [a man]. To approach God with the intimate *Thou* and then to retreat in confusion into the more remote *He* is one way, one stereotype, by which the Rabbis give expression at once to both intimacy and awe and indicate their recognition that God is like none other. Words are, at best, a clumsy tool with which to express the mystical experience of God. The *Berakhah,* the distinctive form of Jewish prayer, makes a real attempt to convey that experience.

"OUR FATHER WHO ART IN HEAVEN. . . ."

The most passionate personal prayers of our liturgy are found in the daily morning service known now, alas, to so few, and in the *Yom Kippur* service read only once a year. They are, for the most part, individual prayers, each recorded in the name of the Rabbi who was wont to recite it before or after the public service.

"*Vihi Ratzon,* May it be Thy will, O Lord our God, . . . that we may acquire the habit of Torah [study] and that we may cling to the *Mitzvot.* Lead us not into the power of sin or of transgression or temptation or shameful deeds. Let not the evil inclination rule over us . . . and give us this day and every day grace, love and mercy in Thine eyes and in the eyes of all men." This prayer, for all that it is an individual appeal, is stated in the plural, and it ends with a plea that God's loving-kindness may be granted to all Israel. It is interesting to note that a famous Christian prayer owes much to the *Vihi Ratzon* found here.

In one of the many periods of persecution suffered by Jews (this time in Persia, in 456 c.e.), public pronouncement of the *Shema* was forbidden to them. Their Rabbis urged them to worship God in private, just as they had been accustomed to do in the public service: "*Le'olam Yehay Adam,* Let a man always remember to worship God in private, as he is wont to do in public." This is a cryptic reminder to say the *Shema* even though government authorities have forbidden it. That is why it is usually printed in smaller letters in the *Siddur.*

Following this plea is a condensation of the *Shema,* to be smuggled in before the service that *was* permitted. But even this short *Shema* was felt to require a proper setting. It is preceded, therefore, by three short introductory paragraphs. The first is a confession, originally said by a Rabbi of the third century, on *Yom Kippur:* "Master of all worlds, not because of our righteous deeds do we lay our supplications before Thee, but because of Thine abundant mercies. What are we? What is our piety? Our strength? What shall we say before Thee, O Lord? Are not all the mighty as nought before Thee, famous men as if they had never been? . . .

"But we are Thy people, . . . children of Abraham who loved Thee. . . .

"Therefore, we are bound to praise . . . and to sanctify Thy Name. How happy are we. . . . How beautiful our heritage. Happy indeed are we, for we can declare . . . twice each day, '*Shema Yisrael. . . .*'"

The *Shema* is followed by a short declaration of God's holiness (a form of the *Kedushah* prayer also forbidden to Jews of that period), "Blessed art Thou, O Lord, Who sanctifies His Name before the whole world." The last phrase expresses the hope that the need for secrecy may speedily pass and that God will then be worshipped openly all over the world.

God's sovereignty over the whole universe is then recounted:

"Thou hast made the heavens and the earth and the sea and all that is in them, and who among all the works of Thy hands, on high or below, can question what Thou doest?" Yet, characteristically, the Jew turns at once—in the same sentence—from God, described as utterly powerful, seemingly utterly unapproachable, directly to God, his Father in heaven! "Our Father Who art in heaven, deal with us lovingly for Thy great Name's sake," the prayer continues. It ends on the hopeful note of God's promise to return the captives to the Land of Israel, a hope made so necessary to them because of the severe restrictions with which they had to contend.

SACRIFICES

Without conducting a scientific opinion poll, one may safely venture the guess that only a small minority of Jews still expects or desires sacrifices to be reinstated in a restored Temple in Jerusalem. Yet Jews continue to recite the accounts of the sacrifices appropriate to each period and occasion as they are described in the *Prayer Book* selections from the Pentateuch and the Mishnah. Mere habit does not explain the stubbornness with which they have persisted in the daily recital of the laws of sacrifice.

Of course, the first reaction in modern times was "to throw out the baby with the bath water," to eliminate from the *Prayer Book* all mention of sacrifices as an unsavory reminder of our primitive past. But a careful reading of this whole section and a deeper penetration into the religious thought of the Rabbis will disclose some interesting implications, not perhaps apparent at first.

It is important to recognize that for the Rabbis of the Talmud, the sacrifices, even when they were available, had no propitiatory purpose. Man could not buy God's forgiveness, as it were, by *any* sacrifice offered upon the altar. Reconciliation with God was always to be from the heart and required repentance, humility, a sense of sin, and the determination not to sin again. In fact, it is because the actual sacrifice had already become for the Rabbis incidental to its symbolic meanings that they could go one step further and feel that the reading of the Biblical verse enjoining sacrifices was sufficient to reconciliation with God.

Psychologically, they were quite ready to allow study of the passages about sacrifices to replace actual offerings as a mode of worship when the loss of the Temple made this necessary. In addition, we must remember that they looked upon the study of Torah itself as a primary way to serve God. We can understand, therefore, why they put the readings from Bible and Mishnah dealing with sacrifices into the morning service, after the Temple was destroyed. In this fashion, the Rabbis were able to keep always fresh and vivid the memory of the Temple service and, at the same time, to make concrete their teaching that the study of Torah is an altogether acceptable substitute for the sacrificial service of the Temple.

But it is not the only substitute. For prayer, too, is equated with the sacrifices. In a comment on Deuteronomy 2, 13, the Rabbis say, "Just as the service of the altar is called *Avodah*, so is prayer called *Avodah*." [7] Prayer, they add, is *Avodah Shebalayv*, the service of the heart, and this service is just as acceptable to God as the Temple service of old. The term used for the sacrifice-service is *Avodah*, literally, work or service, and today we still use the word *services* in its enlarged rabbinic sense to mean *worship*, even in English.

In the year 70 of the Common Era, the Romans were convinced that Judea had been permanently destroyed, never to rise again. Yet the Jews did not cease longing for Jerusalem and their dream of the Temple Rebuilt never died. It remained a verdant hope during two millennia of exile because, among other things, the Rabbis had inserted reminders of that hope into various rituals—into the daily prayers, the Grace after Meals, the wedding ceremony, and others. But no expression of their confidence in the ultimate revival of Jerusalem was as convincing as the constant reiteration of the details of the sacrifice-service. For that service alone, that institution among all their institutions, could exist only in Jerusalem. One can eat and pray and marry anywhere, but the sacrifices may be offered only in the Temple in Jerusalem. Thus every recall of the sacrifices made real and conscious again their expectation of an early return to "Jerusalem Rebuilt."

All these ideas and associations cluster around the recital of the passages from Numbers, Leviticus, and from *Mishnah Zevahim* on the sacrifices. Perhaps it is less than the part of wisdom "to throw out the baby with the bath water."

LOGIC FOR THE LAYMAN

There has never been a prayer book quite like the *Siddur*. No wonder people today find it strange and hard to understand. All the minutiae of animal sacrifice are carefully set down and then, without a word of introduction or a pause, as if it were the most natural sequence in the world, there follows a list of tersely stated, highly abstract rules of logic. For that is what the *Thirteen Middot* or Principles of Exegesis are —the logical principles by which new laws may be inferred from statements in the Pentateuch. And these laws of logic are meant for the layman to recite and to think about every day while he is at prayer. This extraordinary juxtaposition of sacrifices and logic is, however, only another instance of the affirmation of the wholeness of life in the Jewish religion which we pointed out when we studied the first *Berakhah* of the day.

The role logic plays in Judaism is peculiar to it. Ordinarily, when a religion employs logic to derive or to "prove" its basic ideas of God, the soul, salvation and so on, it produces a philosophy of religion, a theology. Such theology is far removed from the competence of the ordinary man. Therefore it remains the domain of specialists, theologians. The people receive the conclusions arrived at by the philosophers and accept them as their religious beliefs—that is, dogmas.

Judaism is quite different. Except for the few famous Jewish philosophers of the Middle Ages, Judaism is, for so intellectual a people, startlingly poor in theology and theologians. Its "basic ideas," its religious or value-ideas, are not derived by logic from agreed upon, fundamental assumptions; nor are its value-concepts anywhere exactly defined. Their ideas of God's mercy, His justice, Torah, holiness, charity, loving-kindness, *Mitzvah,* and the other value-ideas that constitute the pattern of Jewish religious thought are completely taken for granted by Rabbi and layman alike; they are simply part of the natural furniture of every Jew's mind.

Moreover, these value-ideas are dynamic. Without benefit of philosophic analysis, they have for centuries been affecting the character and conduct of many peoples through the teachings of Judaism and its daughter religions. But it is only in very recent times, with the development of the social sciences, that these basic values have come to be recognized as ultimates, integral to a society and incapable of logical derivation or proof.[8] Leading thinkers of our time increasingly espouse the view that "the final values of the moral life are as exempt from experimental proof or disproof as are the postulates of scientific method." [9]

But all this is not to say that logic plays no role in Judaism. On the contrary, careful logical thought is essential to Judaism. Its role is to develop law—that is, to apply the value-concepts to life, to an ever increasing number and variety of specific, concrete situations. *Tzedakah,* love or charity, is a Jewish value-idea. The religious authorities nowhere in the vast literature of the Talmud record any concern with defining just what *Tzedakah* is, nor with "proving" that it is a necessary virtue. But the most careful kind of logical thought is expended on developing all the ramifications of the laws of charity: Who must give charity? Even a poor man? How poor, exactly, must a man be to be free of the obligation to give to others? How much should a man give? Should all the needy receive the same amounts, and if not, what is the proper basis for allotment? Need, previous estate, or what? These questions and the answers to all of them are *Halakhah,* law. *Halakhah* is found in the Talmud and every Jew is expected—indeed, required—to study some Talmud every day.

In the Talmud, logic, then, is directed to the solution of concrete, actual problems. Even a man of moderate intellectual capacity, given proper training, can follow the application of logic to this kind of problem. For he is accustomed to using logic in the same way to solve the ordinary problems of his daily life, of his craft or his business. Moreover, until very recently, all but the dullest-witted among the Jews were given training in the uses of logic through the study of Talmud in the normal course of their religious education.

For these reasons, it was assumed that ordinary men would find no difficulty in understanding the long excerpt from the *Sifra* [10] on the thirteen principles of logic by which additional laws may be inferred from statements in the Torah. Study of

Torah was considered a mode of worship, as we have seen, and therefore a man who perused these difficult rules carefully every day was also worshipping God.

In the Jewish religion, logic is the handmaiden of life; it is employed to discover more and newer ways to put religious values and ideals into practice. Life is full and well rounded in Judaism and nothing human is alien to it. The *Siddur* reflects that wholeness.

The first part of the morning service ends here with a short prayer for the restoration of the Temple—a fitting close to the section dealing with sacrifices.

Tefillin

In the days of the Temple, pomp and ceremony, pageantry and drama, characterized its service. The Levites were the chorus, the Priests were the actors, the High Priest, the hero. In an ascending scale of elaborateness, each was dressed in special ceremonial robes as they played out the drama of the sacrifice-service. But all this came to an end with the destruction of the Temple. In the synagogue every Jew plays a part—an equally modest part, it is true—in a service that is intense but not very colorful. Nevertheless, something of the drama of worship is recaptured when all the men don *Tallit* and *Tefillin* for the daily morning service. Women, by the way, are not required to put on *Tefillin* but some women were known to have done so in rabbinic times. History records a few instances in later years as well, and, as far as we know, no law forbids it even now.

The *Tefillin* consist of two small leather boxes, to each of which is attached a long leather thong. One box is to be fastened on the forehead, the other, on the left arm above the elbow. As each is set in place, a benediction on the *Tefillin* is recited. The thong of the arm box is then wound seven times around the arm and three times around the middle finger like a ring. The words accompanying this action were added in the seventeenth century. They are from Hosea, 2, 21-22: "And I will betroth thee unto me forever. . . ." The symbolism here is very bold and its intent is made even more obvious in the last part of these verses: "I will betroth thee unto *me* [traditionally, *Me* is taken to mean God] in justice and righteousness, in loving-kindness and in mercy."

Each box contains bits of parchment on which are inscribed four passages from the Pentateuch: two from Exodus 13 (1-10 and 11-16), and two from Deuteronomy (6, 4-9 and 11, 13-21). For the *Tefillin*, just as for the Scroll of the Torah, these verses must be handwritten very carefully on specially prepared parchment, and only a perfect copy will serve. Each passage contains a reminder of the miraculous deliverance from the bondage of Egypt and of the sign to be worn on the head and the forehead: "And it shall be for a sign unto thee upon thy hand and for a memorial [literally, reminder] between thine eyes . . . ; for with a strong hand hath the Lord brought thee out of Egypt" (Exodus 13, 9). "And these words which I command thee this day shall be upon thy heart; . . . and they shall be for frontlets [*Totafot*] between thine eyes" (Deuteronomy 6, 6-8).

Many theories have been advanced to account for their origin. The name, *Tefillin*, itself offers no clue to its history for it is not used in the Bible at all and is very probably of later origin. It is merely a form of *Tefillah*, prayer. The key word for our purpose is *Totafot*, frontlets. According to Cassuto,[11] *Totafot* were well known in Bible times as signs, indicators of some sort, worn on the forehead that all might see them and remember something. They were, in other words, a mnemonic device, a memory-aid. Israel was commanded to wear *Totafot*, inscribed with the words of the Torah, that they might always remember the Exodus from Egypt and the commandments of the Torah.

An earlier and more primitive origin is suggested by Kaufmann in his monumental work on the history of the religion of Israel.[12] The word *Totafot*, Kaufmann contends, means *drops*, from the verb, *Taftef*, to drip. And the evidence indicates that in very ancient times worshippers would put drops of blood from the paschal lamb or other sacrifice on their foreheads, on their hands and on the doorposts of their houses as protection against plague and other evils. A striking instance is the blood sprinkled on the doorposts of the houses of the Israelites in Egypt on the night the firstborn of the Egptians were stricken.

Generally, however, by the time of the Bible—with the exception of the example just cited—these ancient blood rites were no longer practiced by Jews. Yet the name *Totafot* persisted, as words do persist, even when they acquire new meanings. And *Totafot* undoubtedly had, by then, become a memory-aid, as Cassuto suggests. When the Israelites were told that the words of the Torah were now to be their *Totafot*, they could understand the command very well. They recognized that these signs were given them that they might keep the Torah constantly before their eyes and continuously in their thoughts. There could be no doubt about the function of these outward "signs," for the Bible itself stated it clearly. The precepts of the Torah are very precious and Israel must never be allowed to forget them: "And these words which I command thee shall be upon thy heart; . . . thou shalt speak of them when thou sittest in thy house and when thou walkest by the way and when thou liest down and when thou risest up. And thou shalt bind them for a *sign* upon thy hand and they shall be for *Totafot* between thine eyes. And thou shalt write them upon the doorposts of thy house and upon thy gates."

The primitive origins of these signs and frontlets and their ancient magical effects had been so far forgotten by the time of the Bible that scholars have had to dig deep to unearth their probable meanings in their pre-Israelitish past.

Though divested of their pagan associations by the Bible, the *Totafot* had not yet become the *Tefillin* we know today. It was not until the rabbinic period that the *Tefillin* became an institution. Their construction, their use in the daily morning prayers, and, above all, the deeply personal significance attached to their regular use were all established during the rabbinic period. It was the Rabbis who gave to this ancient ritual a broader meaning in addition to the "reminder-function" it had had of old. They made the act of putting on the *Tefillin* a signal for each man to scrutinize his own acts every day and to repent every day. For many years, *Tefillin* were worn all day by the pious; in later generations, they became the common "garb" of all Jews at morning prayers. Some pious Jews still wear the *Tefillin* all day.

The *Tefillin* are not a simple symbol with one correct meaning. An institution with a long history never has one, single "meaning." All the old associations cling to it and more significance can always be added. Thus the *Tefillin* have acquired for the Jew a cluster of varied meanings. Maimonides, in his code of Jewish law, in the section on *Tefillin*, says, "Great is the sanctity of the *Tefillin*, for while the *Tefillin* are on a man's head and about his arm, he is humble and God-fearing; . . . his heart does not entertain evil thoughts, but he fills his heart with ideas of truth and righteousness."

Very few objects in Judaism are considered holy, holy in themselves. Of the objects used for ritual purposes, such as the candles for the Eve of Sabbath, the *Sukkah,* the *Kiddush* wine, and so on, none are holy. They are merely the means to an end —and that end is to induce the experience of holiness in the person who uses them in the performance of a religious rite. It is not the *Kiddush* wine that is holy; it is the man who experiences a sense of holiness, when he makes *Kiddush* and pronounces the benediction over wine.

However, the Scroll of the Torah *is* considered holy, and by the same token, so are the *Tefillin* and the *Mezuzah* which contain portions of the Torah, written as scrupulously as is the Torah. Yet even this holiness *in objects,* it is important for us to recognize, is unlike any apparently similar quality found in other and more primitive religions. For in Judaism the holy object has no physical or spiritual power that can be used for any purpose whatsoever. Contact with, or kissing or touching the Scroll of the Torah, for example, is not believed to heal or to protect or to save from anything. The holiness of the Torah Scroll implies only that it is to be treated with very grave reverence. In other words, even that most holy object, the Scroll of the Torah itself, has no mystical powers. If the Torah has no such powers, it is clear that neither the *Tefillin* nor the *Mezuzah* have any special protective power, and they cannot possibly have been intended to be used as amulets to safeguard the user in any magical way. In fact, such use would be considered a *Ḥillul Hashem,* a desecration of the Name of the Lord.

The *Tefillin* are a reminder, it is true, but a reminder of many things—of the Exodus from Egypt, of the words of the Torah, and a reminder to each individual to examine well into his own deeds and carefully into his own heart every day.

PASSAGES OF SONG—THE "SHORT PSALTER"

The public service begins at this point, with a benediction introducing the section known as *Pesukay de Zimra*, Passages of Song. Included are the last six Psalms of the Book of Psalms —numbers 145 through 150. All of them are joyous, all exult in God's majesty and power and His goodness to man. To convey this mood the Psalmist employs five different words for *joy* within a few verses. Nature itself and all manner of men must appreciate God's work and sing His praises. Do not put your trust in princes, says the Psalmist, in mere men from whom no help can be expected. But the Lord Who made heaven and earth, Who feeds the hungry, succors the oppressed, supports the widow and the orphan, He is our help. "He heals the broken in heart and binds up their wounds." "Let everything living praise the Lord. Hallelujah!" This is the last verse of the last Psalm.

Included among the Passages of Song, we find several long, composite hymns made up of verses chosen from various Psalms, all of them on the theme of praise and thanksgiving to God. Even the verses from Chronicles and Nehemiah included in this section are, in a sense, also psalms, for both are songs of thanksgiving and praise, one of them a variant of Psalm 105. The "Song of Moses" at the Red Sea is the last hymn included in this "Short Psalter" and that, too, is a song of praise recounting God's great power as demonstrated in His rescue of the Israelites from destruction on the shore of the Red Sea. The great army of Egypt advanced, but horse and rider (the invincible military device of that time) were drowned in the sea, while Israel, a pack of unarmed slaves, walked dry-shod across to safety, with the help of God.

So greatly was every verse of the Torah revered that a benediction of gratitude was recited before each reading from the
Bible, and another benediction followed that reading. The
Pesukay De Zimra are no exception. They are preceded by the
long blessing, "*Barukh She'amar,* Blessed be He Who spoke
and the world came into being. . . . O God, merciful Father,
praised by the mouth of His people. . . . Blessed art Thou, King,
extolled in Psalms of praise." After the Passages of Song are
completed, this section of the service closes with another benediction, "*Yishtabakh,* Praised be Thy Name, O our King. . . ."

HALF-*Kaddish* [13]

No prayer is as widely known among Jews, at least by name,
as the *Kaddish,* and none remains quite so thoroughly misunderstood. Perhaps its many forms, the radically different occasions on which it is recited, the lack of any reference to the
dead or to death in a prayer ostensibly devoted to the dead,
and its queer-sounding Aramaic phrases may account for the
misconceptions about it.

Something of the *Kaddish* is probably familiar to many people—though not recognized for what it is—through the *Magnifi-
cat* (May He be magnified) of the Catholic Church, and more
particularly as the *Pater Noster* (Our Father), in which both
the phrasing and the order of ideas closely resemble the first
sentences of the *Kaddish.*[14]

Just how and when the *Kaddish* originated is not altogether
clear, but it is certain that not all of it was composed at the
same time. Each sentence, sometimes each phrase, comes down
to us through devious routes, from different times and as parts
of prayers for different occasions.

The oldest part of the *Kaddish* is probably not the first paragraph beginning, "*Yitgadal,* May His great Name be magnified," but the short response of the congregation, "*Yehay Shemay Rabba Mevorakh.* . . , May His great Name be blessed for ever and ever to all eternity." This sentence, which is Aramaic, as well as its Hebrew equivalent, are both found in the Talmud and in other rabbinic sources. The Hebrew form is, of course, the older of the two; it antedates the Talmud and goes back to the days of the First Temple. At that time, before 586 B.C.E., whenever the priests would pronounce the Name of God, the people who stood in the Courts of the Temple used to bless His Name in a response very similar to the *Yehay Shemay Rabba.*[15] Their response was the *Amen,* the reaffirmation of the greatness and holiness of God. Thus it became a formula very well known to everyone through frequent repetition.

After the destruction of the Temple, the Tetragrammaton (the four letters that represent the Name of God) was no longer pronounced. Nevertheless, when the greatness and holiness of God's Name was declared in any assembly, people continued to respond with the old formula, by now probably familiar in its Aramaic form as "*Yehay Shemay Rabba.* . . ." The Rabbis accounted it very meritorious to make this declaration in public—that is, in the presence of a quorum of ten men (a *Minyan*)—and occasions were eagerly sought for its appropriate repetition.

The first short paragraph of the *Kaddish* creates such an occasion, for it reads, "*Yitgadal Veyitkadash* . . . , May His great Name be magnified and sanctified in the world which He created according to His will. And may He establish His Kingship during your lifetime and your days and during the lifetime of the whole House of Israel, speedily and soon and say ye, Amen." We do not know just when this part of the *Kaddish* was composed or when it came into general use, but the first time it is mentioned is in the second century of the Common Era by Jose ben Halafta.

Jose ben Halafta, having been ordained Rabbi in spite of the interdiction of the Roman rulers of Palestine, had to flee for his life. In Sepphoris (in northern Palestine), he established a school for the teaching of Torah which attracted some of the most brilliant young scholars of the day. Jose, a tanner by trade, was not only one of the most penetrating minds among the creators of the Mishnah, he was also famous as a remarkable religious preacher. It is he who records that in his time it was the custom to close every lecture or sermon with a prayer sanctifying the Name of God and voicing the hope that the Days of the Messiah might be very near, when not only Israel would engage in the study of Torah and worship God, but all the world would come to recognize Him and accept His Kingship. To this closing prayer the students would respond, "*Amen, Yehay Shemay Rabba* . . . , Amen, May His great Name be blessed for ever and ever." This prayer and the response to it in essence comprise the *Kaddish* as we know it.

Jose does not tell us who composed this prayer or where it came from. He seems to take for granted that everyone knew it very well. But there can be little doubt that it was an adaptation of the messianic vision of Ezekiel, as stated in his thirty-eighth chapter, verse 23: "I will be magnified and sanctified and made known in the eyes of many nations and they shall know that I am the Lord." Here we have the familiar phrase, *Yitgadal Veyitkadash* in a slightly different grammatical form. And here, very likely, is the original source of the *Kaddish* which extols God's Name and looks forward to a new world, united under His Kingship.

Since the language spoken by Jews all over the Middle East was, during the rabbinic period, largely Aramaic, most of the teaching was in Aramaic. It was therefore natural for the lecturer to close his session with a prayer in the same language. That is how the *Kaddish* happens to be recited in Aramaic rather than in Hebrew.

From the *Bet Midrash* to the *Bet Kenesset*, from the House of Study to the House of Worship, was a very short step at that time, and so the *Kaddish*, with which every period of instruction had ended, soon was taken over by the synagogue to mark the close of a religious service. In the course of time, it was added at the close of each section of the prayers, as well. That is why the Short or Half-*Kaddish* is found at the end of the Passages of Song which complete the Preliminary Prayers in the morning service.

We said above that the Rabbis accounted it very meritorious to say the "*Yehay Shemay Rabba. . . .*" in public. It is not always easy for us today to understand the urgency the Rabbis felt, the overwhelming importance they attached to the *public* declaration of God's holiness. Such declaration, we must remember, was for them an instance of *Kiddush Hashem*. God, Creator of heaven and earth and its only King, was known to them, experienced by them, but quite obviously not recognized by the pagans around them. To make God more widely known in the world, in a variety of ways, that is *Kiddush Hashem* (literally, Sanctification of the Name). Most of us think of *Kiddush Hashem* as martyrdom. To die rather than to bow to idols, to die rather than to deny God, is the supreme, the final instance of *Kiddush Hashem*. But it is far from the only one.

The broad ramifications of the concept of *Kiddush Hashem* can be understood only if we recognize that *Kiddush Hashem* is Judaism's answer to the pagan world. In rabbinic times under the Romans, the Jews were a tiny but stubbornly resistant minority, devoted to the worship of the One, Invisible God in a pagan world. Yet, according to Jewish theology, God deals with every man, any man at all, according to his deeds. "And," says a Midrash,[16] "this rule [that repentance transforms a sinner into a righteous man] applies to all the peoples of the earth, whether among Israel or among the nations." And another Midrash boldly declares, "I call heaven and earth to testify for me: whether Gentile or Israelite, whether man or woman, whether male-slave or female-slave, according to the deed done, thus does the Holy Spirit (*Ru'ah Hakodesh*) rest upon him." [17] Moreover, a non-Jew need only observe the basic ethical laws—the Seven Laws of Noah, they are called—to inherit a share in the World to Come. For a religion with such ideas, according so generous a recognition to the ethical stature to which any human being can attain, within or outside of the religion of Israel, there is patently no need to engage in an intensive missionary campaign.

But this does not exempt a Jew from the obligation to try to bring home to men a greater awareness of God, to demonstrate *Kiddush Hashem*. He can do this not only, as in exceptional cases it becomes necessary to do, by laying down his life as a martyr but continuously in his own daily life. When a Jew acts honorably in all his dealings with his fellowmen, being even more scrupulous than is required, he thereby sanctifies the Name of God, teaching others by his superior ethical behavior that God is indeed God in the world. In fact, in one Midrash is found the statement that Israel has been deliberately dispersed by God, in order that by their behavior toward their neighbors "they shall declare My Glory." And if, on the other hand, an Israelite is dishonest, he commits two sins at once. He steals and in addition, he discredits, profanes, the very Name of God; he is guilty of *Hillul Hashem*, of Profanation of the Name (of God). Unethical conduct is thus not only sinful in itself—it is, in addition, a negation of *Kiddush Hashem*, of the opportunity to make God known in the world. By nobility in the everyday transactions of life, a Jew can demonstrate God's effectiveness in the world—and that is *Kiddush Hashem.*

But God, the Invisible, requires manifold and continuing demonstration that He is indeed King over the whole world. And Jews themselves need to be reminded that God rules the world in justice and love. Meticulously ethical conduct is especially incumbent, therefore, on the man who knows Torah. For he who is learned in Torah can prove by his actions that the Torah does have efficacy in establishing very high standards of behavior, and thus he sanctifies the Name. Many a tale is told of one Rabbi or another, himself a poor man, who refused to accept a normal opportunity for gain lest there be, in such a transaction, the remote possibility that he was taking unfair advantage of another. *Caveat Emptor* (Let the buyer beware!) is a Roman, not a Jewish, proverb. The *Talmid Ḥakham* (literally, the learned) was expected to be not only a repository of theoretical knowledge of Torah, but also a man of saintly character, a living demonstration of *Kiddush Hashem.*

Public expression—that is, in a *Minyan*—of an articulate statement about God's greatness is also *Kiddush Hashem* because it constitutes another way to make God manifest in the world. So necessary is this public avowal felt to be that one Rabbi, speaking as it were in the name of God, says, "If ye are not My witnesses, then I am not God." To respond wholeheartedly, "*Yehay Shemay Rabba* . . . , May His great Name be blessed for ever and ever," is therefore *Kiddush Hashem;* it is witnessing publicly, in the presence of a *Minyan,* to God's greatness and holiness. Since without a *Minyan* the declaration of God's Kingship is not a public statement, a *Minyan* is always required for reciting the *Kaddish.*

How the *Kaddish* became a Mourners' prayer is another, related tale which will be told when we reach the Mourners' *Kaddish* in the course of the morning service, after *Alaynu.*

6

The Morning Service—
The *Shema* and Its Escort
of Benedictions

THE CALL TO PRAYER

A ll of the service that has gone before was added relatively recently, for it became part of the regular public service somewhat less than fifteen hundred years ago. As we have seen, most of these preliminary prayers had, for generations before that, been said at home prior to attending the synagogue. That is why we come upon the formal Call to Prayer here. Once it had marked the beginning of the public service. We can trace this ancient call to bless the Lord back to Temple days. Then as now, the people responded, "Blessed be the Lord Who is to be praised forever and ever." This is the response to the Name of the Lord, so reminiscent of the response in the *Kaddish*.

THE TWO BENEDICTIONS THAT PRECEDE THE *Shema*

The *Shema* is so important, so central to the service that it is not to be casually introduced. Moreover, as a direct quotation from Torah, it is necessarily preceded by a benediction of gratitude for Torah. In this case there are two benedictions, each describing a different manifestation of God's love.

The first *Berakhah* is called *Yotzer Or,* Creator of light. The most startling experience of the morning is that it is again light. The sun is shining and life can begin anew. Fearful was an eclipse of the sun to early man. The "Connecticut Yankee" traded on that terror. How wonderful, then, the renewal of light each day, when God "in mercy lights up the earth for them that dwell upon it and in His goodness renews creation every single day." Two words set the mood for this long benediction: *Berahamim,* with mercy, used often in rabbinic literature in the sense of (God's) love or compassion, and *Betuvo,* in His goodness. God's goodness, His mercy, His love for man is the dominant theme of this *Berakhah,* but not the only one. Several other ideas are associated with the major theme. In fact, a rich variety of ideas interwoven in a complex pattern is characteristic of the prayers of the *Siddur.* This quality gives them depth and interest and it helps to explain their age-long appeal to many sorts of men in all kinds of moods.

The prayer *Yotzer Or* emphasizes the fact that *God* created the sun and its light. Surrounded by the highly developed civilizations of Egypt, Persia, and Rome, Israel nevertheless continued to reject their pagan ideas completely. No culture, however intellectually or esthetically attractive, could influence Israel in favor of a belief that the sun and the moon were deities with power over men's lives. Instead, they persisted in teaching that it is *God* Who created the heavenly bodies, that all of them move or stand still only at His command and give light to man only through their Creator's mercy.

In these few sentences of the *Yotzer Or* we find also the pregnant idea that God "renews creation every day, always." Man can find the courage to begin life anew each day, freed of the barnacles of yesterday's errors, burdens, and sins, since he faces each morning a fresh new world that God has just created!

It is thus not only God's love on which the *Yotzer Or* dwells. It is on His power, majesty, and holiness as well. But the unadorned starkness of the Jewish conception of God, entirely without images, made it very difficult to conceive and to describe His majesty and greatness. One way in which Judaism succeeded in concretizing God's power and holiness, without trespassing on His absolute imagelessness, was to surround Him with a court of myriads of beings, angels who serve Him, act as His messengers, and celebrate His majesty and holiness twice every day, singing, "Holy, holy, holy is the Lord of hosts; the whole earth is full of His glory." Unique to Judaism are *these* angels, shadowy beings with a sort of half-life, not very clear even to those who first imagined them.

There are many names for angels in Hebrew. There are *Malakh* and *Shaliah*, both of which mean messenger; there are ministering beings, living beings, holy ones (also applied to saintly men), *Serafim* and *Kheruvim*. English retains the Hebrew terms, written Seraphim and Cherubim, which literally mean fiery beings and winged beings. The connotation of Cherub, in English—an angelic young child—is derived from a specific Midrash in which the Rabbis, in a play upon the Hebrew *Khe-ruvim*, say it means "like a young child." But names are rarely given to individual angels. They are usually referred to as a class of beings with no personal identity or individuality.

In rabbinic writings, moreover, angels are never mentioned in and for themselves. They are always used to make concrete or to dramatize an important religious idea such as God's love or His justice, Torah or Israel, or other value-ideas.[1] The angels act as a foil to highlight God's loving-kindness, for when they accuse man or Israel of having committed some wrong, it is God Himself Who defends man against the angels' accusations. When the angels helped rescue the little children of the Israelites at the crossing of the Red Sea, God told the angels that they had been created solely for that purpose. So shadowy and unreal are the angels that in the World to Come, says a Midrash, when sin will be no more, there will no longer be any necessity for the Angel of Death and he will cease to exist. Clearly, angels in Jewish theology have no independent existence. They sing the praises of God, surround Him as a court and act as His instruments in punishment as in reward, but they can initiate nothing by themselves.

These vague beings, though myriad in number, in no way multiply God or detract from His oneness. They are not even conceived to be supra-human, for man and indeed all the creatures on earth, are said to be more precious to God than the angels. Angels possess no life or being or will of their own. They remain always messengers and servants of God, a poetic device for making concrete and dramatic some of the highly abstract ideas of the Jewish religion. The rabbinic notion of angels is far from being dogmatic or even very clear, for there are wide differences of opinion on their constitution, description and number, and on what angels may have done in any given case. Some people undoubtedly did believe in angels as real beings but "a great part, if not all of the angelology in the Babylonian Talmud is folkloristic." [2]

The second *Berakhah* preceding the *Shema* begins, "*Ahavah Rabbah,* With abounding love hast Thou loved us, Lord our God . . ." and it continues in this vein: Thou gavest our fathers the Torah and taught them the rules of life. Show us Thy love, O God, and give us the mind to understand, learn and teach all the precepts of the Torah. Open our eyes and strengthen our will to carry out all its *Mitzvot* for we have always trusted in Thy holy, great and awesome Name. Gather us, we pray, from the four corners of the earth and bring us up into our Land again. Thou hast shown us Thine especial love in bringing us close to Thy worship. Blessed art Thou, O Lord, Who hast loved His people Israel with so great a love.

This benediction expressing gratitude for the precious gift of Torah quite naturally serves as an introduction to the *Shema*, since the *Shema* consists of several selections from the Pentateuch. It is not only when a man is called up to the reading from the Scroll of the Torah that he recites a blessing on God's love for Israel as demonstrated in His having given them the Torah. Every selection from the Bible is preceded by and closed with a benediction, even when that reading is part of the text of the prayers.

THE *Shema* AND "MONOTHEISM"

The *Shema* is the first prayer a Jewish child is taught, the last a man says on the approach of death. It is the climax of Jewish prayer. It is taken from the Bible and, as literally translated as it can be, it says, "Hear, O Israel, the Lord our God, the Lord is one." A vast literature has grown up around these words, but exactly what they do mean in the Bible and exactly what the connotations of the word *Ehad* (one) may be in that context, no one can be quite certain. To say, as some do, that this is a declaration of the unity of God, a statement of belief in monotheism, is to pull it entirely out of focus. That *Ehad* here means unique, different from other gods, is the contention of many careful scholars.[3] But that the *Shema Yisrael* does *not* imply an awareness of or an interest in the philosophic problem of monotheism is certainly obvious—from the great antiquity of the prayer, if for no other reason—and there are other reasons.

For our purposes here, it is more relevant to inquire into what the verse means as it is used in the *Prayer Book*. We must ask what it had come to mean to the Rabbis, since it was they who made it a major theme of the Siddur. And there, we are on firmer ground. We have not been left in the dark by the Rabbis, for they have inserted a short explanatory statement into the body of the *Shema*, between the first declaration and the following excerpt from Deuteronomy. This sentence becomes a rabbinic comment on the *Shema*, though its words are from an old Temple response. It reads, "Blessed be the glory of *His Kingship* for ever and ever." It is said silently by each member of the congregation and is intended to help him understand and feel the full intent of the *Shema*. When he recites the *Shema*—with eyes covered to bar any intruding distractions— each Jew is expected to accept the yoke of the Kingship of God upon himself, to try to experience God's Kingship at that moment. *Malkhut Shama'yim*, the Kingship of God (literally the Kingship of Heaven), has often been incorrectly translated as the Kingdom of God. It is used in Christian texts in that sense, as in the phrase *Thy Kingdom Come*. In Judaism, *Malkhut Shama'yim* is no Kingdom of God in some far future time; it means the Sovereignty of God over all the world, here and now. The implications of God's sovereignty over the world are vast and subtle, entering into the life of every individual who accepts it. To accept that Kingship daily is for the individual to try to rise to a mystical experience of God. That is why saying the *Shema* is in a sense the apex of the service. With these words every Jew "makes God King" as it is put poetically, in the Talmud. In these words, each individual expresses his wholehearted acceptance of a God-ruled world. Philosophical proofs that more than one Final Cause is impossible, were, it is safe to say, as remote from the minds of the Rabbis and as irrelevant to their needs as the Third Law of Thermodynamics! But a deep experiential awareness of God's undisputed govern- ance of the world dominated all their thoughts and all their teachings. This they expressed when they recited the *Shema*.

"STUDY OF TORAH"

The term "The *Shema*" is sometimes used to refer to the *Shema Yisrael*, the single sentence we have just been discussing, but more often it means that and all three paragraphs which fol- low the *Shema Yisrael*, as well.

The first paragraph (which includes the *Shema Yisrael*) is that famous quotation from Deuteronomy 6, 4-9. It tells a man to love God with all his heart and all his might and to express that love through continuous study of the Torah from earliest morning until he lies down to sleep at night, and no matter where he may be, both at home and abroad. It admonishes him to be sure to teach it to his children, too, as his richest gift to them. The phenomenon of a whole people passionately de- voted to the study of a book is peculiar to Israel and requires explanation. That the Jews were natural students, somehow more interested in the pursuit of knowledge for its own sake than other peoples, not even their greatest admirers would claim for them. Yet the highest aim in life for every Jew was the study of Torah. Social caste was determined by one's knowledge of Torah and no man was more despised than an *Am-Ha'aretz*, an ignoramus.

From the very earliest times, the drive to study Torah was part of the mind and the tradition of Israel. But study of Torah was not for them a form of intellectual play nor was it even a purely academic enterprise. In Judaism—beginning with the rabbinic period and until very recent times—"study of Torah" always implied a spill-over into action, into "doing Torah," as they expressed it. "If there is Torah in a man he takes care that he come not to transgression and sin," says a Midrash. Study of Torah, then, was motivated by the full force of the drive to live an upright life. Study of Torah meant study plus the efficacy of Torah in life; it led to the practice of *Mitzvot* and *Good Deeds* (*Ma'asim Tovim*). Only if we recognize this twofold meaning of Torah, can we appreciate its overwhelming influence on the life of the Jew.

REWARD AND PUNISHMENT

Many people are not quite certain what to make of the second long paragraph of the *Shema*. It is a quotation from Deuteronomy 11, 13-22, "And it shall come to pass if ye shall hearken diligently to My commandments," to love your God and to serve Him with all your heart, that I shall give your land rain, your crops shall prosper and you shall eat well. But if you stray away and worship other gods, the land will yield no fruit and you shall perish rapidly from off the good land which the Lord has given you. (Beyond the quotation marks, this is a free translation.) The simple cause-and-effect relation expressed here between good conduct and peaceful plenty on the one hand, and idol worship with all the immorality it implied, and banishment from the good land on the other, has mortified some modern rationalists. This section of the *Shema* has therefore been omitted from the Prayer Books of several large sections of Jewry.

But the religious man must feel, must he not, that God's

justice does operate in the world, that good must somehow triumph and that evil must in the end be doomed. What matter if this conviction about the necessary effects of good and evil be expressed in simple pastoral terms. The magnificence of the idea is in no way impaired. We do not try to rewrite the Prophets' messages because they are stated in terms of this same simple society. Moreover, no one who has lived through the terrible days of Hitler, no one who remembers how well prepared he was and how very nearly he conquered the world, how unready we were in anything but faith in the justice of our cause, can fail to find support for his confidence in God's justice. For the outcome of the war *was* the terrible debacle of the Fascists; Israel has risen like a Phoenix from its ashes, and the democracies of the world have been given another chance to build a better world.

THE *Tzitzit*—THE ROLE OF RITUAL

The last paragraph of the *Shema* is from Numbers 15, 37-41. It is another of those paragraphs that some people skip over very rapidly, almost in embarrassment, because it tells about the *Tzitzit*, the fringes a Jew is commanded to wear on his garments. It has been the fashion, for some time now, to despise the ritual laws of Judaism as relics of a primitive past and at the same time to profess admiration for its advanced ethical ideas. Many have shed the rites, intending to retain the ethics. But it is not easy to disentangle the ethics of Judaism from its ritual practices. In the Pentateuch and in the rabbinic view, both are the commands of God. The ritualistic *Mitzvot*, for example Sabbath observance, or the various tithes for the priests and for the poor, or the washing of the hands before a meal, all

these are hedged about with numerous, specific ritual regu-
lations. Yet they have become the means for the cultivation of
the inward life. They provide numerous situations in which one
is made conscious of the possibility of achieving holiness even
in the ordinary experiences of day-to-day living. In short, these
rituals surround the daily life of the Jew with an aura of holiness.

But in addition, these and many other apparently ritual observances are, in effect, powerful aids to social and personal
morality. For the tithes meant also giving food to the priests
and the poor. The ritual handwashing before meals, which was
originally part of the priests' process of purification, was, by
the Rabbis, extended to include every Jew, thus raising *all* the
people to the estate of the priests, as it were. Through a ritual
act, holiness, now no longer the exclusive prerogative of priests,
could be acquired by every Israelite. This simple ritual dram-
atized the democratization of his religion for the Jew whenever
he washed his hands in preparation for a meal. The Sabbath, of
course, because it enjoins rest on all men, master and servant
alike, and even on domestic animals, is clearly an institution of
vast social and personal moral power.

Yet it would not be fair to leave the impression that, for the
Rabbis, a sense of the ethical is only a by-product of ritual.
On the contrary, the Rabbis seek out ethical "reasons" for many
ritual commands of the Bible, indicating, thus, their recognition of the priority of the ethical. They classify *Mitzvot* as
"grave" or "light"; they call the love of God and charity "grave"
Mitzvot but *Tzitzit* a "light" *Mitzvah*, unquestioningly assign-
ing greater importance to the ethical commandments. They
prove that they are well aware of the purely ethical whenever
a clash of interests between the ritual and the ethical arises.
Then the ritual must always give way. Where human life is in
jeopardy, all the injunctions of the Sabbath are in abeyance,

for "The Sabbath is given to you, but you are not surrendered to the Sabbath," say the Rabbis in a famous Midrash.[4] Perhaps it is not as widely recognized that they abhor a man who performs a ritual act meticulously but neglects his ethical duties.[5] To those who brought choice turtle-doves to the Temple as sacrifices but who failed to do their parents' bidding, the Rabbis refer as men "who despise My [God's] Name!"

For the Rabbis, the whole of the religious life was one, and that is why they usually equated ritual and ethical commands. Both, they felt, come equally from God. But they were at the same time keenly aware of the realm of the ethical, as such. This apparent contradiction was never logically resolved by them because their religious outlook was not a logically contrived system. As the situations of human experience warranted, they emphasized now the ethical, now the ritual demands of their religious life. Ritual acts in Judaism are intended to be acts that, even when performed daily, convey with exquisite poignancy an experience of holiness. And holiness is "the imitation of God," demanding of man at once the most ethical and the most completely ritualistic behavior of which he is capable.

Now let us return to the light *Mitzvah* of *Tzitzit* as it is described in the last part of the *Shema*. The *Tallit*, originally a large toga-like garment similar to the *aba'ya* of the Beduin today, was the daily dress of the inhabitants of the desert. It has shrunk from toga to shawl, from practical garment to symbol worn because of its fringes, the *Tzitzit*. Make fringes for your mantles with a thread of blue running through them and *look* at them, says this section of the *Shema*, so that you are reminded to do all God's commandments and don't go straying off into every enticing by-path your eye lights on. In order to be able literally to fulfill the command to *look* at the *Tzitzit*, men wear the *Tallit* with its fringes only by daylight, at the morning, but not at the evening service. The *Tallit* is not worn at the afternoon service, because the *Shema*, including the section on *Tzitzit*, is not recited at that service. Even a man's clothes are enlisted in the service of God, a continuous reminder and a prod keeping him always "holy unto your God."

The last sentence of this paragraph reads, "I am the Lord your God Who brought you out of the Land of Egypt to be your God. I am the Lord your God." Thus the idea of God Who redeemed Israel from Egypt is the link between the *Shema* and the benediction on God, the Redeemer of Israel, which follows the *Shema*.

THE CLOSING BENEDICTION

The closing benediction after the *Shema* begins, "*Emet Veyatziv*, true and firmly established" are the words of the Torah, a reaction to the passages from the Torah just read. But two adjectives never suffice. A long and ardent flow of descriptive phrases is added, as if once Torah has been mentioned it cannot be left without adequate praise. In English translation the passage is not only unimpressive, it seems almost in poor taste. Yet we must remember that each language has its own style modes and post-Biblical Hebrew never spares an adjective! In the original, therefore, this short panegyric seems natural; its effect is heart-warming; it works up to a crescendo of feeling, leaving the reader, too, glowing with enthusiasm for the Torah.

The prayer then moves into its major theme. God is our King and our Redeemer, the King and Redeemer of our fathers. He has been the Help of our fathers (*Ezrat Avotaynu*) and the Shield of their children through every generation. Other than

God, we have neither king nor savior. He redeemed us from Egypt and delivered us from slavery. Their first-born perished, ours were saved; to a man, the army of the master-race drowned in the Red Sea, but the beloved, Israel, passed safely through. God has brought low the haughty and delivered the meek. At the brink of the Sea, Moses and the Children of Israel made a new song to celebrate their deliverance. "*Mi Khamokha* ... *Adonai*, Who is like unto Thee, O Lord, ... doing marvels." This long paragraph is the elaborate introduction to the benediction after the *Shema:* "Blessed art Thou, O Lord, Who has redeemed Israel."

7

The Morning Service—
The *Amidah*

INTRODUCTORY

The essentials of the prescribed service as established by the Rabbis for the morning service on week-days, Sabbaths and Festivals consist of the *Shema* and the *Amidah*. The *Amidah*, literally the Standing Prayer (because one remains standing while reciting it), has several names in addition to this one. It is called the *Shemoneh Esray*, the Eighteen, from the fact that it was originally a series of eighteen benedictions; the name was not changed, however, when another blessing was added, making the nineteen we now have in our prayers. But the *Amidah* is also called by the Rabbis *Hatefillah*, *the* Prayer, indicating its importance in the service.

These nineteen blessings were not composed by one man or in one period. Like much of the *Prayer Book*, they have a long history. The first three and the last three benedictions are very old, going back to the early days of the Second Temple when they were recited daily by the Priests. Most of the other benedictions date from the second century before the Common Era —and some scholars place them even earlier.

They are divided into three groups: The first three are blessings of Praise, the last three, of Thanksgiving. The middle thirteen, the most recent are interestingly enough, benedictions of Petition.

94

THE FIRST THREE BENEDICTIONS

The Mishnah calls the first blessing *Avot*, Fathers, from the fact that in it God is addressed as the "God of Abraham, God of Isaac and God of Jacob." This reference to our ancestors implies no nostalgia for the "good old days," nor does it indicate a sophisticated interest in history. It is instead, an expression of the rabbinic idea of *Zekhut Avot*, the Merit of the Fathers. *Zekhut Avot* represents the moral link between the generations, the idea that we are all, in some sense, involved in each others' lives. It insists that the good or ill we do reflects on our parents and on our children and, in ever larger circles, on the society in which we live; in short, that there is such a thing as "corporate personality." Associated with an awareness of a corporate personality, is the firm belief in "corporate responsibility." [1] These, we may point out, are not merely theological ideas. The responsibility of society for the sins of its members is beginning to affect social legislation increasingly in our time. Delinquency, prison management, housing, are only a few areas in which we have come to accept the implications of corporate responsibility.

The second *Berakhah* is in praise of God's love. God's "quality of mercy is not strained." It is available, says the *Berakhah*, to everyone, to the fallen, to the sick, the imprisoned, and even to the dead. For who, they felt, was more in need of God's mercy than the helpless dead! All these are examples of *Gemilut Ḥasadim*, Deeds of loving-kindness. *Gemilut Ḥasadim*, in rabbinic thought, are deeds of love done without any expectation of reward, when, in fact, no reward is possible. The concept of *Gemilut Ḥasadim* is nowhere so strikingly illustrated as in deeds done for the dead. Burying a man properly, protecting

his good name, caring for his bereaved family, all these are
Gemilut Ḥasadim, Deeds of loving-kindness, for the departed
has no power to repay kindness.

HOLINESS AND MAGIC

The third *Berakhah* is on the recurrent theme of God's holiness, amplified into the longer *Kedushah* when the Reader repeats the *Amidah* at a public service. As we have already
pointed out, holiness in Judaism is not a quality usually inherent in things. It is a quality of God himself. That the Jewish
idea of holiness represents one form of the revolt against magic
may seem surprising. Yet the difference between religion and
magic lies fundamentally in the answers one gives to these questions: What *is* holiness? And, what does magic *do?* Magic,
like science, must produce results. Holiness, on the contrary,
has no efficacy. It cannot be used to produce anything, except
perhaps more holiness. Nor is holiness a weird, awesome power
to be wielded only by a priest; at least, not in Judaism. You and
I, any Jew, or any man for that matter, can himself acquire
holiness when he imitates God. As God is merciful and gracious,
say the Rabbis, as God is long-suffering and abundant in loving-kindness, so be thou long-suffering and abundant in loving-
kindness, and merciful. What has been omitted from this list
of qualities of God which man must strive to imitate is very
significant, for we are not told to imitate God's quality of
justice—only His mercy, His love. Yet the cultivation of these
qualities of character is only one facet of the discipline required for the cultivation of holiness. Holiness itself can be acquired only through constant effort. The whole spectrum of
Jewish religious practices and the ideas that inform them are

intended to help us become more sensitive to that dimension of life known as holiness.

THE MIDDLE SECTION—PETITIONS

The fourth *Berakhah* expresses our gratitude for the distinctively human gift of wisdom and understanding: "Favor us, from Thy store, with knowledge, understanding and wisdom." To grasp a new fact, to acquire some new understanding of relationships or causes, just to be more aware of the world we live in, is an itensely creative experience.

God's help in the striving for repentance, for a return to Him through Torah and worship is the theme of the fifth benediction. The sixth is the short daily confessional which closes on the hopeful note: "Blessed art Thou, O Lord, gracious and abundantly generous in forgiving." The fifth and sixth blessings deal with Torah both as study and as practice. For the Rabbis use the term *Torah* in the double sense of study of Torah and its pragmatic effect on conduct. For example, they contrast an individual who "did Torah" with one who "did evil." But even when Torah is not used in the sense of good conduct, it is very often coupled with proper behavior in the rabbinic cliché, "Torah and *Ma'asim Tovim*, Torah and Good Deeds." Study of Torah spills over into action; it teaches a man right conduct and keeps him from evil: "Blessed be the Omnipresent . . . Who gave the words of Torah to Israel that they might learn from them ethical conduct in order that their sins should not multiply in the world." [2] Moreover, Torah is a means of repentance and reconciliation with God. A Midrash, speaking in the name of God, says: "My children, come and penetrate into the words of the Torah, and see what I have written for you [in order] to forgive your transgressions and to take away your iniquities and to cause your sins to pass away from before My countenance." [3] These implications of the idea of Torah explain how a *Berakhah* on Torah came to be included in the prayers for repentance and forgiveness. A lapse in devotion to Torah is at the same time a lapse in good or proper behavior.

The seventh blessing is on God as the Redeemer of Israel, an idea we have already met at the end of the *Shema*. Through the generations, it was God alone Who fought the battles of Israel against its overwhelmingly powerful enemies. Jews regularly recall the Exodus from Egypt on Passover and on many other occasions, the Maccabean War on *Hanukkah,* and the fight against Haman on *Purim*. We, in our time, witnessed the victorious outcome of the War for Independence in 1948. Thus Israel's vivid personal sense of God as the Redeemer of Israel has led them, in every dark hour, to turn to Him, their Redeemer, as their first and only Savior.

The eighth *Berakhah* is a plea for good health and healing, and special prayers for the very sick may be introduced at this point. Good health is normally basic to human happiness but to make of religion a monolithic instrument designed only to promote man's health is to debase religion. It is to wash out of it the variety of motives and ideals that enrich and dignify human life. In Judaism, the desire for good health is considered perfectly justifiable, and God, the Source of all bounty, is also looked to as the supreme Healer. But the prayer for health remains only *one* of the nineteen benedictions of the *Amidah*. Because the Jewish religion turns our minds to the needs of our fellow-men and to the needs of Israel as a whole, because it does not encourage the individual to become preoccupied with himself and his own needs, even with his own spiritual needs, the notion has gotten about that Judaism has no interest in the private anguish of the individual soul or in the troubles and problems he must face daily. This is, of course, an entirely mistaken notion. There are many examples of profoundly personal prayers in the Jewish liturgy. Several of them are here in the *Amidah,* where personal petition is given expression in the fifth, sixth, eighth and ninth benedictions, and before the close of the sixteenth.

The ninth *Berakhah* is the prayer for a beneficent nature. We live today so sheltered from heat and cold and storm, so independent of the elements, that only in a year of drought or when some catastrophic upheaval of nature overwhelms us, do we become aware of our dependence on God's mercy for the conditions necessary to life on earth. Only when hurricane and flood remind us of our tragic helplessness do we sense our need for God's loving care, His *Middat Rahamim,* in the management of natural forces. Only in such crises are we apt today to feel the full force of this *Berakhah* on a beneficent nature.

The tenth *Berakhah* treats of the *Kibbutz Galuyot,* the Ingathering of the Exiles. Not since Ezra's time (about 450 B.C.E.)—and even then on a much smaller scale—has any generation of Jews seen so tremendous an ingathering of exiles, come together from the four corners of the earth, as have we in our time. It is nearly unbelievable—this prayer has been answered now, after two thousand years of daily repetition!

The meaning of the eleventh *Berakhah* is not altogether clear, but it may be related to the preceding prayer for the return of the exiles and the establishment of an independent government for Israel with its own just courts. Unfortunately most of the translations miss some of the connotations suggested by the repetition of the word *Tzedakah* (and its verb form). Since this is a rabbinic prayer, *Tzedakah* here means *love,* and the prayer should be rendered thus: "Restore our judges as of old. . . . Rule Thou alone over us, O Lord, in loving-kindness and in compassion and deal lovingly with us in judgment. Blessed art Thou, O Lord, King Who loves [both] charity [in the sense of charitableness, love] *and* judgment." An interesting confirmation of this interpretation is the fact that during the Ten Days of Repentance, between the New Year and the Day of Atonement, when man and his acts are being judged on High—at that time, the word *Tzedakah* is omitted, and the benediction ends, "God, King of judgment."

The twelfth *Berakhah* is the latest to have been added to the *Amidah*. It was inserted probably some time during the first century of the Common Era, and brought the total number of benedictions to nineteen, though the name of the prayer remained, as we have said, the *Shemoneh Esray*, the "Eighteen." Its wording has so often been modified and corrected by Jews and by Christian censors that it is no longer clear what the original text may have been. Whatever the terms used, we do know that this *Berakhah* was so worded as to make it impossible for a member of any of the various Jewish sects of the time to lead the community in prayer. Israel seethed with numerous splinter groups and religious sects in those days, at the turn of the era, and the problem of the dominant group, the Pharisees, was to keep Judaism from becoming clouded and confused by the extremes of religious opinion and practice then rife. Something of the activities, beliefs and practices of several of these sects has been revealed in the Dead Sea Scrolls.

Unfortunately, in the Middle Ages, Jews were sometimes the victims of Jewish informers, traitors who reported all kinds of Jewish "crimes" to church or government officials. The wording of this twelfth *Berakhah* was changed, therefore, to signify an appeal for divine help against these *Malshinim*, slanderers.

JUDAISM AND THE IDEA OF CONVERSION

The thirteenth *Berakhah* turns abruptly to a far pleasanter theme. It is a special blessing for the choice spirits of Israel, for the righteous (*Tzadikim*), for the pious (*Ḥasidim*), for the elders of the people and for the righteous (or true) converts —and all these are classed together. The *Ger Tzedek,* the true convert, was indeed lovingly regarded in Judaism.

The very notion of *Ger,* convert, was a rabbinic novum. In polytheism, conversion was unnecessary, for if a man changed his abode, he could worship the god of the new place with no strain on his conscience—there was always room for one more, among many gods! When a land was conquered, its gods gave way to the rulers' gods, or a simple syncretism obtained. But when God is conceived as God alone in the world, and other gods are only idols of wood and stone, without power or reality, then one either worships God or remains a pagan, an idol-worshipper; no compromise, no syncretism is possible. This, of course, accounts for the intransigence and martyrdom of the Jews in the face of the demands of Antiochus and their later Roman rulers that the Jews as loyal citizens bow before the image of the Emperor. Quite naturally, other peoples regarded the Jews as merely unnecessarily stubborn.

In the Bible, when a non-Israelite had lived in Israel for some time, he was called a *Ger,* a sojourner. He had certain rights and privileges as a *Ger* under Jewish law, but he was not a convert in our sense. It is in rabbinic times that we first find the idea of a convert, a man who may live anywhere, but who, by changing his ideas about God and the world, and by changing his habits of life, can become a Jew. There were many converts to Judaism from among the Romans and the

Near Eastern peoples in the first centuries of the Common Era. It is ridiculous to think that honest proselytes ever were or are unwelcome in Judaism. The very notion of conversion is a Jewish invention!

The fourteenth *Berakhah* is on God, Builder of Jerusalem, another aspect of the prayer for the return to the Land. God's return to His Temple on Mt. Zion is at once the symbol and the motive for the reëstablishment of Israel on its land and the restoration of the House of David to its throne.

The fifteenth *Berakhah* reiterates the idea of restoration to Zion but stresses the messianic aspect of the return of "the Shoot of David."

The sixteenth *Berakhah* closes this middle section of the *Amidah* with a prayer for the favorable acceptance of the first fifteen benedictions and a reiteration of our confidence that God hears and will give heed to our prayers.

It is here, before the close of this benediction, that provision is made for each man to pour out his heart in prayers of a private nature if he feels the benedictions of the *Amidah* have not adequately expressed all his feelings or all his needs. We must not forget that the *Amidah* is said silently by each man alone, guided by the community prayers, but not limited to them.

THE CLOSING SECTION—THANKSGIVING

The seventeenth *Berakhah* repeats the theme of God's return to Zion.

The eighteenth *Berakhah* is given in two forms, one to be said silently by the individual when he recites the *Amidah* by himself, the other to be said by the congregation during the Cantor's public repetition, though the second, slightly different version is not strictly a *Berakhah* in form. "*Modim Anahnu*," it says, "We acknowledge that Thou art our God and the God of our fathers. . . ." Once again we express our gratitude to God for our very lives, for all "His *Nissim* [necessarily but incorrectly translated miracles] that are with us every day" and at all times. The term *Nissim* is one of those Hebrew words that it is almost impossible to translate. The meaning of *Nissim* is twofold. It does sometimes refer to what we call miracles, events which cannot be explained by natural law. The most striking example of a *Nes* (singular of *Nissim*) in the literal sense of miracle is the parting of the Red Sea to allow the Israelites to pass over dry shod and its equally miraculous flooding over when the Egyptians tried to follow them across.

But there is another sense, for which there is no equivalent in English, in which rabbinic Judaism uses the term *Nissim*. *Nissim* also refers to those normal events of our daily lives in which God's providential care is evident. In the Midrash, are found examples of the "*Nissim* that are with us every day:" A man recovers slowly from a serious illness; another walks in the woods and just escapes a poisonous snake that suddenly flees instead of striking him. And all of us, in an experience not at all cataclysmic, get our daily bread; we live in a world that is full of the things we need for our comfort. In these things, the Rabbis saw the Hand of God, His "full, open and generous Hand," as they put it in the Grace after Meals. "Every day Thou doest *Nissim* and wonderful things for us and no man [even] knoweth [of them]," says a Midrash.[4]

The *Modim* prayer in the *Amidah* (the eighteenth benediction) indicates how widespread among the people was the recognition of the place of normal *Nissim* in their lives. They regarded it as perfectly natural to say, "We will give thanks to Thee . . . for Thy *Nissim* which are daily with us . . . and for Thy wonders and benefits that are with us at all times. . . ."

When the Reader repeats the *Amidah,* he recites the priestly blessing between the eighteenth and the nineteenth benedictions. In the Temple, it was the Priests who recited this blessing daily, at the end of the *Amidah.* After the destruction of the Temple, and as late as the ninth century (in Saadia's time), the descendants of the *Kohanim* (Priests) continued to recite the blessing as part of the regular synagogue service every day. That custom, for one reason or another, seems to have fallen into neglect except in Israel where the *Kohanim* still recite the priestly blessing every Sabbath. What we have now in the Reader's recital of the blessing is in the nature of a substitute for the blessing by the Priests, a vestige of the Temple service.

On the Festivals, however, it is still the Priests—that is, their contemporary descendants everywhere—who continue to exercise the privilege of calling upon God to bless His people. For, it is important to note, it is not the Priests who bless the people at a service; it is God. The Priest merely invokes God and calls upon Him to bless the people. The words of that benediction are, "May *the Lord bless* thee and watch over thee, may *the Lord* make His countenance to shine upon thee. . . ." In Judaism, only God can bless, as only God can forgive. No man, layman or Priest, ever acquires these powers.

The last *Berakhah,* the nineteenth, is the prayer for peace. The *Kaddish* and the Grace after Meals, as well as the *Amidah,* all close with a fervent plea to God to bring peace "upon us and upon all Israel."

But Jews seem never to have had enough of prayer and so, after the last benediction, we find a "private meditation." Many private meditations, added to the prescribed prayers of the *Amidah,* have been recorded in rabbinic literature. They were composed by men of unusual sensitivity and devotion, and often of great poetic gifts as well. The one chosen for inclusion in the *Prayer Book* is characterized by a gentle and humble spirit. It was written by Mar ben Rabina in the fourth century of the Common Era. "O my God," he prays, "guard my tongue from evil and my lips from speaking with guile. Even to those who curse me, let me be silent. May I be as the dust before everyone. Open my mind to Thy Torah and let me pursue Thy commandments with my whole soul. . . ." Later, a few sentences were added from another source and the whole was closed with an appropriate verse from Psalms, "May the words of my mouth and the meditations of my mind find favor before Thee, O Lord, my Rock and my Redeemer." Contrary to the usual English translation of *Layv* as *heart,* in this prayer, we have translated *Layv* as *mind;* for ancient peoples, among them the Jews, looked upon the heart, not the brain, as the physical seat of the mind. It is therefore misleading to use the word heart in English, where it has entirely different connotations.

PRAYERS AND REPETITION

Ours is the age of the jet plane, of spot announcements and condensed books. The slow pace of the prayers, the long time required for their recital, and the repetition of the same themes are unappealing to many people today. Most revisions of the *Prayer Book* have, therefore, begun as abridgments and ended as a series of brief statements with little emotional drive to recommend them. We misunderstand the nature of prayer if we demand brevity of it. An essay makes its point as clearly and as briefly as possible, but prayer is not an essay, not even an essay on theology. It aims not to explain but to produce a mood through the medium of words. All mood-inducing speech is rhythmic, repetitious. Poetry is rhythmic speech. It often repeats a word or a phrase, achieving its emotional impact by form as well as by idea. Song has recurrent refrain, producing its feeling-tone in part through repetitive form.

Prayer is poetry—at least great prayers are—but all prayers repeat their themes and their key phrases again and again until we begin to respond to their mood, until our natural preoccupation with our own worries, irritations, and limitations yields to the larger outlook of the prayers. Slowly, our perspective broadens and we begin to feel a little of the great universe around us, perhaps even to catch a glimpse of what is meant by an experience of God and a sense of His nearness. This may be the explanation for the healing effect of repeated periods of prayer. Each repetition reinforces the mood only imperfectly achieved when first we come to pray.

8

The Morning Service
(Concluded)

CONFESSION AND SUPPLICATION

For centuries the *Amidah,* concluded the formal service. Gradually, a few of the many individual devotions available were made part of the service itself—and there were many to choose from, for everyone who could, wrote prayers. A natural sifting process probably retained the most inspired of them, for this part of the service was not fixed until after the invention of printing.

The private daily Confession of our *Siddur,* so moving in its stark simplicity and brevity, is, however, of rather early origin. "O Merciful and Gracious One, I have sinned before Thee. O Lord, full of mercy, have compassion upon me and accept my supplications." Until the thirteenth century Jews still prostrated themselves, face to the ground, when they said this prayer. Now, complete prostration is reserved for *Yom Kippur* during the recital of the *Alaynu.*

It may seem odd to find the confession here near the end of a long service, but in fact it is wisely placed, for in this way, one comes to it properly prepared. Wholehearted confession which involves much more than merely reciting a formula is not easily achieved, especially by modern man, and a long period of preparation is a necessary prelude.

107

Psalm 6 follows. It is an appropriate complement to the short confession for it continues in the same vein and intensifies the effect of that simple statement. David pleads for God's mercy with the violence and passion so characteristic of him. "Be gracious unto me, O Lord, for I am withered away. Heal me, O Lord, for my very bones are terrified. . . . I am weary with my groaning; every night I make my bed swim; I melt my couch with my tears. . . ." But at the end of the Psalm, "The Lord hath heard my supplication; the Lord will accept my prayer. . . ." David is comforted, calmer after his confession, certain now of God's compassion and forgiveness.

READING THE TORAH

Reading the Torah at the service is not relegated to one day a week, on the Sabbath. The Torah is also read, of course, on Festivals, on *Purim,* on Fast Days (both morning and afternoon), and on *Rosh Ḥodesh* (First Day of the Month) but special readings are assigned to those days and we refer here only to the occasions when the regular weekly Portion is read. The first section of the portion for the following Sabbath is read at three services before the full reading on Sabbath morning—first, at the previous Sabbath Afternoon Service, then on Monday morning, and again on Thursday morning. These days divide the week into nearly even parts and it is thought that the second and the fifth days were chosen because on those days people were in the habit of gathering in the nearest large town for business, for court sessions, and perhaps just to exchange a word with their isolated neighbors. It seemed like a good time to read some of the Torah at these services so that more people would hear it. And this has remained the weekly pattern of Torah reading to this day.

On Mondays and Thursdays—that is, on the week-days the Torah is read—additional penitential prayers and supplications are also included in the service, except on personal or general Jewish days of rejoicing. Strangely enough, the penitential prayers are also omitted in a house of mourning or on Fast Days, as if the sorrow of those days is too great to suffer these mournful prayers in addition.

When the Torah is read in the synagogue on Monday and Thursday mornings and on Sabbath afternoons, only three men are called up to the Scroll to "read." These three are a *Kohen,* a *Levi* and an Israel.

On the blessings before and after the reading, and on the implications of Torah as part of the service of worship, see the discussion below, in Chapter 13, on the Sabbath Morning Service.

CONCLUSION OF THE SERVICE

Whether or not the Torah is read at a service, *Ashray,* Psalm 145 (and several verses from other Psalms) is recited by the congregation at this point. Like most of the Psalms, it is universal in scope. Israel is not once mentioned in it; there is no Jewish "local color." It tells of God's beneficence to all creation, "Gracious and loving is the Lord, slow to anger and great in loving-kindness. The Lord is good to all and His tender mercies are over all His works. . . . His Kingship is eternal and His rule continues in every generation. . . . The Lord supports all that fall and raises up all that are bowed down. . . . The Lord is nigh to all who call upon Him, to all who call upon Him in truth. . . . Let all flesh bless His holy Name for ever and ever." No wonder many peoples and many religions have borrowed from the Psalms for their liturgies.

After *Ashray*, the *Kaddish Titkabal* is recited. *Titkabal* means literally, "May it [this service of prayer] be accepted." This *Kaddish* is recited by the Reader as a fitting close to the service. The text is essentially the same as in all forms of the *Kaddish*, with the addition of the sentence, "May the prayers and supplications of all Israel be accepted by their Father Who is in heaven." Here again we see that the *Kaddish* is not a prayer for the dead but a hymn of praise that marks the close of a service.

"*Alaynu Leshabay'ah*, It is our duty to praise the Master of all and to tell of the greatness of the Creator. . . ." Thus begins a prayer which is part of every service. We discussed some aspects of the idea of God's Kingship when we studied the *Shema*. But a single prayer does not exhaust all the nuances of meaning in so grand a conception as God's Kingship. There is a phrase in rabbinic Hebrew which means the "Yoke of the Kingship of Heaven." The Yoke of God's Kingship is a heavy one and it needs to be lifted up anew each day, many times, and in many different ways. In the *Alaynu* prayer the meaning of God's Kingship is spelled out in some detail. It is He, says this prayer, Who made heaven and earth and He is King over all the world; there is none else. All false gods and all idolatries will one day be recognized for the vanity they are and will be utterly destroyed. All the wicked will turn to God and at that time "*all* the inhabitants of the earth . . . will accept the Yoke of Thy Kingship." The prayer conjures up a vision of one mankind united under the Kingship of Heaven.

It is easy to give at least intellectual assent to so noble a conception as the one contained in this second paragraph of the *Alaynu*. But its first paragraph has not always been as sympathetically understood. Israel, in the introductory section, seems to be filled with smug satisfaction over its good fortune, over its superiority to other peoples. "We must praise the

THE MORNING SERVICE (CONCLUDED)

Master of all," the prayer begins, ". . . since He did not make us like the peoples of all other lands [idol-worshippers] . . . nor is our portion like theirs, nor our fate like that of their multitudes." Let us not forget that these words, this delight in their own happy lot is expressed by the hounded, the persecuted, the already scattered remnant of Israel. Yet there is no intent to delude themselves here. They explain at once why they believe these words to be no less than the literal truth. "For *we* bend the knee and prostrate ourselves and acknowledge the King of the kings of kings, the Holy One, blessed be He." This, they claim, is their unique good fortune, for this they are grateful, and not for any peculiar virtue or privilege which is available to them alone.

On the contrary, far from trying to remain in sole possession of their exalted privilege of worshipping God, Israel always looked forward to the day when "All the inhabitants of the earth will recognize and know that to Thee every knee must bend. . . . Before Thee, O Lord our God, will they fall and prostrate themselves . . . and all of them will accept the Yoke of Thy Kingship. . . . At that time will the Lord be [recognized as] one and His Name one [for all mankind]."

Some time in the twelfth or thirteenth century, this prayer was taken from the service of *Rosh Hashanah* (the New Year) and appended to the daily prayers. So many of the Jewish martyrs of the time, contemporary records report, died intoning the *Alaynu*, proclaiming God's Kingship with their last breath, that it was deemed right for everyone to recite it every day. Martyrdom had unfortunately become for the Jew an almost daily occurrence.

MOURNERS' *Kaddish*

The Mourners' *Kaddish* is recited by the mourners in a congregation after *Alaynu,* very near the end of the service.
Mourners are those who have lost a close relative within the
past eleven months or those who are remembering the anniversary of the death of such a relative. Originally, as we have
seen,[1] the *Kaddish* was a hymn to the greatness and holiness
of God's Name, recited after a lesson devoted to the study of
Torah or at the close of a service of worship. We must now
trace the steps by which it became also a mourners' prayer to
be said in memory of the departed.

The key to the problem lies in a recognition of two important ideas that are involved in a recital of the *Kaddish.* One is
the mighty role of Torah in Jewish spiritual life and the other
is the great merit attached by the Rabbis to the recital of a
formula that constituted *Kiddush Hashem,* Sanctification of
God's Name. *Kaddish,* recited at a public service, offered such
an opportunity because it created the occasion for the response
made by the congregation: "May His great Name be blessed
for ever and ever."

At one time, lectures on Torah were given in the house of
mourning during the week after the death of a learned man as
a means of honoring his memory; later, this period was pro-
longed and the lectures were continued for a whole year. At
the end of each discourse the lecturer would naturally close
with the *Kaddish,* and the mourners and visitors present would
respond with: "May His great Name be blessed for ever and
ever." But in order not to shame anyone, this way of honoring
the memory of the learned was extended to include everyone.
This was perhaps the beginning of the associaton of the *Kaddish* with paying respect to the memory of the dead.

A single social "accident" seldom produces a new institution. Several events, ideas, or previously accepted modes of behavior converge to produce the new institution. The development of the *Kaddish* for Mourners is an excellent case in point. We can glean more of the processes by which it expanded in meaning from the discussion of two related matters in the Midrash. When the father dies, a Midrash says, his influence lives on in his son; how do you know what manner of man the father was? Look to the son; if he takes an active part in the discussions at the House of Study, if he repeats some Torah his father taught him, then he honors his father's memory. For people will say, "So-and-so must have been a man of learning and good deeds to have taught his son thus." After the discussion of Torah in which the son had taken a leading part, he would naturally recite the *closing Kaddish* and those present would respond as usual, "May His great Name be praised. . . ." But in the course of time, the custom of studying Torah in honor of the dead lapsed, and only the recital of the *Kaddish* by the bereaved son remained as the expression of his respect. In effect, the *Kaddish* had become a short cut, the prayer for mourners.

In this way the son was still able to honor the memory of his father—just by reciting the *Kaddish*. For though study of Torah is so important, certainly *Kiddush Hashem* (Sanctifying God's Name) is also a very "grave" *Mitzvah*. And this *Mitzvah* the son performed when he recited the *Kaddish* at a public service and elicited from the congregation the response, "*Yehay Shemay Rabba*, May His great Name be praised. . . ." Then the people would ask, in the language of the Midrash, "Who was his father who taught him thus?" In this setting, too, the point is made that when the son recites the *Kaddish*, he causes God's Name to be sanctified by the congregation and he thus recalls to himself and to others the father who taught him Torah and *Mitzvot*.

The first specific mention of the *Kaddish* as a mourners' prayer is found in the *Mahzor Vitry*, a thirteenth century compendium of Jewish prayers. Though the *Kaddish* had probably been accepted as a mourners' prayer some centuries earlier, the fact that it is called the "Orphans' *Kaddish*" for the first time in the thirteenth century does mark it as a relatively late institution. It was in the Middle Ages that it gained such a strong hold on the people and became, in popular practice, so completely a prayer for the dead. This was no doubt in part due to the fact that masses for the souls of the departed were so much part of the religion of the people around them and that Judaism had no equivalent institution.[2]

The Rabbis of that time struggled against the growth of popular notions that the *Kaddish* was of some intercessionary value to the dead. For example, Rabbi Abraham ben Ḥiyya Ha-Nasi (who died in 1136) wrote, "All who think that the deeds of his sons . . . which they do for his sake after his death —that is, when they pray for him—that these help him, such thoughts are pure imagination and vain hopes in the eyes of all the wise [*Ḥakhamim*] and all people of science." (Quoted in Hebrew by Pool, in his book *The Kaddish*. Mine is a very literal translation.)

Abraham Hurwitz, a learned Rabbi of the sixteenth century wrote, "Let the son keep a particular *Mitzvah* which his father commanded him to hold to and if he carries it out, it is accounted more than the Kaddish. The same is true also of daughters. For the Kaddish is not a prayer that the son should say for the father before God that He may raise him from *Sheol* [Limbo, or the gave] but it is merit . . . for the [name of] the dead when his son sanctifies the Name [of God] and [causes] the congregation to respond after him, '*Amen. Yehay Shemay Rabba Mevorakh*, Amen. May His great Name be blessed for ever and ever.' "[3]

THE TEN COMMANDMENTS

The Ten Commandments were read in the Temple every day just before the recitation of the *Shema*. Surprisingly enough, they are no longer part of the prescribed service, though they are still recited in some synagogues at the end of the morning service. An interesting bit of the history of the Jewish religion can be read between the lines in the story of the eclipse of the Ten Commandments.

They were removed from their place in the service by the Rabbis! For so drastic a step there must have been a very good reason—and there was. During the years just before, and for several hundred years after the Common Era, Judaism was plagued by sectarians of various kinds. Some left the fold but continued to be a problem to the parent group. Those who remained within continued to create difficulties of all sorts. Apparently some of the sectarians, notably the early Christians, taught that only the Ten Commandments were to be accepted by everyone as God's will, but that the rest of the Bible had been given only to Israel as punishment for its sins and it was therefore now superseded by the new revelation, the New Testament. In order to prevent derogation of all the rest of the Torah by placing undue emphasis on the Decalogue, the Rabbis then removed the reading of the Ten Commandments from their usual place in the service just before the *Shema*. And there, at the end of the service, recited only in some synagogues, and then only after the *Tallit* and *Tefillin* have been removed, is the Decalogue to this day.

The Ten Commandments are apodictic laws against sin, and such laws are unique to Israel. Apodictic laws are laws for which no reason is given other than that God wills it so. They represent a recognition that moral laws are as indigenous to the structure of the universe as are the laws of physics, and that, like other axioms, they are not subject to proof. No one can really *prove* the validity of these basic moral laws. Any reason advanced to show that they are necessary or true will always depend upon another moral law for its justification. This is an endless chain, or a circular one, for finally one reaches a statement so general that all meaning has been washed out of it—or one returns to the beginning again. In other words, all moral values are axioms; one accepts them or rejects them. And there the matter rests. The Ten Commandments are such final moral laws. Their influence on human society, through the teachings of Judaism and the religions which took them from Judaism, has been enormous. This is due not only to the terse, vivid way they are stated but to the laws themselves and to the motivation upon which they rest—on God's will alone.

"The formulation and the spirit of the apodicitic laws are unique and original in Israel." [4] They reflect a much more advanced standard of conduct than is found elsewhere in contemporary civilizations, according to Albright. He points out that the personal reflections on wrongdoing and the lists of sins found among Babylonians or Egyptians of the second millenium before the Common Era—the probable period of the Decalogue—are "repetitious . . . and lacking in any sense of balance between important and unimportant things." [5] Archeological research, far from undermining our regard for the Ten Commandments, has only succeeded in increasing our wonder that these noble laws should have come, not from the great civilizations of Babylonia and Egypt, but out of Israel, their weakest and least important neighbor.

The Thirteen Principles of Faith of Maimonides, which appear in the *Siddur* at the end of the Morning Service, were discussed earlier in connection with *Yigdal*, a hymn based on these Principles.

9

The Afternoon Service— *Minḥah*

EVOLUTION OF THE NAME

The sun has passed the zenith and man turns again to God in prayer. Perhaps because the work of the day must go on and *Minḥah* is only a pause for spiritual refreshment, this service is the shortest of the day.

The name *Minḥah* has an interesting history. Literally, *Minḥah* is a gift or an offering; it is the name of the cereal part of the sacrifice offered twice daily in the Temple, morning and afternoon. After some time, however, the *Minḥah* came to mean only the afternoon sacrifice. Oddly enough, this came about because the victory of Elijah over the prophets of Baal occurred in the afternoon at *Minḥah* time. The story is told in the Second Book of Kings (Chapter 18) where it is said that, after the prophets of Baal had failed to prove the reality and effectiveness of their gods, it was "at the time of the offering of the *Minḥah* that Elijah, the prophet, came near and said, 'Lord God of Abraham, Isaac and Jacob, let it be known this day that Thou art God in Israel.' " And He did!

The evolution of the meaning of *Minḥah* is, then, from a twice-daily offering in the Temple, to an afternoon offering, to the afternoon prayer. This is the explanation usually given, but there is no certainty that it is the "real" one. There is another which derives the name *Minḥah,* not from the word meaning *an offering* but from a similar root meaning *to rest.* According to this explanation, *Minḥah* refers to the fact that the day is waning, coming to rest as it were. Nachmanides, the great medieval philosopher and Bible commentator, gives this explanation, and it too sounds reasonable. But which of these is correct, no one knows. Both are possible and both are poetically appealing.

THE ORDER OF THE SERVICE

No new or special prayers have been introduced for the Afternoon Service. The order of the prayers is this: Psalm 145 (*Ashray*), the *Amidah* as in the morning (with one minor change), Supplications, *Alaynu* and the Mourners' *Kaddish.* This is the form set down by Rav Amram in his *Siddur* in the ninth century and thus it has remained to our day. For a description of these prayers, see the previous chapters on the Morning Service.

On Fast Days, such as *Tishah Be'Av* (the 9th of Av), the Afternoon Service also includes a reading from the Torah, constant for all Fast Days except *Yom Kippur.* It consists of two sections from the Book of Exodus. The first is from Chapter 32, 11-14, in which Moses pleads with God not to be angry with His people, to remember His promise to Abraham, to Isaac, and to Jacob that He would cause their descendants to multiply until they were as numerous as the stars of the heavens, and to give them the Land of Israel as an inheritance. The section read ends with the verse, "And God repented Him of the evil which He had intended to do to His people." The second passage is from Chapter 34, 1-10. It is in this section that we find the famous "description" of God as He passed by Moses: "Lord, Lord God, merciful and gracious, long-suffering and abundant in goodness and truth, keeping mercy unto the thousandth generation, forgiving iniquity and transgression and sin."

The *Haftarah* (the section from the Prophets read after the portion from the Torah) is also the same for all Fast Days— again, except on *Yom Kippur*. It is from Isaiah, Chapters 55, 6 to 56, 8. It is a call to return to God "for He will abundantly pardon." It is a promise of joy and peace to come, joy and peace alike for Israel and for the stranger in the Land who seeks God. "For My house shall be called a house of prayer for all peoples." Only those who are entirely unacquainted with the Jewish liturgy can fail to appreciate its twin emphases on God's tender love and on Israel's acceptance of all mankind as equally sharing in God's love.

Minḥah was one of the first casualties of our age of hustle. But as long ago as in the rabbinic period, the Rabbis of the Talmud expressed a fear that men might overlook *Minḥah*, coming as it does in the busiest time of the day. They therefore made a particular point about not forgetting it. The Mishnah says that a man must not go to bathe or sit down to eat or even begin to study near to the time for reciting *Minḥah* before he says the prayer; "lest he forget and not pray," adds Rashi in explanation.

10

The Evening Service—*Arvit*

Ma'ariv

The Evening Service is ordinarily called *Arvit* (of the evening) in the *Prayer Book* but it is most often spoken of as *Ma'ariv*. This more popular name is also derived from a word related to the Hebrew for *evening*. It is the key word of the first benediction of the Evening Service; "*Ma'ariv Aravim*, God, Who at His word brings on the evening twilight." *Ma'ariv* in this sentence is a verb and it means *causes it to become evening*, but long ago it acquired another personality and became a noun, the name of the Evening Service.

THE ORDER OF THE SERVICE

Once we have mastered the Morning Service, the evening prayers are easy to follow. The same general pattern is closely adhered to, though the service is shorter at night.

The preface to the Evening Service is the very brief appeal for pardon, "*Vehu Rahum*, For He is merciful, forgiveth iniquity, and will not destroy. . . ." The day is done, its quota of failures and of our own inadequacies faces us as if to say, "Another day lived, and what have you done with it?" Shamefaced, we turn to God and appeal to Him for forgiveness and mercy.

Barakhu, the Call to Prayer, follows directly after this confession. It allows no time for brooding. It directs men's minds away from too much introspection and calls attention to the core of the service which is the *Shema* in its frame of four blessings. There are two benedictions before the *Shema*, as in the morning, but at the Evening Service, there are two at the close as well.

The first *Berakhah* before the *Shema* is the response to the darkness of the night, as was the parallel benediction of the morning to the wonder of the new day. At night God's love is made evident in the regularity and therefore the dependability of nature. For night always follows day and the stars are ordered "in their watches in the firmament" in complex but never erratic courses. God, Who in His wisdom and understanding directs all this rhythmic play of the great forces of nature, will continue to rule over us forever. The Rabbis never tire of telling of God's goodness to man in this as in other ways.

"*Ahavat Olam*, With everlasting love hast Thou loved the House of Israel. . . ." This is the counterpart of the second benediction before the *Shema*, the *Ahavah Rabbah*, of the Morning Service. It has been misinterpreted as an expression of great pride or of a spirit of exclusiveness on the part of Israel to say that God loves His people, Israel, with everlasting love, as if they thought themselves better than other men. But indeed that is not so. This *Berakhah*, it must be understood, is in the nature of an introduction to the *Shema* which is a reading from the Torah. How wonderful, says the *Berakhah*, that we have been given the Torah with its laws and *Mitzvot*. We rejoice in its guidance and shall study it day and night, for life and length of days are to be found in its pursuit. It is a mark of God's love that He has given us this precious gift of Torah to live by.

But, of course, *anyone* who chooses to, anyone at all, may study Torah, live the life it prescribes, and thus himself acquire the Torah, thereby becoming the recipient of God's gift as fully as if *he* had stood at the foot of Mount Sinai! A man certainly need not, according to Jewish thought, have been born a Jew to earn or possess this manifestation of God's love. Torah was given first to Israel, but not exclusively to Israel. Absolutely no inherent or biological superiority is ascribed to Israel in this benediction. The praise and the glory are all for the Torah, not for themselves.

THE DOGMAS OF JUDAISM

The first benediction after the *Shema* in the evening is very similar in theme to its counterpart in the Morning Service. It begins by asserting confidence in the Torah (the *Shema*) which has just been read and then proceeds at once to the major theme of the *Berakhah,* God as the Redeemer of Israel. God, our King, it says, redeemed us from the grasp of tyrants and has done wonderful things for us, marvels without number. He rescued us from the slavery of Egypt and caused us to conquer our enemies; He performed miracles for us in the land of Pharaoh and brought us out from among the Egyptians into everlasting freedom.

The idea of the *Yetziat Mitzra'yim,* the Exodus from Egypt, is so crucial in Judaism that belief in the fact of the Exodus through God's intervention is one of the few clearly enunciated dogmas of the Jewish religion. But one should not, for that reason, conclude that Judaism is after all a dogmatic religion with a creed its adherents are required to accept.

We must admit that there are a few dogmas in Judaism, but

nowhere in rabbinic literature—we may safely say, nowhere in the whole of the Talmud and the Midrash—are these dogmas marshaled into a creed. And there is a vast difference, psychologically and intellectually, between a few scattered dogmas and an officially established creed. Though the Rabbis invented the institution of conversion, they did not require assent to a creed, or to any beliefs for that matter, as a condition for becoming a Jew. Nor do we find any instance of a Jew who denied (*Kofer* is the Hebrew term for "one who denies") a dogma and who was then excommunicated for his denial.

Nevertheless, there are a few religious beliefs, as we have said, which Jews are expected "to acknowledge." *Modeh* is the Hebrew word for it. Yet even a dogma in Judaism does not have the completely static character we usually associate with dogma. *Mattan Torah,* Giving of Torah (by God) and even *Teḥiat Hamaytim,* the Resurrection of the Dead, are ideas handled with a marked degree of flexibility in rabbinic literature. And it is not accidental that in their discussions of the Exodus story, the Rabbis achieve no consensus on many aspects and details of the event.

Obviously, a belief is not a dogma if it represents something a man has himself experienced. But when one is asked to accept as true something he has *not* himself experienced, then that belief becomes a dogma. Now, the belief that God brought Israel up out of the land of Egypt is such a dogma. However, the Rabbis do not allow it to remain an event experienced only by someone else. Most striking is their attempt to make every individual, in every generation, so completely relive the experience of the Exodus as to make it, at least in imagination, a matter of personal experience. The Order of Service for the home for Passover Eve is called the *Haggadah.* It relates the story of the Exodus through quotations from the Bible, the rabbinic interpretations of these verses, and their explanations of the ceremonies and symbols of the Festival. Stimulated by the dramatic recital of the *Haggadah* and by the symbols for the events of the Egyptian sojourn and the Exodus presented at the *Seder,* every Jew is invited "to look upon himself as though he had gone out of Egypt . . . saying to his son, 'It is because of that which the Lord did for *me* when *I* came out of Egypt.'" There is a definite attempt here to take the events of the Exodus "out of the sphere of belief and into the sphere of experience." [1] It almost seems as if the Rabbis were struggling to escape from the confining net of dogma.

When a religion is based upon dogmas and creeds, sooner or later it will also produce its "heretics." But so minor is the role of dogma in Judaism that there is no word for heretic in Hebrew. The word nearest in meaning is probably *Apikoros,*[2] a word, be it noted, that is of Greek, not Hebrew, origin. *Apikoros* is occasionally used in the sense of a sectarian or an infidel (one who is no longer a Jew) but *Apikoros* usually means a skeptic, not strictly a heretic at all. *Min,*[2] literally another *kind* (of person), means a sectarian; it is the specific word for one who belongs to an unacceptable splinter group, separated from the main body of Judaism by its beliefs and practices. But the Jews no longer had occasion to use this word after the early centuries of the Common Era and it disappeared from use after the time of the Mishnah (about 200 C.E.).

Heretic-hunting was not a sport Jews indulged in, nor was it, for them, a state of mind which their religion encouraged.

In summary, we may say that rabbinic dogmas are few in number, are never presented as a systematic creed, and are never stated as if they were the basic principles of Judaism. On the other hand, the Rabbis do state clearly that the proper attitude toward certain beliefs is "acknowledgment," but imaginative personal experience and some room for individual differences erase the static quality of dogma in rabbinic Juda-

ism and prevent the flexible pattern of its religious thought
from being constricted into a few dogmatic beliefs.

In the evening, there are two benedictions after the *Shema*.
The second one is the prayer called *Hashkivaynu* (Cause us to
lie down), from its first word. It is the benediction on God
as the Watchguard of Israel. One of the most touching figures
of speech in the *Siddur* is found in this prayer for God's protection. What dangers and troubles does a man not conjure
up in the weary hours of the night! From them all, he seeks
surcease in the safest place he can imagine, near to God. "Hide
us in the shadow of Thy wings," he prays every night, "for
Thou art God, our Guardian and our Deliverer; Thou art God,
a compassionate and merciful King."

The rest of the Evening Service is substantially like the
morning prayers.

11

Welcoming the Sabbath

Shabbat BEGINS AT HOME

Judaism has always been a uniquely home-centered religion. Perhaps this is so because it is an old religion with an unusually long, unbroken tradition reaching back into patriarchal times, when the firstborn, the eldest of the clan, was also its priest. But whatever the historical reason, for many centuries the father, the mother, and even the children of a family have been their own functionaries in the performance of Jewish ritual. And the setting has been quite simply, their own home.

Though a *Minyan* or quorum of ten—that is, a synagogue—is desirable for the conduct of a service, and a few prayers do require the presence of a *Minyan*, yet each Jew can recite a complete service of prescribed prayers at home three times a day "without benefit of clergy." Benedictions on bread, on wine, on the *Lulav*, on the *Sukkah*, on *Matzah*, the *Kiddush* and Grace after Meals, all these and many more prayers are recited at home. The *Seder* on Passover is conducted at home and a large part of every Festival's ritual is its home celebration. The Sabbath begins with a *Berakhah* recited by the wife when she lights the Sabbath candles at home and ends with the benedictions of the *Havdalah* Service conducted by the husband, at home. These are some of the religious ceremonies that enrich Jewish home life.

Any notion that the religious status of woman in Judaism is an inferior one must be modified by the recognition of her share in creating "the Holiness of the Day," *Kedushat Ha'yom*, for the Sabbath in her own home and for the members of her own family. For when she lights her Sabbath candles and recites the benediction, "Blessed art Thou, O Lord our God, . . . Who has hallowed us . . . and commanded us to kindle the Sabbath light," at that moment a woman causes the Sabbath to begin in her home, by her will, as it were. Though there are, according to Jewish law, some conditions that modify this statement, they do not nullify it.

She covers her eyes as she says the benediction to create a legal fiction! Ordinarily a *Berakhah* precedes the act which it celebrates. For example, the blessing on bread (*Hamotzi*) precedes the act of eating the first morsel, the blessing on the *Tallit* precedes putting on the *Tallit*, and so on. But the benediction on the Sabbath candles cannot precede the act of *lighting* the candles, for the benediction ushers in the Sabbath and once the Sabbath has begun, it would not be permitted to kindle the fire for the candles. Therefore the legal fiction. A woman lights the candles, covers her eyes so that for her the candles are not lit, says the *Berakhah*, uncovers her eyes and lo! there are the candles, properly burning, and the *Berakhah* said at the right time.

Often we hear this candle-lighting ceremony referred to as "blessing the candles," an expression literally translated from the Yiddish, *Benschen licht*. This is a singularly inept description of the rite. For as we have pointed out several times, there are in the Jewish religion no holy objects other than the Scroll of the Torah, or objects which contain parts of the Torah on parchment, such as the *Tefillin* or the *Mezuzah*. The Sabbath candles, however, are certainly not holy and no benediction is intended to make them so. The words of the blessing themselves clearly describe its intent. The *Berakhah* says, "Blessed art Thou, O Lord our God . . . Who has *hallowed us* by His

commandments and commanded us to light the Sabbath light."
It is we who are hallowed in the rite, obviously, and not the
candles. The *Mitzvah*, the ritual act, like every ritual act, is
intended to serve us as a stimulus for experiencing holiness and
is not meant to invest objects with holiness. The expression
"blessing the candles," in Yiddish or in English, is an interpretation of the rite borrowed from other religions and does not
reflect the significance of ritual in Judaism. The formula used
in every benediction accompanying a rite says, "*Kiddeshanu
Bemitzvotav,* He [God] makes *us* holy through His *Mitzvot.*"
These words clearly limit the operation of the idea of holiness
in Jewish ritual to its human impact.

For the Rabbis the source of God's commands was, of course,
the Torah—that is, the Bible. When they said, in a benediction, "God commanded us," they meant just that. And this is
what we find in the benediction on lighting the Sabbath light.
"Blessed art Thou, O Lord our God, . . . Who has hallowed us
and *commanded* us (*Vetzivanu*) to kindle the Sabbath light."
But the Bible does not ordain the kindling of the Sabbath light!
There is not even the suggestion of such a ceremony in the
Bible. In spite of this, the blessing does say, ". . . and He commanded us. . . ." How could the Rabbis allow this to be said?

The custom of lighting a special ceremonial light for the
Sabbath was well established by the second century of the
Common Era,[1] but the inclusion of a blessing in the ceremony
came generations later and the Rabbis of the Talmud themselves composed that blessing. They seem to have had no hesi-
tation about couching it in the same terms they used for blessings ordained in the Torah, boldly wording it, ". . . and He
[*God*] commanded us. . . ." They took it upon themselves to
legislate for Israel, feeling their own laws also to be the commands of God because they so vividly experienced the living,
continuing nature of Torah. Torah, for them, had not been

given just once, in the past. "In their eyes, the rites ordained by them too, are *Mitzvot* of God and not only those rites that are ordained in the written Torah." They stated this position unequivocally in their famous dictum, "Weighty are the words of the Ḥakhamim [the Rabbis], for he who transgresses their words is like him who transgresses the words of the Torah." [2]

Social ideas are never created anew, out of nothing. They always arise out of existing ideas, and are often broader, more inclusive, and at the same time more differentiated than their predecessors. The ideal of democracy which flowered in these United States in the eighteenth century is an excellent example of the growth of a social idea. Democracy was not born in America. Its history goes back to Greece in the centuries before the Common Era. It expanded in meaning and acquired new vigor in revolutionary France. Again it grew immeasurably in breadth when it was distilled through the minds of the Founding Fathers. And it is still growing. No strait-jacket of final definition by social philosophers can keep it from continuing to develop new applications and additional connotations, now and in the foreseeable future.

The Rabbis of the Talmudic era had in remarkable degree the creative capacity for enriching the meaning of the ideas they inherited from their past. The development of the concept of Torah is another instance of the effect of genius on social ideas. As the Rabbis use it, Torah grows in scope until its meaning is vastly enlarged. Its outlines do not become blurred as it grows, because the process of finding continually new and concrete applications of the concept goes on side by side with, indeed as an integral part of, this organic growth. That is how the Jewish religion, without destroying its native character, was able to develop within its own framework from the Biblical to the rabbinic period.

It was not until Judaism was confronted with medieval philosophy that it froze—first, into terms carefully defined and therefore arrested in growth; then, into statements of belief, "logically" derived and therefore ostensibly unalterable; and finally, into creeds, permanently fixed. By then, Judaism had almost lost its capacity for natural, organismic growth. Had all Jews of that time been philosophers, Judaism would by now probably have become merely an archeological curiosity. Fortunately most Jews, even most Rabbis, were not philosophers and persisted in their devotion to the evolving, nonphilosophical social tradition of their fathers. The philosophers' interpretation of Judaism was not generally accepted and the flexibility of the tradition persisted in spite of their efforts. That is how it happened that the living stream of Judaism has managed to trickle down to us—perhaps for new philosophers to try to organize into new logical schemas.

WHAT MAKES TIME HOLY?

After *Shabbat* begins at home with the lighting of the candles, it is joyously welcomed with song and prayer at the Evening Service. Though the Sabbath recurs every week, Jews greet it on each occasion as an event they have longed for during all of the six preceding days. It is not easy to pinpoint the source of its power to inspire such devotion or to state it in so many words. For the Sabbath is all of a piece with the rest of Judaism; it cannot be understood as a solitary, discrete phenomenon.

The institution of the week, punctuated by one day of rest, is so old and so much part of the rhythm of our lives, whether we are Sabbath observers or not, that we are apt to overlook the fact that it is a social invention of the first magnitude.

Somewhere in its very early history Israel carved out of the sameness of all time a fixed period and invested it with special significance.[3] *Shabbat Kodesh*, Holy Sabbath, they called it. The social feat of making a unit of time holy cannot be accomplished without some unusual means. The day has to be distinctly marked off from other days. This is achieved in various ways. No work is done on these holy days, and the more holy the day, the more kinds of work are forbidden. On the Festivals, Passover for example, using fire and cooking are permitted, but on the Sabbath this, too, is forbidden. On *Yom Kippur,* the Day of Atonement, the Sabbath of Sabbaths, everything comes to a standstill. Every usual, normal activity of life is eliminated and the whole day is given over to penitence and prayer.

Cessation from normal activities, however, is not the whole story. Special prayers and specific rites are designed for each holy day; a cluster of social ceremonies, particular foods and even appropriate clothes have become part of the constellation of habits that mark off each time of holiness. These help to establish its unique character and to separate this period from the rest of life. The Sabbath is made holy, according to the Rabbis, by especially good food and especially fine clothes, as well as in other, more generally recognized ways.

Limited as its forms of celebration are, Thanksgiving has profound significance for Americans. Much richer in rites and therefore much more evocative and more meaningful are the old, the traditional religious festivals to the professing adherents of any religion. But among all the festivals of the Jewish calendar, the most potent vehicle of holiness is the weekly Sabbath Day. It had so many facets of significance for the Jew, it invested his life with so much meaning and gave him so many opportunities for the experience of holiness that he tried to prolong it as much as he could. He began to celebrate the Sabbath always even earlier than sundown and did not

allow it to depart until three stars were clearly visible in the
sky, accounting it a "*Mitzvah* to add [time] from the weekday
to the holy day." [4]

We tend today to be overstimulated and oversatiated at the
same time. We want so much and find innumerable means for
satisfying our most extravagant wants. As a result, many of the
delicate nuances of living escape us. Soon every day becomes
like every other, whether we are at work or not. We live in a
"week of Sundays." How monotonous life can become if we
miss the artifacts of time that make certain periods holy!

THE SERVICE OF *Kabbalat Shabbat*

In rabbinic times, the service on Friday night used to begin
with Psalms 92 and 93, but in the seventeenth century six
Psalms (numbers 95 through 99, and number 29) were introduced as a preface to the service. No shadow of sin or sorrow
darkens the mood of these Psalms; they are almost exuberant
in spirit. An abounding joyousness and a sense of release per-
vade the hymns, as if every burden of the week had been cast
aside and man could now give himself over to experiencing
God's just and beneficent rule over all the world.

Somewhat earlier, in the sixteenth century, the service had
already been expanded by the addition of several contemporary poems. The most famous of these is "*Lekhah Dodi,*
Come, my Beloved, to meet the Bride." It was written in 1540
by Rabbi Solomon Halevi Alkabetz and it is now included in
the Friday Evening liturgy of almost every Jewish community
in the world. Various intricate literary devices, the more complicated, the more admired, were much in vogue in those days.
Jewish liturgical poetry was no exception; it was cut after the
same pattern. *Lekhah Dodi* is an excellent example of that

ornate style. The first letters of each verse spell out the author's name, acrostic fashion, and numerous quotations and paraphrases from the Bible are woven into his own words. But this artificial, highly stylized form has not prevented the poem from having great charm and grace. With mounting intensity it conveys the moving idea that the Sabbath is God's own gift to us, that she is the Bride, the Queen, the source of joy and many blessings.

The contrast between this almost gay religious poem and the very next line in the *Prayer Book* is therefore nothing short of startling. For here we find the greeting to those mourners who are in the synagogue for the first time since they have sustained their loss. In many synagogues to this day, the mourners wait in an anteroom during the recitation of the introductory Psalms and the singing of *Lekhah Dodi;* they enter only after these have been concluded. This custom gives us a hint of the reason for placing a sad duty rather inappropriately right after a joyful hymn. Originally, the mourners were greeted as they entered the synagogue, at the beginning of the service. But when the prefatory Psalms and hymns were introduced, comforting the mourners remained fixed just before the original beginning of the service. And that is why the mourners now wait apart, and enter just as we are ready to extend to them the formal greeting to mourners. "May the Everywhere-Present God [*Hamakom*] comfort you among the other mourners of Zion and Jerusalem." These words offer the mourner the comfort of God's love and indirectly remind him that he is not alone in sorrow. The fact that the greeting is offered shows that the community is not indifferent to the individual's trouble, but its brevity and restraint are determined by the fact that it is part of a public service.

Here the prefatory Welcome to the Sabbath (*Kabbalat Shabbat*) closes and the Evening Service begins.

12

The Friday Evening Service

It has come to pass that for many Jews the chief, perhaps the only, service of the week comes on Friday night. This emphasis distorts the simple fact that the Evening Service is essentially the same seven nights a week, for daily prayer constituted a regular part of the life pattern of every Jew. The Friday Night Service is the usual *Ma'ariv* with a few brief additions in recognition of the Sabbath and some very interesting omissions on which we shall comment later.

On Friday Evening, the service begins with the recitation of Psalms 92 and 93. Psalm 92 is called a "Song for the Sabbath Day" because it was sung by the Levites in the Temple on the Sabbath; but very early, according to Maimonides, it became customary to recite it on Friday night instead. Only its title specifically mentions the Sabbath. Its theme is a reaffirmation of confidence in God's justice. The style is vigorous, staccato, piling up examples without pause and making its point by a series of concrete images. The wicked spring up as grass (and in Israel, a dry land, grass is very short-lived) but God has increased my strength to that of the wild ox. The wicked, though they flourish, are soon scattered and destroyed but the righteous grow like a date palm (long-lived, tall and strong, in contrast to the ephemeral grass); they stand firm as a cedar of Lebanon. Even in old age they blossom; green and full of the

134

sap of life, they demonstrate *Ki Yashar Adonai,* that the Lord is just and that there is no unrighteousness in Him.

Psalm 93 follows and after this, the Evening Service proceeds as on weekdays until just before the *Amidah.* It might be helpful to review here the general plan of the Evening Service up to the point at which the special Sabbath prayers begin.

The Daily Evening Service, *Ma'ariv*

1. The Call to Prayer, *Barakhu.*

2. The two benedictions before the *Shema:*
    a. The first benediction—On God Who creates light and darkness;
    b. The second benediction—On God's love for Israel, as witnessed by His having given them the Torah.

3. The *Shema,* in three paragraphs:
    a. The first paragraph—"Hear, O Israel . . ." and "Thou shalt love the Lord, thy God. . . ."
    b. The second paragraph: On reward and punishment—God's Justice;
    c. The third paragraph: On wearing the *Tzitzit*—the role of ritual *Mitzvot.*

4. The two benedictions after the *Shema:*
    a. The first benediction—on God's Kingship, introduced by the prayer, *Emet Ve'emunah,* and ending with the *Berakhah* on God, the Redeemer of Israel;
    b. The second benediction—*Hashkivaynu,* on God, our Guardian through the night.

These prayers are discussed in some detail in the chapter on the Daily *Ma'ariv* Service. This outline carries the service only up to the *Amidah,* the "Eighteen Benedictions." Thus far there is very little deviation on Friday night from the daily Evening Service. But here, just before the *Amidah,* is inserted the injunction to keep the Sabbath. To give it proper authority, it is quoted from the Bible, Chapter 31 of Exodus, verses 16 and 17. The Sabbath, it says, is an eternal covenant between God and Israel, a sign that it was God Who created the world. It is an encouraging sign (*Ot,* in Hebrew) a reminder of God's creation of and merciful governance of the world.

THE SABBATH *Amidah*

The peculiar delicacy of feeling which made the Rabbis consider it "bad manners"—bad religious manners, as it were—to ask for any of their daily needs on the Sabbath, may strike us as quaint or over-refined, but to them it was a serious consideration in the choice of prayers appropriate to the holy day. The Talmud says, "It is forbidden for a man to ask for his needs on the Sabbath."

The weekday *Amidah,* as we know, is also called the *Shemoneh Esray,* the "Eighteen," because at one time it consisted of eighteen benedictions. On the Sabbath, the middle thirteen have been omitted on the ground that they "ask for a man's needs." It is unfortunate that some of the most appealing and most intimately personal of the blessings are thus crowded out on the Sabbath when so many Jews do read their prayers. The first three *Berakhot,* and the last three, however, are repeated in all forms of the *Amidah*—daily, Sabbath, and Festivals. These are the most ancient of the blessings, going back to the days of the Temple.

On Friday night, the fourth *Berakhah* is the Sabbath benediction. It relates that God Himself "blessed the Sabbath . . .

and hallowed it above all [other] times." Support for this statement is naturally sought in the Bible and the relevant quotation (from Genesis 2, 1-3) follows in the next paragraph. "And
the heaven and the earth were completed and all their host.
And on the seventh day, God had finished His work which He
had done and He rested on the seventh day from all the work
He had done and He blessed the seventh day and He made it
holy. . . ."

It is difficult to overestimate the profound importance of the
institution of the Sabbath in the culture pattern of Judaism.
This statement from the Bible which is repeated in the prayers
and in the *Kiddush* on the Sabbath, means that for the Jew
Shabbat is no mere social contrivance for achieving more leis-
ure. It is for him inherent in the universe from the very beginning. And because God hallowed the Sabbath, it has a special quality of holiness which is, nevertheless, accessible to
the man who observes the day properly. Only from this point
of view can one understand how the Sabbath actually func-
tioned in the life of the individual.

The third part of the fourth benediction begins, "Our God
and God of our fathers, accept our rest . . . and purify our
hearts to serve Thee in truth." Strive as they might to study
Torah and to do *Mitzvot,* the Rabbis who fashioned these prayers had no sense of their own religious perfection. They certainly never implied that they were "good Jews," a self-con-
gratulatory claim one hears advanced often nowadays. Nor
is there any just ground for the accusation that smug satisfaction in the performance of the "letter of the law" characterized
the religion of the Pharisees, the Rabbis of the Talmud. One
of the many possible rejoinders to their detractors is this humble
Sabbath prayer for a pure heart, for the achievement of the un-
mixed motive in serving God.

Just as vital a part of rabbinic religion as the idea of *Mitzvah* (the religious act itself) is the idea of *Kavanah*, the motivation of the act, or the spirit in which it is performed. Like other rabbinic ideas, *Kavanah* is not readily translatable into a single equivalent English word. It connotes intention, devotion, dedication, single-minded concentration on. After a discussion on the relation between the performance of a *Mitzvah* and the *Kavanah* which motivates it, the decision of the Talmud is that "a *Mitzvah* requires *Kavanah*." The act alone is not enough. Devotion, intention, spirit too, are essential to a religious act, if it is to be properly carried out and religiously acceptable. "Purify our hearts to serve Thee in truth," we pray every Sabbath. It is a plea for help in achieving a spirit of prayer free of any ulterior motive, in which the intention will be as pure as the words.

So dear to the heart of the Jew are these words that they have been made into a liturgical folk-song, chanted not only in the synagogue but wherever Jews gather. "*Vetaher libaynu le'ovdekha be'emet*, Purify our hearts to serve Thee in truth" —with *Kavanah*.

The sixth *Berakhah* (the fifteenth of the daily *Amidah*) is called *Modim*, as usual from its first word. The importance of the *Modim* prayer is indicated by the fact that a variant form of it is recited by the congregation during the Reader's repetition of the *Amidah* at Morning and Afternoon Services, though no other part of the *Amidah* is so repeated by the people. The *Modim* is particularly interesting to us because it demonstrates again the inadequacy of a translation as a substitute for the Hebrew original. Most translators render the prayer into English thus, "We thank Thee for Thou art the Lord our God. . . ." Now the root of the word *Modim* in the Bible does mean *to thank*, but in rabbinic literature it more often means *to acknowledge*.[1] In fact, there is every reason to believe that the Rabbis intended the *Modim* prayer to be an acknowledgment of God's Kingship. The basis for this conclusion, drawn from rabbinic sources, is as complicated as a jig-saw puzzle, but the conclusion itself is very simple.[2] The Mishnah reasons that it is forbidden to say *Modim* twice in this benediction lest the suspicion arise that one is acknowledging "two powers," lest there be any shadow of doubt that it is God alone Who is the King to be acknowledged. The correct translation, then, of the *Modim* prayer should read, "We acknowledge Thee that Thou art the Lord our God and the God of our fathers . . . Thou art the Rock of our lives . . . for generation after generation. . . ."

Indeed, only if we recognize that this prayer is an acknowledgment of God's Kingship can we understand why it is customary to bow profoundly when it is said, just as we bow when we say the *Alaynu* (where, by the way, the same word *Modim* is used) and on other occasions when God's Kingship is acknowledged.

We bow and take three steps backward at the end of the *Amidah* and at the end of the *Kaddish* as well. All prayer is addressed to God, but when we profess our allegiance to Him by acknowledging His Kingship, as in the *Amidah* or in the *Kaddish*, we are conceived to be, as it were, in His very Presence. When the prayer is concluded with the salute, "May He Who makes peace in His high heavens . . . ," we retire from the Presence of the King. Obviously, a casual retreat is hardly appropriate. That is why we bow to the left (the King's right), bow to the right (the King's left), bow directly toward the King, and retire respectfully by walking three steps out of His Presence!

We mentioned above that at the Morning and the Afternoon Services, the Reader repeats the *Amidah* after the congregation has read it silently, each person alone with his prayer. Several reasons are given for this procedure. One is that books were few and precious in the days before printing and not everyone knew all the prayers by heart. Another is that some people might have come late to the service—not a modern failing only, it appears—perhaps even too late to have been able to say the *Amidah* privately. Since the *Amidah* is an obligatory part of the prescribed service both in the morning and in the afternoon, the Reader repeats it to make sure that no worshipper will miss sharing in it, at least by having heard it read. In the evening, though the *Amidah* is now an essential part of the service, there was for a long time some question as to whether it was to be considered *Hovah* (obligatory) or not. Because opinion was divided on this point, other, more practical, considerations influenced the final decision against repetition of the *Amidah* by the Reader, at night.

In Babylon, the synagogue was located outside the town in which the Jews lived, since Persian law did not permit a synagogue to be erected within the city walls. When the men returned home at night, after the Evening Service, their long walk through dark fields was fraught with danger. The service was, for that reason if for no other, made as short as possible to avoid undue delay.

On Friday night, however, the Reader does chant a short summary of the *Amidah* which is known as "*Magen Avot*, Shield of [our] Fathers." It is a compromise between a full repetition of the *Amidah* by the Reader and the alternative of skipping the repetition altogether because of the need to make the service as brief as possible. Moreover, the short repetition allowed the tardy ones to "catch up" with the congregation— to recite the first part of their prayers quietly by themselves while the Reader was chanting the summary. Thus, all the worshippers could go home together, and this was an important safety measure.

WHY JEWISH PRAYERS RARELY HAVE NAMES

Magen Avot is one of the very few prayers to have received a real name. For, almost universally, other prayers are known by the first word or phrase of the prayer they designate; for example, there are *Kol Nidray, Shalom Alaykhem, Lekhah Dodi, Ayn Kelohaynu, Modim* and so on. Some recent revisions of the *Prayer Book* have tried to improve on this apparently meaningless way of identifying prayers by their first words. These new Prayer Books give a title to each prayer, intended to summarize its content, or to convey its central idea for the guidance of the worshipper. But we must remember that any rubric necessarily interprets, and interprets from the vantage point of the person who composes the rubric. Now, wedding a contemporary conception to an old prayer is not always a happy union. The lack of a proper title implied in the traditional use of the first words is not an oversight to be repaired by us. Instead, it has a negative significance of great importance. For every prayer contains a number of concepts, each with many connotations, and a title must necessarily fix on *one* meaning. Even when that title points to one of the meanings actually to be found in the prayer, it confines the worshipper to seeing only one idea there. That is why the Rabbis, and Jewish tradition after them, refrained from giving descriptive titles to the prayers, thus limiting their meanings to a fixed interpretation. *Magen Avot,* as we said, seems to be an exception. It is a summary of the seven benedictions of the Friday Evening *Amidah,* and according to the usual custom, it is known by its first two words. But in this case the Rabbis went so far as to give the prayer another, an explanatory title—*Mayayn Sheva,* Of the Nature of the Seven—that is, of the seven benedictions of the *Amidah.* That the *Magen Avot* is a summary of the *Amidah* is all they cared to specify in their title; not a very descriptive or limiting title at that!

It may seem like a small thing, this refraining from interpretive titles, and taken by itself it is unimportant. But each detail in the structure of the *Siddur* contributes its share to the mounting effect of the whole. For the *Siddur* is the articulate expression of a strangely nondogmatic religion, one which is a self-sustaining organism, quite capable of growth, but soon distorted if it is forced into a mold foreign to its own peculiarly flexible nature.

Kiddush ON FRIDAY NIGHT

The *Kiddush* has been recited both in the synagogue as part of the Friday Evening Service and at home, for well over two thousand years. Perhaps that is why there is no unanimity among scholars as to which came first—the synagogue ceremony or the home ceremony. The Bible tells us to "Remember the Sabbath to keep it holy," and very early in Jewish history this command was implemented in a specific, verbal declaration of the holiness of the Sabbath, called *Kiddush Ha'yom*. This declaration is made in the blessing said in the public *Kiddush* at the synagogue and by the man, over a cup of wine before the Sabbath meal in his own home. If there is no man in the household, it is the duty of the woman to make *Kiddush* and similarly, by the way, if there is no woman in the household, the man is required to light the Sabbath candles and to recite the appropriate *Berakhah*. The preponderance of evidence seems to point to the *Kiddush* as originally a home ceremony. The simple fact that the benediction on wine (or on bread if no wine is available) is an essential part of the *Kid-*

dush indicates clearly that it was originally an integral part of the meal and that it must have begun as a home ritual.

If that is so, it seems strange that the *Kiddush* should be recited also in the synagogue at the end of the Friday Evening Service. It is almost impossible for us who live so well in America to appreciate the severity of the living conditions that our ancestors of fifteen hundred years ago had to cope with; it is difficult for us to imagine how terribly meager their resources were. In those days, in Babylon, wayfarers were frequently lodged and fed in the synagogue or in a room adjoining it. Wine was a luxury and *Kiddush* at the service was an ingenious and practical economy measure. When *Kiddush* was recited for the benefit of the visitor-lodgers at the end of the service, just before their meal, one cup of wine sufficed for all. In addition, those too poor to afford wine at home were able to hear *Kiddush* and to share in the *Mitzvah*—still at the cost of only the one cup!

By the time the synagogue had ceased to be a part-time lodging house, *Kiddush* had been recited at the service for so many generations that no Rabbi was willing to take the responsibility for removing it. And so, through inertia or habit, there it has persisted stubbornly to this day (except in Chassidic synagogues). Almost providentially, we might add. For now, so many centuries later, when we can afford all the wine we need or want, *Kiddush* at the synagogue has again acquired a useful function. It serves those who would never hear *Kiddush* were it not recited as part of the Friday Evening Service.

On the Eve of the Sabbath, just as on weekdays, the service closes with *Alaynu,* followed by the Mourners' *Kaddish.* In most synagogues in England and the United States, *Yigdal* or *Adon Olam* is sung as a closing hymn.

"FAMILY NIGHT" ON *Shabbat*

In Jewish tradition and according to Jewish law, the Friday Evening Service is meant to be conducted at sundown. The exigencies of modern life, however, have made it very difficult for people to attend a service at sundown, the hour varying from four in the afternoon of a winter day to eight o'clock or later on summer evenings. This situation created a demand for a service late in the evening when more people would find it possible to attend. And so, in Conservative and in many Reform Temples as well, the Friday Evening Service has been delayed until after dinner.

In any event, the home ceremonies for the Eve of Sabbath need not be displaced from their traditional hour. Long before sunset the dinner table is laid in stately white; candles stand at attention ready to be lit; the two white loaves (*Hallot*), prepared for *Hamotzi* (the blessing on bread), are hidden under their own cover at the head of the table, and the goblet and wine are set out for *Kiddush*. Then, if the candle-lighting ceremony remains firmly anchored to the half hour before sunset, at least at home the Sabbath can begin on time.

From the days of the Patriarchs, almost two thousand years before the Common Era, it has been the custom for a father to bless his sons. When the blessing was given on his deathbed, as so often it was in very ancient times, it constituted an important part of the inheritance he left them. This may be the origin of the custom of blessing the children regularly each week on Sabbath Eve. When the father returned from Evening Service at the synagogue, he would place both hands on the head of each child in turn and pronounce whatever blessing his heart dictated. But by the sixteenth century, the words of the benediction had become formalized and the beautiful *Berakhah* found in the *Prayer Book* came to be generally accepted. In a sense, it is the priestly blessing that the father invokes for his children, and another demonstration of the ancient priestly role played by the head of the family. In the absence of the father, the mother gave the children her blessing. In some synagogues today, the Rabbi blesses all the children present on Friday night at the service. Though tradition permits this deviation, modern psychological insights favor the older Jewish custom of parental blessing. Who can measure how much it means to a child, what sense of security, what assurance of love he gains when he feels his father's hands laid on his head in blessing! And this effect begins long before he is old enough to understand the words or the meaning of the ceremony. Perhaps only a certain self-consciousness on the part of many modern parents prevents them from continuing this ancient and psychologically valuable custom.

After this ceremony, the whole family joins in singing the hymn, "*Shalom Alaykhem*, Welcome to You, Ministering Angels." In a *Baraita*,[3] it is related that "Two ministering angels escort a man home from the synagogue on Sabbath Eve, one good and one evil. When the good angel comes [to a] home and finds the candles lit and the table set, he says, 'May it be His will that the next Sabbath be [also] thus.' And the evil angel answers, 'Amen,' against his will. And if not [if nothing is prepared for the Sabbath], the evil angel says, 'May it be His will that the next Sabbath be also *thus*.' And the good angel answers, 'Amen,' against *his* will." On this imaginative parable, the song *Shalom Alaykhem* is based. It was introduced by the Kabbalists in the sixteenth century, but the author is unknown. Unknown, too, is how it happened that singing it on Friday night spread so far and wide, but it is now nearly universally accepted and sung by Jews on the Eve of the Sabbath.

It is no accident that dictates the order of ceremony on Friday night at home. The "script" is very old and very beautiful, and it clearly defines the procedure. Just before he makes *Kiddush,* every Jewish husband turns gallantly to his wife and toasts her in the words of the ancient "Ode to a Virtuous Woman" (Proverbs 31, 10-31). The first words of this poem, *Ayshet Ha'yil,* a Woman of Virtue (or Valor), have entered the daily speech of Jews through the Yiddish and have become the symbol, indeed the name, for the ideal woman. That ideal is no ornamental, lily-white Maid of Astolat but in many ways a modern woman. She is strong, competent, and wise, yet filled with tender loving-kindness to all those in need. She is devotedly loyal to her husband and her family and worthy of praise because "the fear of the Lord" is in her.

There is another custom which grew more popular under the influence of sixteenth century mystics—the singing of songs during and after Sabbath meals. The number of melodies to which these songs are sung is legion, and their variety is as wide as the world. Every country and often every family have their favorites. There are Gregorian chants, Arab shepherd tunes, German drinking and marching songs, lugubrious Russian love songs, and even "God Save the King" borrowed from the English! But the words, most often in Hebrew, occasionally in Aramaic, celebrate God's Kingship, Israel the Beloved, Zion the Holy City, God's love, and His continuing bounty. Intermingled with these themes of rabbinic Judaism are some esoteric, mystical ideas inspired by the Kabbalah.

Two of the best known of these songs (*Zemirot* as they are called) are "*Yah Ribon Olam,* God, Master of the Universe," and "*Tzur Mishelo,* Rock from Whose Store We Have Eaten." *Tzur Mishelo* is a poem of unknown origin; its verses are based on the benedictions of the Grace after Meals, making it particularly appropriate for a table song. *Yah Ribon Olam* is written in Aramaic with scriptural references to the Book of Daniel, one of the later Books of the Bible, the language of which is in part Aramaic. *Yah Ribon* was written in the sixteenth century by Israel Najara whose first name (Yisrael) is spelled out in the initial letters of the verses.

The Grace after Meals on Sabbath and Festivals is preceded by Psalm 126, *Shir Hama'alot*, which joyously sings of the return of the exiles from Babylon to Palestine in 537 B.C.E. So marvellous was this return to those who had actually lived through the experience, that it seemed unbelievable—a dream. "When the Lord brought back those who returned to Zion, we were as in a dream. Then were we filled with laughter and our tongues spoke our joy. . . . They that sow in tears shall reap in joy. . . ." Jews took great comfort from the fact that God had, on this occasion, allowed them to return to the Land. They loved to relate this wonderful event for the courage it gave them to bear the woes and hardships of their life in the dispersion. It was as if they were saying, "God did this for our ancestors on one occasion; it can, it will happen again." The long, dark night of the Exile was eased for them by the hope of another redemption. Zionism was not born with Herzl nor nurtured by modern propaganda alone. The State of Israel is the precipitation of a religious idea in which the concepts of Israel, *Ge'ulah* (Redemption), the Land of Israel, *Kibbutz Galuyot* (the Ingathering of the Exiles) and God's Love loom as large as the concepts of modern nationalism.

For comment on the Grace after Meals, see Chapter 16 on the Grace.

13

The Sabbath Morning Service

IN BABYLON

Saadia Gaon says that on *Shabbat* the Jews of Babylon rose very early and spent half the day in prayer, in reading the Torah, and in explanations of matters relating to the Sabbath. Perhaps it was only the scholars or the very pious who spent so much of the Sabbath day engaged in prayer and in the study of Torah. But there is no doubt that a sense of freedom from the oppressive burdens of the week allowed everyone more time for prayer and for Torah on the Sabbath. "More time" must be understood in terms of a people that prayed three times *every* day and, from our point of view, at considerable length every morning. Everyone was accustomed to take much time for himself—that is, for the expression of his aspirations and his ideals through prayer. Moreover, the range of his intellectual life was determined by the amount and depth of Torah he was capable of grasping. In this setting we can perhaps understand why, to the already full morning service, so much more was added on *Shabbat* when no one was in a hurry.

The service on the Sabbath, then, includes more Psalms and hymns than on week days, one very much longer benediction before the *Shema*, and two whole sections found only on the Sabbath: the full reading of the weekly portion of the Torah from the Scroll and a prayer of benedictions similar to the

148

Amidah, called the *Musaf,* or Addition. There are a few omissions on the Sabbath too. Most interesting is the fact that the *Tefillin* are not worn on *Shabbat.* The reason given is that the *Tefillin* are, in the Torah, called a "sign" (*Ot*) and the Sabbath is also referred to as a "sign" (*Ot*). The first paragraph of the *Shema,* referring to the *Tefillin,* reads,". . . and ye shall bind them for a *sign* upon thy hand . . . ," while, in the quotation from Exodus found in the fourth benediction of the Sabbath *Amidah,* it is said, "It [the Sabbath] is a *sign* between Me and the children of Israel. . . ." Since it was felt that it was not necessary to have both "signs" at the same time, the *Tefillin* were dispensed with on *Shabbat.* Because no thank-offering was made in the Temple on the Sabbath, Psalm 100 which refers to the thank-offering is not read on *Shabbat.* The thirteen middle benedictions of the *Amidah* are also omitted on Sabbath morning as they are on Friday night, and for the same reasons.

THE IDEA OF GOD IN THE *Siddur*

On Sabbath morning the service begins with *Yigdal* and proceeds as on weekdays, with no changes other than the omission of the benediction on the *Tefillin,* as far as the "Passages of Song." Like every other reading from Torah—and of course Psalms are Torah—this section of the service is introduced by its own benediction, "*Barukh She'amar,* Blessed be He Who spoke and the world came into being." This introductory blessing ends: "Blessed art Thou, O Lord, King, extolled in Psalms of praise."

Now, strange as it may seem, Blessed-be-He-Who-spoke-and-the-World-came-into-being is a name of God found more than occasionally in rabbinic literature. But there is at least a score of other names used in the prayers. The one just quoted is less familiar but many other rabbinic names for God are well known even in English. Our Father in heaven, Creator, Rock of Israel, Merciful Father, the Merciful One, Master of the universe, God most high (*Melekh Elyon*), God of our fathers, our Redeemer, our Savior, King, or King of the kings of kings (the titles oriental potentates arrogated to themselves were always exaggerated; many a conqueror of other kingdoms, large or small, called himself the King of Kings; but God was the Supreme King, above all the kings of kings; He was the King of the kings of kings!). These are some of a long list of names for God which we find in rabbinic literature. The Above, Heaven, the Word, the Glory, the Place (*Hamakom*), the Holy One blessed be He, are also found in rabbinic sources; and Friend, Brother, Beloved are not unknown. The import of all these appellatives is of vital significance to an understanding of the Jewish idea of God.

In the discussion of the *Berakhah* we pointed out its peculiar form of address, directly to God as *Thou* in the first clause of the blessing, and more remotely, more reverently as *He* in the last part of the same sentence. This peculiar form is an expression of the normal mystical experience of God in Judaism, of a relationship like none other and therefore very difficult to put into ordinary patterns of speech. Normal mystical experience is so intrinsic a part of the Jewish religion that it must rise to expression in more than the *Berakhah*, it must break through into other channels of expression. And it does—in the epithets applied to God in reverence and love, in adoration and in intimacy. It is not a God-concept these various names denote, an abstract generalization about a Being with certain carefully defined characteristics or "attributes." Such a Being is the product of philosophy which aims to describe God in terms of

His possible attributes, and sometimes, in terms of His "negative attributes"—that is, of qualities He cannot logically be conceived to possess. This Being, in philosophy, is designated by
a single term, God or First Cause. Instead of such a carefully
defined God-concept, we have here in the religion of the Rabbis
a mystical *experience*, a poignant awareness of God. No one
quality of God, no one relationship-word can tell the whole
story of such an experience. Nor is that experience always the
same. That is why there is so wide a range of names: *King of
kings* side by side with *Merciful Father*, and *Master of the universe* with *our Father in heaven*. Each epithet seems to try to
express a private and unique experience, so unique as to defy
generalization in any single philosophic term or name for God.

In the Bible God has one particular Name, the Tetragrammaton, the four letters spelling out His Name. This Name is
so specific as to be almost "personal." But Israel lived among
pagans, people who worshipped many gods. In order to be able
to communicate in any way with these peoples, Israel had to
have some general term for "gods." That term was *Elo'ah*, a
god. Sometimes *El* or *Elohim* is used in this sense, usually with
a possessive, as, "their gods." But these words are not indicative of a general concept of God, for the pagan gods are always
conceived as "false gods," "idols," "no-gods." When the Rabbis
find (in Exodus 20, 3) "other gods," they ask, "But are they
gods?" *Elohot*, the plural of *Elo'ah*, is the term they use there.

The Biblical and rabbinic idea of God is a peculiar one. It
is, and is not, a generalized idea. They had an idea of the "no-
god" but never included God in any classification. God is reacted to, experienced rather than conceived because He is
unique, other than anything else. He is differently experienced
at different times and in different moods. An effort to catch
this uniqueness and these varied experiences of God is reflected in the numerous names or appellatives of God [1] we find

so frequently in rabbinic literature, and therefore also in the *Siddur.*

We usually think of the special Sabbath prayers as beginning in the morning with "*Nishmat Kol Hai,* The breath of all living shall praise Thee." This is a long and passionate prayer that asks for nothing; instead, it is directed to God in sheer gratitude for all His beneficence. The first part of the prayer is as old as Temple days. The second part, beginning with the sentence, "*Lekha Levadkha,* To Thee alone we give thanks . . . ," is a hymn of the first century before the Common Era. It was written, according to tradition, by Simeon ben Shetaḥ, leader of the Pharisaic party. If no other evidence were available, this hymn would be proof enough of the spirit that animated the Pharisees. There is no dry legalism here. The author reaches after every figure of speech he can think of to suggest the magnitude, the intensity of our gratitude to God and our own inadequacy, and after all is said, our own helpless inability to express the thanks that are due Him.

For all its hyperbole, it is one of the most beautiful prayers in the *Siddur.* Though stated in the plural like most rabbinic prayers, it is profoundly personal in feeling for it is indeed the unrehearsed outpouring of a great religious soul.

The *Nishmat* prayer is the introduction to the blessing after the *Pesukay de-Zimra.* The preliminary section of the service closes with that benediction, followed by Half-*Kaddish,* as on week days. The next section is also substantially the same in structure on *Shabbat* as on every other day. The "Call to Prayer" is repeated at every service of the year, morning and evening, and so is the *Shema.*

On the Sabbath, however, much embroidery embellishes the first benediction before the *Shema.* Each word or phrase of the daily blessing has acted as a peg on which to hang decorative elaborations. On the Sabbath the benediction begins, "*Hakol*

Yodukha, All will acknowledge Thee. . . ." It is a hymn to the goodness, mercy, loving-kindness, greatness, and wisdom that are God's. In the heavenly bodies He created, the Rabbis see His wisdom. It is not the marvels of the natural world they stand in awe of, not Nature they adore for its beauty and intricacy of design, but God Who created it.

The third paragraph of this long excursus on the first bene-diction before the *Shema* is a hymn on the Sabbath Day. There are seven special Day-Hymns—one for each day of the week, recounting the things created on that day, and each based on a parallel Psalm for the day. The one recited on *Shabbat* takes its theme from Psalm 92, "A Song for the Sab-bath Day." The Sabbath is precious and important because God Himself rested on the Seventh Day and then gave that same Day, made holy by Him, to His people Israel for a day of rest. The word used for *rest* here is *Menuḥah,* which means more than just cessation from labor. It connotes quiet, relaxa-tion, peace, as well as rest. After introducing the Seraphim and other angelic beings to sing the *Kedushah* ("Holy, holy, holy is the Lord . . ."), the blessing closes, as it does on week days, with the words: "Blessed art Thou, O Lord, Creator of the luminaries [the sun and the moon]."

THE "CHOSEN PEOPLE"

The second *Berakhah* is the one directly preceding the *Shema* and it deals therefore with Israel's good fortune in hav-ing been given the gift of Torah. "With great love hast Thou loved us, O Lord our God," it begins. It goes on to say, "O our Father, our King, for the sake of our fathers who trusted in Thee and to whom Thou didst teach the laws of life, in the same way, have compassion upon us and teach us. O our

Father, loving and compassionate Father, . . . put it into our hearts to understand, be wise in, obey, learn, teach and fulfill all the words of Thy Torah with love. . . . Blessed art Thou, O Lord, Who takes delight in His people Israel with love." And because He loves them, He gave them the Torah. The Torah is God's gift to Israel, a mark of His love for them.

We have translated the last part of this benediction: ". . . Who takes delight in, or loves (*Ha-Boher*) His people Israel. . . ." The difficult word here is *Boher*. It is usually rendered, "[Who] chooses," but the idea of selection is, in this context, misleading. A careful analysis of the way *Boher* is used in the *Prayer Book* will show that it usually means *to love, to take delight in, to be pleased with,* but very seldom *to choose, to select* from among others. For example, in the closing benediction after the Passages of Song, the final sentence is, "Blessed art Thou, O Lord, God, King, great in praises . . . Who [*Ha-Boher*] loves, or takes delight in, or is pleased with song and Psalm." Surely these words cannot mean that God *chooses* His favorite songs! In the same way, in the benediction before the *Shema* which we have been discussing, Israel expresses the feeling that the fact that God gave them the Torah is an indication of His love.

The three paragraphs of the *Shema* itself are constant for all morning and evening services.

THE ROLE OF THE TEACHER IN JUDAISM

If the *Berakhah* is the most characteristic *form* of Jewish prayer, the *Shema* is certainly one of its most important single statements. It is an acknowledgment of God's Kingship. Moreover, the first paragraph of the *Shema* calls attention to an aspect of Judaism peculiar to it alone—the obsession with Torah, with studying, teaching, and "doing" Torah. The benediction which introduces the *Shema* deals with Torah and pleads with God for the wisdom to learn and to teach Torah and for the strength of will to obey its commandments. In the *Shema* itself the people are commanded to carry the words of the Torah always in their minds and to "teach them to your children . . ." and to discuss them everywhere.

The role of Torah grew even greater during the rabbinic period and beyond it, and profoundly influenced the structure of the Jewish group. The command to teach Torah was as important as the command to study. "Everyone who teaches his fellow one verse [of Bible] or one *Halakhah* [law] or one word, it is as though he places life before him," says a Midrash.[2] Torah tells a man how to live. No boon can be greater than to teach him Torah. The teacher thus became indispensable to the community. He was paid, of course, but also treated with marked reverence. "To what may he [the teacher] be compared? . . . to a tree in whose shade all sit, and he is like the candle which gives light of eyes to the multitude." [3] The community saw to it that teachers were hired for the specific purpose of teaching children. Simeon ben Shetah (to whom the second part of the *Nishmat* prayer is ascribed) established schools for the young in the first century before the Common Era and teachers for *Tinokot* (little children) are referred to in the Mishnah. The tradition that Jewish parents deny themselves so much to pay for their childrens' education did not begin in the ghettos of Eastern Europe. *Seder Eliahu*, a Midrash of the Mishnaic period from which we have often quoted, says: "Recall how many blind there are in Israel who have no food [blindness was endemic in the East until very recently] and yet they give money that their children may study Torah. Recall how many little lads there are in Israel who know not their right hand from

their left yet engage in Torah every day continually." Children
began their schooling at the age of five or even younger.

The whole of Jewish social organization revolved for centuries around the need for a synagogue and the equally indispensable need for schools for the children. In the light of the
standards of education set for everyone—no economic or social
class distinction was tolerated—we can appreciate how thoroughly the study of Torah penetrated into every nook and
cranny of the religious life.

Torah was read in the synagogue, studied daily, bound on
the arm and the head as a visible reminder to scrutinize one's
conduct daily; and it was posted on the doorway of every
house that all who entered might see it at once. This *Mezuzah*
(literally, doorpost and, by association, the ritual object which
we shall describe here) is, like the *Tefillin*, a bit of parchment
on which the *Shema* is carefully handwritten. The parchment
is enclosed in a small oblong case of no prescribed material or
design but so made that through glass or an opening the parchment within is visible. The *Mezuzah* in its case must be firmly
affixed to the upper right side of the door frame—that is, the
right side, as you enter.

Since it contains a part of the Torah, the *Mezuzah*, like the
Tefillin and the Scroll of the Torah itself, is holy. But it is not
an amulet meant to ward off evil spirits from one's door, any
more than the *Tefillin* are amulets. The *Mezuzah* must be understood in the setting of Torah, of the never flagging emphasis
on Torah. To wear a *Mezuzah* as an ornament or a charm
smacks of *Avodah Zarah*, idol worship, paganism. Judaism
never sanctioned such use of the *Mezuzah*. When, on going into
or out of a house, some people touch the *Mezuzah* and then
put their fingers to their lips, the gesture must be understood
as one of respect for Torah—or that is what it was originally
meant to be.

As on weekdays, there is on Sabbath mornings one long benediction after the *Shema;* it is the *Berakhah* on God as the Redeemer of Israel.

THE SABBATH MORNING *Amidah—*
THE ROLE OF MOSES IN THE JEWISH RELIGION

The Sabbath morning *Amidah* is shorter than the daily one, consisting of only seven blessings. The first three and the last three, so ancient that their inception goes back perhaps twenty-five hundred years, remain as the permanent frame of every *Amidah*.

The middle or fourth benediction declares the Sabbath to be a fundamental institution of Judaism. Since the authenticity of an institution in the Jewish religion is best established by reference to the Bible, a quotation from Bible in support of the Sabbath is required at this point. But a quotation from Torah is seldom set down abruptly in the *Siddur*. It is introduced with ceremony, formally, by a *Berakhah*. And this is what the first paragraph of the fourth benediction does. It is a prelude to the quotation from Exodus to follow. But a note is struck in this paragraph, most unusual in the *Prayer Book*. "Moses," it says, "Moses rejoiced in the portion he was given, for Thou didst call him a faithful servant. When he stood before Thee on Mount Sinai Thou didst give him a crown of glory for his head. And he brought the two Tablets of Stone down in his hand, and on them was inscribed the observance of the Sabbath."

This simple little vignette describing Moses to whom God gave exceptional honor, made visible in the "crown of glory" is an astounding thing to find in the *Siddur*. For, with conscious deliberation, Jewish tradition from the days of the Bible has always been careful to humanize its greatest leaders and heroes. The greater the man, the more conspicuously were his faults pointed out. It was their way of making sure that no man would be deified. Even Moses, the greatest of the prophets—Moses, who had come nearer to seeing God than any other human being—even Moses was only a fallible human being. He was a man of short temper; he had killed an Egyptian. In fact, he had struck the rock in anger, disobeying God's clear command, and as a result he was not permitted to enter the Promised Land.

In rabbinic tradition there are numerous tales about Moses. They tell of his marvellous deeds, but at the same time the Rabbis are very careful not to exaggerate his importance. In the *Haggadah* of Passover, for example, Hamlet is played without the Prince of Denmark! It is no accident that in this rabbinic text, the long special service for the Eve of Passover, Moses is not mentioned even once. While the paragraph we have been discussing contains the only glorification of Moses in the liturgy,[4] the Rabbis have allowed his name to be mentioned in the *Siddur* on two more occasions. When the Ark is opened to remove the Scroll for the Torah reading, a verse from the Book of Numbers quotes Moses briefly. The point of emphasis in the quotation, however, is not Moses but his call to the Lord: "Rise up, O Lord, and Thine enemies . . . shall be scattered from before Thee." Just once more is Moses mentioned. Before the Torah is returned to the Ark it is raised up for all to see, and the congregation says, in the words of Deuteronomy, "This is the Torah which Moses set before the Children of Israel *according to the command of the Lord,* by the hand of Moses." It is interesting that on both these occasions the name of Moses enters only because the relevant Biblical quotation includes it. Though he is the greatest of the prophets, we are made to understand that Moses acted in these instances merely as God's instrument. For it is God Who brought us up out of Egypt and God Who gave us the Torah, not Moses. A clear line is drawn between reverence for so remarkable a leader and raising him to the status of a demi-god. That line Jewish tradition was extremely careful not to cross.

The last words of the paragraph introducing the fourth benediction read, "And inscribed on them [the Tablets of Stone] is the command on observance of the Sabbath and it is also written in Thy Torah." Though it is to the Tablets of Stone that the whole of this section directs our attention, and we therefore expect the Fourth Commandment on the Sabbath to be quoted now, there is, instead, a sudden shift in the last phrase, to the Torah outside of the Decalogue. This is another instance of the tendency in rabbinic literature to underemphasize the Decalogue as against the rest of the Torah.[5] What follows is an excerpt from the Torah (Exodus 31, 16 and 17), "The children of Israel shall keep the Sabbath . . . as an everlasting covenant. It is a sign between Me and the children of Israel forever. . . ." A sign, like the sign of the *Tefillin*, of God's love and of a covenant between Him and Israel.

The third part of the Sabbath benediction is a happy commentary on this "sign" that was given only to Israel. "The idol worshippers do not have the Sabbath nor do the wicked enjoy its rest. But Thou gavest it to the seed of Jacob in whom Thou didst take delight, the people who hallow the Seventh Day and bask in Thy goodness. . . ." The contrast between this exultation and the last part of the benediction is striking. Now, instead of pride in their possession of that priceless treasure, the Sabbath, Israel prays humbly to God to accept them and their rest as a fit offering. "Our God and God of our fathers," they pray, "accept our rest, hallow us by Thy commandments, and may our portion be in Thy Torah. Satisfy us with Thy goodness and give us joy, with Thy help. Purify our hearts to serve Thee in truth and may we inherit, O Lord our God, Thy holy Sabbath."

"NORMAL MYSTICISM" IN THE JEWISH RELIGION

The fifth benediction of the Sabbath *Amidah* (which is the seventeenth in the Daily Service) reads, "Blessed art Thou, O Lord, Who returns His Presence [*Shekhinato*] to Zion." *Shekhinato*, the form used here, means His *Shekhinah*. Now *Shekhinah* is one of the very many rabbinic names for God, and the root of *Shekhinah* means *to dwell*. Because of this derivation, this literal meaning of *Shekhinah*, some scholars have concluded that this name refers to the "in-dwelling God," or to the "God within man" as they phrase it or, as certain philosophers have put it, the "immanence of God." But derivation of a theological idea from the literal meaning of a root-word is open to several serious sources of error. The literal meaning of a word often gives way to new ones, very far afield, and the old root then ceases to be a dependable guide to the richly connotative later idea. Or, on the contrary, more recent ideas are sometimes read back into a climate of thought in which they did not exist, merely on the basis of an apparent connection between the later idea and the literal meaning of the older word, thus thoroughly distorting the native, intended significance. In the case of the word *Shekhinah*, this kind of reasoning may result in introducing into rabbinic Judaism ideas which are entirely foreign to it or which became common theological coin only centuries after the Talmudic era.

It is important, therefore, to inquire whether the Rabbis who were responsible for the term *Shekhinah* did in fact possess the idea of an in-dwelling God; whether, by *Shekhinah*, they intended to imply "immanence" as a quality of God; whether, indeed, it is conceivable from their point of view that God might in any sense dwell within a man. A careful analysis of the contexts in which they use the name *Shekhinah* will reveal exactly what it does mean to the Rabbis and what it cannot possibly connote in the framework of rabbinic Judaism.[6]

The Rabbis use the term *Shekhinah*, as they use the many other appellatives for God which we discussed above, as a name for God Himself, equating it with other Biblical and rabbinic names. "When David heard this [that he was not to build the Temple], he bowed down . . . and came and sat before the *Shekhinah* and said, 'My *Father in heaven*, may Thy great Name be blessed for ever and ever.'"[7] Here it is *Father in heaven*, often it is the *Holy One blessed be He*, which is used interchangeably with *Shekhinah* as a name for God, but the passages are numerous and varied.

Unlike other appellatives for God, the name *Shekhinah*, however, does have a special connotation, that of the nearness of God to man. David, in the Midrash just quoted, ". . . came and sat down before the *Shekhinah*." Again, "He who prays ought to regard himself as though *Shekhinah* were in front of him," says the Talmud.[8] And the *Ethics of the Fathers* asserts that the *Shekhinah* "rests on" two persons who interchange words of Torah. In the *Mekhilta*, another Midrash, *Shekhinah* is described as sharing (as it were) in the affliction of the community and even of the individual, and *Shekhinah* hovers over Israel, or as the Rabbis say it, Israel is gathered "under the wings of the *Shekhinah*." In all of these examples *Shekhinah* is used as a name for God and all of them reflect a sense of the nearness of His Presence.

Now this sense of God's nearness is another aspect of the normal, mystical experience of God that characterizes Juda-

ism. The *Berakhah* expresses it, the variety of appellations for
God expresses it, and the name *Shekhinah* expresses it, too.
For *Shekhinah* is the name of God used in statements reflect-
ing that normal mystical experience in prayer, in the study of
Torah, in connection with manifestations of God's love or His
holiness, when God is experienced as very near to man.

The philosophers' conception of the immanence of God is
not found in rabbinic writings. For, although *Shekhinah* is
conceived by the Rabbis to be *near* to man, *with* Israel, it is not
understood to be *within* man or *within* Israel as a permanent
resident principle. Their figure is that of Israel "under the
wings of the *Shekhinah*;" but if there are wicked ones among
them (among Israel), they "crowd off the feet of the *Shekhinah*" from the people. *Shekhinah*, in other words, is not permanently or necessarily even *with* the people of Israel; nor
does God, the *Shekhinah*, dwell always in the Temple in Jerusalem. Though the *Shekhinah* dwelt in the Temple, God was
not immanent in it, for He left it when the Temple was destroyed. "At that hour [when the Temple was burned]," says
a Midrash, "the Holy One blessed be He wept, saying, 'Woe
is Me! What have I done! I had caused My *Shekhinah* to dwell
below for the sake of Israel, but now that they have sinned, I
have returned to My original place.'"

God is other than anything in the world, governs it in love
and in justice, according to rabbinic Judaism, but He is not a
principle within the world nor is He in any sense, within man.
Shekhinah is the term used for God when His near Presence
is experienced. But there is another meaning in which the
term *Shekhinah* is employed and it is this second connotation
to which the fifth benediction of the Sabbath *Amidah* alludes.
The whole of the *Berakhah* there reads, "May our eyes behold
Thy return to Zion in mercy. Blessed art Thou, O Lord Who
restores His *Shekhinah* to Zion." When Israel voiced the hope

that their "eyes might behold Thy return to Zion,"—that is, the Lord's return to the Temple—they meant just what they said, quite literally. For this second, much rarer use of the name *Shekhinah* implies not only the sense of God's nearness but clearly indicates an actual experience of seeing or hearing Him. This use of the term *Shekhinah* is usually associated with the Presence of God in the Temple on Mount Zion. It is hinted in rabbinic sources that the pilgrims who came up to the Temple in Jerusalem three times a year for the Festivals, came actually to *see* God, as well as to appear before Him, that is, to *be seen* there.

But this kind of "abnormal" experience was not entirely in consonance with the normal mystical experience so characteristic of rabbinic Judaism. And some outstanding Rabbis, notably Rabbi Akiba, practically denied the possibility of such "abnormal" visions, for they claimed that even the angels did not *see* God. Nevertheless, some references to visions and locutions are found in rabbinic literature. Yet it is very rare to find an experience of this sort described as occurring in their own times by the Rabbis. Such extraordinary phenomena are instead referred to happenings in the remote past, are described as having taken place in the lives of the Patriarchs or the Prophets. And sometimes such unusual events are imagined as occurring in the future, in the Days of the Messiah perhaps, or when the Temple will be restored. To that future possibility does the fifth benediction refer when it says, "May our eyes behold Thy return to Zion. Blessed art Thou, O Lord, Who returns His Presence (*Shekhinato*) to Zion."

THE EXPERIENCE OF TORAH

On Sabbath morning, the service has two foci: *Avodah,* the Service of Prayer, and *Torah,* the reading of the Torah from the Scroll. This reading is not a purely academic exercise. Neither is it read merely for edification. Great reverence is shown to the Torah, and the handling of its parchment Scroll is surrounded by rules intended to make that reverence part of the consciousness of every Jew. A Jew is enjoined to bind Torah on his head and arm, to fasten it on his door, meditate on it and talk of it day and night, teach it to young and old. Is belief in a single, final Revelation the basis for the supreme value and holiness ascribed to the Torah?

We must make it quite clear that Revelation is *not* a Jewish religious term and that, in fact, there is no equivalent for the word Revelation in Biblical or rabbinic Hebrew. *Mattan Torah* (giving of Torah) *is* a rabbinic term and it means the giving of Torah "from Heaven" on Mount Sinai *and* upon other occasions. It is a Jewish belief, a dogma of the Jewish religion. But, on the other hand, it is important to realize that *Mattan Torah* to the Jew is not just a one-time event that occurred in the past. Not only was the Torah given on Mount Sinai, the Rabbis imply, but it is given to the individual here and now and he must make it his own personal experience, through his own actions. There are many, many statements in rabbinic literature that bear this out. For example, ". . . he who is engaged in Torah [that is, the Study of Torah] and observes it, it is as though he received it from Mount Sinai." [9] Moreover, the Rabbis extend the notion of the divine origin of Torah to the Oral Torah (the *Torah Shebe'al Peh*), to the laws and interpretations which they derived from the (written) Torah. They go even further than that. They attribute divine sanction to laws and institutions which they themselves have made and which they recognize were not derived at all from the Bible.[10] Yet these purely rabbinic enactments are considered by them to be also "Torah."

Mattan Torah represents a belief that on a few specific occasions in the distant past God gave Israel Torah. But *Torah* itself is a much larger and more dynamic idea; for the teachings of the Rabbis are also *Torah* and are also conceived to be authorized by God. Thus, the more dogmatic idea of *Mattan Torah* is modified by the idea of *Torah,* Torah which is continually being developed by the Rabbis, which each man can himself experience "as though he [had] received it from Mount Sinai" when he studies it and when he practices its commandments. It is the continuous, actual, personal experience of Torah which is emphasized in the rabbinic teachings and which accounts for the place of Torah in the service and in the daily life of the Jew.

"THIS IS THE TORAH. . . ."

The Scroll of the Torah is housed in an Ark, a cabinet, so placed as to make it visible all over the synagogue. The Ark is set on a platform in the far wall, usually but not necessarily, in the East wall of the synagogue, toward Jerusalem. For many generations—and in some Orthodox synagogues to this day—there was a second platform in the center of the synagogue. The Torah was carried in state from the Ark to the central platform and placed there on a table for reading. The architecture of the interior of the synagogue with its central reading desk reflected the importance of the Torah in the service and, at the same time, permitted the Torah to be brought close enough to the people so that everyone could hear clearly every word as it was read aloud. Today the central reading desk has been eliminated from most synagogues because the problem of acoustics can be so much more efficiently managed. But the custom of carrying the Torah around the synagogue has remained in symbolic form. The Torah is carried from the Ark, down from the platform, and around to the opposite side before it is placed on the desk and unrolled for reading. Although the Ark is called the *Aron Hakodesh*, the holy Ark, we must remember that the Ark and the platform on which it stands do not constitute an altar. There is no altar in a synagogue, only the Torah, a table for unrolling it for reading, and the Readers' lectern. And the Ark is called the *Aron Hakodesh*, the holy Ark, only because it houses the Torah, which is a holy object.

As the Ark is opened, the congregation chants those verses from Numbers (10, 35-6) which tell of what Moses said when the Ark moved forward at the head of the Israelites on their long march from Egypt to the land of Israel, "Arise, O Lord, and Thine enemies shall be scattered and those that hate Thee shall flee from before Thee." The hymn concludes with a verse from Isaiah, "For out of Zion shall go forth the Torah and the word of the Lord from Jerusalem."

The Reader then takes the Torah from the man who has lifted it out of the Ark and says the *Shema Yisrael*, after which the congregation repeats the *Shema*. Then, in different words, not from the Bible, the theme of the *Shema* is chanted again by the Reader and the congregation. And a third time, the Reader calls upon the people to magnify the Lord and to exalt His Name (*Gadelu Iti*). Their response is, "Thine, O Lord, is the greatness and the power and the glory, the victory and the majesty. . . . Exalt ye the Lord our God."

We cannot help but notice that just as the Torah is being

taken out of the Ark with more pomp and ceremony than is found elsewhere in the service, all the hymns, responses and chants lay stress not on the Torah, but on the glory and the power and the majesty of the Lord! And the reason for this apparent incongruity is quite simply that just at this point it is important to counter the danger of Torahlatry, worship of the Torah. It is as if, by these passages in praise of God's greatness, the Rabbis meant to make clear that though the Torah is to be revered and honored, we must not forget that it is the Lord alone Who is to be worshipped.

On the Sabbath seven men are called up to "read" from the Torah, first a *Kohen*, then a *Levi* and then five "Israels." Since the Scroll contains no vowel marks and no guide to its proper cantillation, it became the custom for an expert to read the whole portion, lest any one of those called up be shamed by his inability to read the text correctly. For no least error in the reading was tolerated; every inflection had to be accurately rendered. Only this meticulous insistence on perfect reading and on perfect copying of the text of the Bible could have preserved the Jewish Masoretic (official) text with such marvellous accuracy through two millennia and in many lands. An interesting confirmation of the accuracy of the Jewish text of the Bible has recently come to light. The very ancient text of those fragments of the Book of Isaiah discovered several years ago among the Dead Sea Scrolls differs in only a few minor details from our present Hebrew text of that prophet! And the Pentateuch was even more zealously guarded, since only absolute perfection was admissible in a Scroll for synagogue use.

In spite of the fact that it is so difficult to read correctly from the unvowelled Torah Scroll, a way was found for every Jew to participate in the reading of the Torah. As each man is called up in turn, he touches the first word to be read with his *Tallit* (out of respect, he does not use his bare finger) and he makes the benediction on the Torah. This blessing is an expression of gratitude to God for having so loved His People Israel that He gave them His Torah. After a man's section of the reading has been completed, he makes the appropriate closing benediction on Torah and steps aside for the next person to be called up. His has been the honor and his the *Mitzvah* of having "read" from the Torah.

The honor of being called up to the Torah is associated with a wide range of personal joys and sorrows. A bridegroom is called up on the Sabbath before his marriage. After his reading, a special *Mishebayrakh* is recited for him and his bride. *Mishebayrakh* means, literally, "May He Who blessed . . . ," but it is used as a noun in the sense of a blessing invoked for someone. When a child is born, the father is called to the Torah and a *Mishebayrakh* is made for the mother and child. If the baby is a girl, she is formally named on that occasion. If someone is very ill, a close relative is called up to the Torah and a *Mishebayrakh* is made after the reading for the recovery of the sick person. And on the anniversary of a death (*Yahrzeit*), a man will request that he be called up to the Torah in order that, at its close, he can have a short memorial prayer said in memory of his loved one. Thus these formal expressions of personal joy and sorrow bring about a community sharing in them, a rich by-product of the association of such events with the reading of Torah.

Bar Mitzvah

Not the least important of the personal events connected with the reading of the Torah in the synagogue is the *Bar Mitzvah*. In recent times, some confusion has arisen as to just

what *Bar Mitzvah* is. The words *Bar Mitzvah* are not the name
of a ceremony and certainly do not mean *Confirmation*. In
Jewish law a boy comes of age, for most purposes, at the age of
thirteen. At thirteen he acquires the rights and responsibilities
of an adult male in matters of ritual, and the moral responsibility for his own conduct. *Bar Mitzvah* is the word that describes this adulthood. It is a peculiar word, half Aramaic, half
Hebrew. *Bar* is the Aramaic equivalent of the Hebrew word
Ben, a son. *Mitzvah* in this combination means, roughly, the
commandments of the Torah. A *Bar Mitzvah* is a *person* who is
now permitted (or required, as the case may be) to perform
those *Mitzvot* which his age and capacity permit him to fulfill. He is now required, like every adult male, to put on *Tefillin*
in the morning, and he is now permitted to be called up to the
Torah in the synagogue and to recite the *Berakhah* before and
after the reading. Since, beginning with his thirteenth birthday,
a boy *may* be honored in this way, it is customary to call him to
the Torah on the earliest possible occasion after his birthday.
But whether he is or is not called up to read from the Torah, he
is, in any case, *Bar Mitzvah* automatically at thirteen.

Judaism, traditionally, has no confirmation ceremony. Confirmation means to be confirmed in some belief or creed. Since
the Jewish religion has no official creed, and since becoming a
Jew does not involve giving assent to a creed, confirmation at
puberty or at any other time was not a Jewish rite. In the early
nineteenth century, however, certain German synagogues introduced a confirmation ceremony for boys only. Later, groups of
boys and girls were taught and confirmed together in the synagogue on *Shavu'ot* (Pentecost). The institution spread widely
in Germany, in France, and then in the United States. Confirmation, especially for girls, has become universal in Reform
synagogues in this country and has won very wide acceptance
in Conservative synagogues as well.

A new institution, the *Bat Mitzvah* (feminine of *Bar Mitzvah*), parallel to the *Bar Mitzvah* for boys, has gained many adherents in recent years. *Bat Mitzvah* was first introduced by Dr. M. M. Kaplan at the Sabbath morning services of the Society for the Advancement of Judaism in New York City, in 1923. As an institution with no history in tradition, it has naturally assumed many forms. Some synagogues have made the *Bat Mitzvah* ceremony exactly like the *Bar Mitzvah*, calling up the girl to the Torah on her thirteenth birthday. Others, unwilling to make so radical a break with tradition, have introduced a variety of ceremonies for the *Bat Mitzvah* at the Friday Evening Service when the question of being called up to the Torah does not arise.

These are the chief personal events celebrated in connection with the reading of the Torah.

THE *Haftarah*

When the reading of the whole *Parashah* (weekly portion of the Pentateuch) has been completed, an eighth man called the *Maftir* or concluder, is called up. He recites the same benedictions on the Torah as have the previous seven men, and the Reader repeats the last verses of the *Parashah* for him. At least three, and sometimes more of the seventh section, are re-read. He remains on the *Bimah* (platform) while two more men are called up. One of them lifts the Torah up high over his head and stands with his back to the congregation, his arms raised and extended so that the Scroll is partly unrolled and the written surface visible to the people. When the Torah is lifted up and everyone can see it, the congregation chants the verse from Deuteronomy 4, 14, "This is the Torah which Moses set before the Children of Israel according to the command of the Lord. . . ." Then the Torah is lowered and the second man rolls it up and dresses it in its protecting robes of silk or velvet.

Now the *Maftir* is ready to read the lesson from the Prophets, called the *Haftarah*, the conclusion. Talmudic statements show that by the first century of the Common Era, it was already the custom to read from the Prophets after the reading from the Pentateuch Scroll. At first the choice of the selection was left to the reader, but little by little, specific readings for each *Parashah* became fixed by tradition.

There is always a reason for the choice of a *Haftarah*, a connection between it and the Torah reading of the week. Sometimes that connection is easy to recognize, for similarity of event, person, or theme has determined the choice of the prophetic lesson. But often the thread of connection is a thin one indeed; only one verse or one word may be the link that binds the Torah portion to its parallel prophetic reading.

By the time of Rav Amram Gaon (the middle of the ninth century), the benedictions before and after the *Haftarah* were well established, as we can gather from the fact that they are included in his *Siddur*. The blessing before the *Haftarah* is especially interesting, because in it we meet again the idea that God loved or took delight in the Prophets of truth and righteousness, in the Torah, in Moses His servant, and in Israel His people. The word used to express this love is *Baḥar* (and its variant form, *Boḥer*). We have already called attention to the mistranslation of *Boḥer* in a similar benediction. There, as here, *Boḥer* meant not "chooses," but "loves, takes delight in." In the context of this benediction before the *Haftarah*, the real meaning of the term *Boḥer* can hardly be misunderstood. God did not "choose" the Torah from among other *Torot* (plural of Torah). Only if one reads the passage, "He [God] took delight in the Torah, in Moses . . . , in Israel . . ." does it make sense.

The *Haftarah* is, in most synagogues, read from a voweled, printed book, not a Scroll. After the *Haftarah*, there are four benedictions:

One—on God Whose promises (in the Torah) are to be depended upon, for every word in it will eventually be fulfilled. This is a message of encouragement for dark days.

Two—on God Who will bring joy to Zion and its inhabitants.

Three—on God Who will restore the House of David, allowing none other to sit on the throne as the Messiah. This is a reminder that the Messiah has not yet come.

Four—on God Who hallows the Sabbath.

Yekum Purkan

Before the Torah is returned to the Ark, a prayer called "*Yekum Purkan*, May salvation arise. . . ." is recited for the long life and good health of the scholars, teachers and disciples who study Torah and expound its precepts. The *Talmid Hakham*, the wise or learned man, was more than a scholar. In his mind and in his character, he embodied the Torah. It was he who made the tradition come alive by demonstrating its effectiveness in the moral life. It was he who applied the Torah to new conditions, social and economic, as the need arose. And it was he who, by raising disciples, saw to it that the tradition continued from generation to generation like the living protoplasm of the genes of heredity. Judaism produced other ideal types: saints and heroes. But if one type must be chosen as the apotheosis of Judaism, that one is surely the *Talmid Hakham*.

The second paragraph of the *Yekum Purkan* is a plea to God to extend the same boon of long life, health of body, strong children, ample sustenance, grace, mercy, and loving-kindness to the whole "holy congregation." The congregation is called holy, *Kadisha*, because of course, Israel is a holy people and the individuals who make up the congregation are therefore holy too; and Israel is holy because it performs the *Mitzvot*, it obeys the commandments of the Torah. But, in addition, when any ten men come together to worship, they constitute a *Minyan* or congregation; and only a *Minyan* can conduct a full, public service at which the holiness prayers may be recited. These are the *Kaddish*, including the Mourners' *Kaddish*, the *Kedushah* which is the responsive recitation of the Trisagion ("Holy, holy, holy is the Lord of hosts") during the Reader's repetition of the *Amidah*, and a few other prayers of similar nature. In short, a congregation is called a "holy congregation" not only because its members are holy but because it enjoys the special privilege, as a *Minyan*, of reciting the holiness-prayers.

When the name of a congregation is given in Hebrew, one will often see it preceded by the Hebrew initials, *Kuf Kuf*. These are an abbreviation of the phrase, *Kehillah Kedoshah*, Holy Congregation, and the reference is to the same phrase, with the same connotations of the word "holy" as is found in the Aramaic equivalent in the *Yekum Purkan*.

ANNOUNCING THE "NEW MOON"

The Jewish calendar is punctuated by a full quota of holidays. Spring and Fall are enriched by frequent Festivals and Holy Days. Winter is marked by *Hanukkah* and summer by *Tishah Be'av*. The Sabbath comes every week and the first day of the new month is also a holiday, an occasion for renewal of hope and renewal of life. It is celebrated as a minor holiday

called *Rosh Hodesh,* the head of, or the first of, the month. On
the Sabbath before *Rosh Hodesh,* the blessing for the new
month is recited in the synagogue, just before the Torah is returned to the Ark. Standing before the people with the Torah
in his arms to give the occasion added weight and solemnity,
the Reader publicly proclaims the day of the week on which
the new month will begin. This custom arose in the time of
the *Geonim* (plural of *Gaon*) and is recorded in the *Siddur* of
Rav Amram in the ninth century. The determination of the
exact time of the beginning of the month assumed great importance in the early centuries of the Common Era, because
on the date of the new month depended the determination of
the dates of all the other Jewish Holy Days and Festivals.

The Jewish calendar is based essentially on the lunar year—
that is, on the phases of the moon. Coordination of the lunar
and the solar years, so that Passover will always come in the
spring and the Day of Atonement in the fall, is achieved by a
system of leap years and added months determined by a series
of compilcated mathematical computations. In the eighth century of the Common Era, a dispute arose between the sectarian Karaites and the Rabbinites from whom the Jews of
today are spiritually descended. The point at issue (and it was
only one among many) concerned the method for determining
the day on which the new month was to begin. The Karaites
insisted on the older method of visual identification of the new
moon, whereas the Rabbinites preferred to compute the exact
day mathematically. For this reason the Rabbis instituted the
custom of announcing publicly the correct time of the new
moon's beginning according to their reckoning. In an old
Roman *Prayer Book* we find this sentence preceding the announcement of *Rosh Hodesh:* "Thus did our Rabbis rule, that
we remind this holy congregation, so that all, adults and children, may know that *Rosh Hodesh* of the month of [So-and-So]

will fall on [this-and-this] day, according to the reckoning of the Rabbis."

THE "FEAR OF HEAVEN" AND THE LOVE OF GOD

The public announcement is preceded by an ancient prayer [11] for sustenance and health, for a "life in which there is *Yirat Shama'yim* [fear of Heaven] and fear of sin . . . , a life in which we shall have love of Torah and fear of Heaven. . . ." This prayer was inserted as prelude to the announcement of the new month only about two hundred years ago. It is one of the many prayers composed for personal use by a Rabbi of the Talmud and later incorporated into the *Prayer Book* because of its aptness, power, or beauty. It includes among its more usual requests, as the quotation here indicates, a peculiar petition, a plea for *Yirat Shama'yim*, for the fear of Heaven. A man normally prays to be free from fear; he does not pray for "a life in which there is fear!" Yet the words "fear of God" or "to fear the Lord" are very frequently found in the Bible and in rabbinic texts as well. A careful survey of the use of these terms in the Bible reveals that to fear God and to love God are phrases employed interchangeably to mean devotion to Him. Certainly in the Bible, no notion of contrasting emotions is suggested, though in English fear and love certainly connote altogether different feelings. In Deuteronomy, the commands both to fear and to love God are repeated again and again in connection with the injunction to keep God's commandments. The two words are used together for emphasis, and separately with the same connotations. The first two paragraphs of the *Shema* are well known examples of the close connection between love of God and devotion to the commandments of the Torah: "Thou shalt *love the Lord,* thy God, with all thy heart. . . . And these words which I command thee this day shall be upon thy heart. . . ." And again in the second paragraph, ". . . if ye hearken to My commandments . . . *to love the Lord,* your God, and to serve Him. . . ." But there are also several parallel passages citing fear of God as the emotional basis for obeying the commands of the Torah. For example, in Chapter 5, 26 (Deuteronomy), God speaks of Israel and says: "O that they had such a heart as this always, *to fear Me* and to keep My commandments. . . ." So completely are the motivations of love and fear identified in Deuteronomy, that in Chapter 10, 12, we find that both love and fear are used in one verse and in the same sense: "What doth the Lord, thy God, ask of thee, but *to fear the Lord,* thy God, to walk in all His ways and *to love Him* and to serve the Lord, thy God, with all thy soul, . . . and to keep, for thy good, the commandments of the Lord. . . ." The full force of the identity of love and fear expressed in this verse is perhaps not apparent unless one is aware of the parallelism so characteristic of the Hebrew style of the Bible. Two phrases or two clauses, each worded a little differently, are frequently employed to convey the same idea; it is a device used for emphasis.

We find this parallel use of love and fear not only in the Pentateuch; it extends to the rest of the Bible as well. It is frequently illustrated in Psalms, where one instance after another can be cited to show that godly men are spoken of as those who "fear the Lord" or as those who "love the Lord," and both phrases connote the same quality.[12]

In rabbinic literature, as in the Bible, both expressions are often used to mean devotion to God. In the Midrash, *Seder Eliahu,* we find that: "[A man] should say to himself, 'I love Heaven and I fear Heaven,' in order not to transgress any of the *Mitzvot* of the Torah."[13] Nevertheless, the Rabbis do sometimes distinguish between loving God and fearing Him, and then the words *love* and *fear* are taken to mean more nearly what they mean in English. When that is the case, the Rabbis always teach that love of God is superior to fear of Him. Rabbi Simeon ben Eleazar says, "Greater is he who acts from love than him who acts from fear." [14] And in another instance, in a Midrashic commentary on Deuteronomy, it is said: "The Torah makes a distinction between the man who acts from love and the man who acts from fear, and the reward of the former is far greater than that of the latter."

However, the specific significance of the term *Yirat Shama'yim* (fear of Heaven) as it is used in the prayer we are discussing is new with the Rabbis. For them, it has several connotations closely related to the general meaning of the phrases in the Bible *to love God* and *to fear God;* it implies piety, care in the observance of the *Mitzvot*. But in rabbinic literature, *Yirat Shama'yim* is also tantamount to the acceptance of the Kingship of God. Now we can understand why a man would pray for *Yirat Shama'yim*. It is not fear of the Lord the prayer entreats Him to grant. It is devotion to God, full acceptance of His Kingship, and careful observance of all His commandments which a man aspires to achieve in the month before him.

After this introductory plea and a short prayer for the redemption of Israel, the ancient formula announcing the new month is pronounced. The closing prayer to "the Holy One, blessed be He" beseeches Him to grant us a renewal of life in the month before us, joy and salvation to the whole House of Israel.

RETURNING THE TORAH TO THE ARK

After the congregation has recited *Ashray*, the Reader takes
the Scroll of the Torah and chants verse 13 of Psalm 148,
"Praise the Name of the Lord for His Name alone is exalted."
This verse exalting God may have been placed here just before the Torah is returned to the Ark, to make it perfectly clear
again that, though the Torah is "true, enduring and precious,"
it is God Who is *Nisgav Levado*, Who is alone exalted. This
is the opinion of a great medieval commentator, known as The
Roke'ah from the name of his most famous book. He was
Eleazar ben Judah ben Kalonymous of Worms (Germany)
who died in 1238, after having been the Rabbi of Worms for
many years. He was a Talmudist of vast erudition, a commentator on the Bible, a liturgist with a clear and lovely style,
an astronomer who knew all the sciences of his day, and with
it all, a Kabbalist who was swayed by visions of legions of
angels and demons! He had suffered terribly during the Crusades. One day, while he was working on his commentary to
Genesis, two Crusaders had entered the house and killed his
wife, their two daughters, and their only son. In spite of this
great tragedy, his ethical works, the best known of which is
The Roke'ah, exhibit gentle piety, great patience, and love for
humanity.

For hundreds of years Jews have called their leading
scholars, not by their own, personal names, but by the names
of their most famous books. The personality of the man is lost
in his best spiritual product; his person fades into such insig-
nificance that even his name is forgotten—but his book is not!
It is The Roke'ah who called attention to the striking fact that,
as the Torah is put away, it is God Whom we exalt lest we

forget that the Torah is only another of God's creations. It is natural, then, to infer that this, very likely, is also the motive for singing the short hymns exalting God as the Torah is removed from the Ark.

Before it is replaced, the Torah is carried again in a procession around the synagogue, while Psalm 29 is chanted responsively by Cantor (or Reader) and congregation. This Psalm, too, tells of God's power and glory as it is revealed in a magnificent storm that thunders in from the sea and strips the forests bare. But through the din and the tearing winds, God sits firmly enthroned in His Temple on High and rules as King forever. He will give His people strength (*Oz*) and bless them with peace. Moreover, according to a Midrash, *Oz*, strength, signifies Torah, and that is why Psalm 29 is chanted here. They read the last verse thus: "God will give *Oz* [that is, Torah] to His people."

As the Scroll is being replaced in the Ark, another hymn is sung in which, at last, Torah itself is mentioned. God says, "For I have given you a goodly portion; do not forsake My Torah. It is a tree of life to them that lay hold of it and its supporters are made happy. Its roads are roads of pleasantness and all its paths lead to peace" (Proverbs 3, 18-19).

Musaf—THE ADDITIONAL SERVICE

The synagogue service is, wherever possible, analogous to the order of the sacrifice services in the Temple. *Minhah,* for example, is the equivalent of the afternoon *Tamid* sacrifice. The daily morning service is also parallel to the regular morning sacrifice offered in the Temple. On Sabbaths, New Moons, and Festivals, an additional offering was brought after the usual morning sacrifice and this was called the *Musaf,* meaning "that which is added." That is why there is a *Musaf* or Additional Service on Sabbath morning after the *Amidah.* The *Musaf* is really, in form, another *Amidah,* and, like the Friday night and the Sabbath morning *Amidah,* it consists of seven benedictions. The first three and the last three are identical with those of the daily *Amidah.*

The middle benediction, the fourth, describes the Sabbath Additional Sacrifice Offerings. The introduction to this *Berakhah* is an acrostic in reverse, beginning with the last letter of the alphabet, *Tav.* "*Tikanta Shabbat,*" it begins, "Thou didst institute the Sabbath." It is a song in praise of the delights of the Sabbath. "Those that *taste* it merit life," it says. There are several interpretations of this odd statement. One commentator takes it to mean that the Sabbath, here and now, is a *foretaste* of the delights of the World to Come, which will be "all Sabbath," as it were, with no workaday days in between. Another commentator explains that it refers to the reward for the *Mitzvah* of eating especially fine food on the Sabbath! His demonstration depends upon a play on the Hebrew words for *taste* and fine or *tasty foods.*

"THERE IS NONE LIKE OUR GOD. . . ."

After *Musaf,* the congregation sings a hymn, "*Ayn Kelohaynu,* There Is None Like Our God." It is a favorite hymn of little children who find it so easy to learn the few repetitive words long before they can have any notion of the theology implicit in them. The doggerel-like music and the arrangement of the words as we have them is exceptionally inappropriate to the meaning of the hymn, which is a solemn profession of God's uniqueness. The original of *Ayn Kelohaynu* must be older than the ninth century, for in Rav Amram's *Siddur* he cites the poem but gives an earlier arrangement of the verses. The original version reads, "Who is like our God [*Mi Kelohaynu*]? There is none like our God [*Ayn Kelohaynu*]." Therefore, "We will acknowledge our God [*Nodeh Laylohaynu*]" by saying, "Blessed be our God [*Barukh Elohaynu*]." Then, for emphasis, it concludes, "Thou art our God [*Atah Elohaynu*]." The rearrangement of the verses as we find them in our Prayer Books must be laid to the door of some acrostic-loving poet of the geonic period, for in its present form, the initial letters of the lines do spell out "Am[e]n," but the clear meaning of the original has certainly been blurred in the process!

14

Minḥah on Sabbath Afternoon

*M*inḥah on Sabbath afternoon is a much more leisurely serv-
ice than it is on weekdays. It begins as usual with *Ashray*.
Immediately following *Ashray*, the prayer "*Uva Letzion Go'ayl,*
A Redeemer shall come to Zion" is recited. This is a collection
of verses from, among others, Isaiah, Ezekiel, and Psalms. On
Sabbath afternoon it was the custom in Babylon during rab-
binic times for people to gather in the synagogue before
Minḥah to listen to a discourse on Torah and to read from the
Prophets and the "Writings." *Writings* includes the Books of
Psalms, Proverbs, Job, Song of Songs, Ruth, Lamentations,
Ecclesiastes, Esther, Daniel, Ezra, Nehemiah, and the two
Books of Chronicles. A few centuries later, in the time of the
Geonim, the passages from Scripture were usually chosen to
emphasize the theme of redemption, and the readings would
close with a *Kedushah,* a holiness-passage. In time the themes
and the choice of passages to be read became fixed and formalized, and that is how *Uva Letzion* came to be put together and
to be recited at *Minḥah* on Sabbath afternoon.

But this same prayer, *Uva Letzion,* is also recited daily near
the close of the morning service, after *Ashray*. There it serves
the function of introducing into the daily service some passages from the Prophets as a kind of *Haftarah,* since no other,
specific provision is made on weekdays for readings from the

Prophets. On *Shabbat* morning, however, since the Torah is read at the service and is followed by a prophetic reading (the *Haftarah*), it is not necessary to introduce the Prophets through the verses quoted in *Uva Letzion* and it is therefore omitted. But, in order not to skip this prayer entirely on the Sabbath, it is read at *Minḥah*. This is the explanation offered by two of the later Geonim, Rav Sherira Gaon and Rabenu Hai Gaon for the "peregrinations" of *Uva Letzion* from one service to another.[1]

This apparently overcomplicated explanation for the presence of one prayer in the daily morning service, its absence from the Sabbath morning prayers, and its reappearance at *Minḥah* on the Sabbath is quoted here quite deliberately. For it is an excellent example of the tightly constructed architecture of the prayers to which we have often alluded. Nothing about the basic, "required" prayers of the *Siddur* is haphazard or accidental. There is always a logical reason, within the given framework, for the choice or omission of certain prayers in any service. It is true that more "recent" medieval prayers, dirges, poems, and hymns have been added, sometimes by whim or by accident, but the original form is like every classic, a thing of beautiful articulation and reasonable structure.

The *Kedushah* in this prayer (*Uva Letzion*) is a quotation from Isaiah 6, 3, "Holy, holy, holy is the Lord of hosts; the whole earth is full of His glory." Immediately following the Hebrew—and this is unique in the prayers—is an Aramaic translation, free enough to be in the nature of a commentary on the verse. The Aramaic reads, "Holy—in the highest heavens, the place of His abode; holy—upon earth, the work of His might; holy—for ever and ever to all eternity is the Lord of hosts; the whole earth is full of the radiance of His glory." It has been suggested [2] that this paraphrase of the Trisagion is an oblique, polemical reference to the Christian use of this verse in its

liturgy, with the implication of support for the idea of the
Trinity in the threefold, "Holy, Holy, Holy." The Trisagion is
repeated in the prayer, *Uva Letzion,* says Mann, together with
its Aramaic Targum (translation), in order to make perfectly
clear that each of the times *Holy* is repeated it refers only to
God Who is God in heaven, God on earth, and God for all time
past and future.

The Aramaic paraphrase of the *Kedushah* (Holy, holy, holy)
to which we have just referred is taken from a Targum, known
as the *Targum Jonathan.* The word *Targum* means a version,
interpretation, or translation, but it is used in rabbinic and in
later Jewish literature to designate specifically the Aramaic
translations of Scripture. The word *Targum* is not Hebrew
in origin. It is derived from the Greek *Tragēma,* meaning "that
which comes after the meal, dessert or sweetmeat." [3] Only its
history can explain the strange connection between *dessert*
and a translation of the Bible. For in rabbinic times, as each
original Hebrew verse of Scripture was read aloud in the synagogue, it was immediately followed by a translation into the
vernacular. The translation was recited by a *Meturgeman* or
translator who stood by during the reading of the Torah for
just this purpose. Thus the translation followed each verse
like a dessert, a *Tragēma.* (The Talmud, by the way, retains the
original meaning of *Tragēma* as well; it speaks of making a
lunch of *Minay Tragima,* of various sweetmeats or desserts.)
Hence this odd name for an Aramaic translation of the Bible!
The Targums were, in effect, not only translations of the Bible
but interpretations of the text prepared for the people of their
day by the Rabbis.

The *Targum Jonathan* is an Aramaic version of the Prophets
made by Jonathan ben Uzziel in Palestine at the beginning of
the Common Era. But the text we have today was reworked
by the Babylonian Rabbis and is therefore probably several

centuries later. It is from this Targum that the Aramaic interpretation of the Trisagion in the prayer *Uva Letzion* is taken.
The prayer continues with verses chosen from the Psalms to
emphasize God's loving-kindness. "For He is merciful, He forgives sin and will not destroy. Again and again He withholds
His anger and does not stir up all His wrath. For Thou art
good and forgiving, O Lord, and abundant in loving-kindness
to all who call upon Thee."

LIFE AFTER DEATH AND THE "WORLD TO COME"

After these verses from the Psalms, the prayer, *Uva Letzion*,
continues thus, "May it be Thy will, O Lord our God and God of
our fathers, that we may keep Thy statutes in *this world* and
be worthy to live to see and inherit goodness and blessing
in the *Days of the Messiah* and in the life of the *World to
Come*." These are rabbinic statements and they call attention
to certain ideas which, in other religions, have played a crucial
role. Perhaps for this reason, and for others into which we
need not enter here, the function of the concept of the World
to Come in Judaism has not been clearly understood in our
time.

The order of "events" described in the prayer just quoted is
this: after this world, come the Days of the Messiah—a time
of "goodness and blessing" here on earth—and then, the World
to Come, with no indication of what that world may be and
only a hint that it will follow the Days of the Messiah.

On Sabbath morning, in the first blessing before the *Shema*
("*Hakol Yodukha*, All shall acknowledge Thee"), we find the
same ideas arranged this time in different order. It reads:
"There is none to be compared to Thee, O Lord our God, in

this world, and there is none other than Thee, O our King, in the life of the *World to Come.* We have none but Thee, O our Redeemer, for the *Days of the Messiah* and none is like Thee, O our Savior, for the *Revival of the Dead.*" Nothing is added here to the description of these states except that, in this case, the *World to Come* precedes the *Days of the Messiah,* and last in the series is added the idea of the *Revival of the Dead.*

There has been much discussion in recent years about what the stand of the Jewish religion is on the question of life after death, whether the ideas of the *World to Come,* the *Days of the Messiah,* and the *Revival of the Dead* are or are not Jewish dogmas, and whether the Jewish religion, like many other religions, is not other-worldly, oriented toward a life after death and motivated in large measure by possible reward or punishment in the hereafter. An examination of rabbinic statements on these subjects will, we believe, show that although some of the ideas named in these two prayers *are* Jewish dogmas, the Jewish religion as a whole is not oriented to the "other world," and, in fact, is decidedly vague on the whole question of the nature of the "other world."

There is no real unanimity among the Rabbis on any of these concepts. But the authorities seem to agree that preceding the Revival of the Dead (*Teḥiyat Hamaytim*), there will be a period called the Days of the Messiah. They do not agree on the duration of this period; estimates run from forty to seven thousand years! There is a variety of opinions, too, on just what will happen during the Days of the Messiah, but all seem to feel that the Days of the Messiah will be a sort of Golden Age here on earth some time in the future. Representative of the trend of opinion in the matter is this statement from the Talmud, "Samuel said, 'There will be no difference between this world and the Days of the Messiah except only [delivery from] subjection to empires.' "[4]

Revival of the Dead is undoubtedly a rabbinic dogma. Those who deny it, say the Rabbis, will "have no portion in the World to Come." But it is not a dogma in the sense in which we ordinarily understand the word *dogma*. It is, after all, a *rabbinic* dogma, and therefore we find that some divergence of opinion exists concerning the way in which the revival will occur, who will be revived, when and where it will take place. There is none of the clarity, unanimity, and definiteness we ordinarily associate with a dogma.

On the World to Come, there is an even greater disparity of views. Some believe that at death the souls of the righteous enter at once into the World to Come; others deny its advent until some far future time. We must conclude that rabbinic authorities have been deliberately ambiguous in their use of the term, the World to Come. Individual Rabbis of the Talmud differ among themselves even about the order in which these various states will occur, and the Talmud itself takes no definitive stand.[5] Certainly, no uniform, clearly defined belief concerning any of these ideas can be discovered from an analysis of rabbinic statements either in the *Siddur* or in other sources.

Must we conclude, then, that Judaism does believe in a life after death? Yes, but when, how, and where are never made very clear. On the contrary, the Jew is continually admonished to observe the *Mitzvot* of the Torah, to obey the commandments of God, not because he will suffer eternal torments in some kind of Hell if he does not obey, not because he will go to some kind of Heaven if he is good, but because *God* commanded the *Mitzvot* and because "its [Torah's] ways are ways of pleasantness and all its paths lead to peace."

THE CYCLE OF READING THE TORAH

On Sabbath afternoon the Scroll is removed from the Ark and the first part of the next week's *Sidrah* (portion) is read. Since the selection is short, only three men are called up to the Torah—a *Kohen*, a *Levi* and one *Yisrael*. The cycle of Torah reading is never-ending. After the whole of one week's portion has been read on Sabbath morning, not one day is allowed to go by before the next *Sidrah* is begun. And so at *Minḥah* on Sabbath afternoon, the new *Sidrah* is read, at least in part. The yearly cycle of readings is also continuous. There is no interval at all between the completion of the last section of the last Book of the Pentateuch and the beginning again of the first chapter of Genesis. As soon as the last verse of Deuteronomy has been read at the morning service on *Simḥat Torah* (the last day of the Feast of Tabernacles called "Rejoicing in the Torah"), a second Scroll is opened and Genesis is begun again, "In the beginning God created the heavens and the earth."

Sidrah and *Parashah* are the terms used to describe the portion of the Torah read each week or at other stated times. *Parashah* means a part or a portion. *Sidrah* is from the same root as the word *Siddur*, meaning order or arrangement. So intimately associated with the synagogue and its customs was the life of the Jew that a week's date was identified by the name of the *Parashah* for that week. *Parashat Noaḥ*, the *Parashah* of Noah, is that week in the year when the weekly reading begins with Chapter 6, verse 9, of the Book of Genesis, "These are the generations of Noah."

The Torah was read and studied continuously. Its ideas and interpretations filled the mind and the conversation of the Jew,

and time itself was measured for him by the weekly readings
from the Torah.

THE *Amidah* FOR SABBATH AFTERNOON—
RABBINIC CONCEPTS OF HISTORY

After the Torah has been returned to the Ark, the *Amidah*
for Sabbath afternoon is recited. Each Sabbath *Amidah,* including this one, has seven benedictions instead of the daily nineteen. The first three and the last three blessings are constant
for every service, but the middle one, the fourth, is the special
Sabbath blessing, and varies for each of the Sabbath services.

At *Minḥah* the fourth benediction is, as we said, devoted to
the Sabbath. Now, in the utterly relaxed peace of a Sabbath
afternoon, awareness is centered on the quiet, tranquility and
joy of the Sabbath. It is the complete rest which God has
vouchsafed His children that is most deeply felt at *Minḥah.*
To make more vivid the happiness and joyousness of the day,
the prayer relates that, "Abraham rejoiced, Isaac was happy,
Jacob and his sons rested on it."

To describe the Patriarchs as enjoying the Sabbath is a
queer inversion of history for, from the point of view of the
Rabbis, the Sabbath was not given to Israel until after the
Exodus from Egypt. Nor is this an isolated instance. Rabbinic
literature is full of anachronisms. They tell of Jacob, "dweller
in tents," sitting in his tent—and studying Torah! Surely the
Rabbis were not primitives; how then can one account for their
historical "blunders?"

If we recognize that the prayers, the homilies, preachments
and Bible interpretations of the Rabbis are little concerned
with what we distinguish as objective facts—except insofar

as these illustrate or point up one of their religious ideas—we will go a long way toward understanding their method of exposition. In the prayer we are considering, it is the joy of the Sabbath they mean to emphasize; in the homily on Jacob, it is Torah; in some of the tales about angels, we saw it was the idea of God's loving-kindness which the Rabbis were trying to convey. Whether they speak of angels or personify the sun and the moon, whether they place Jacob in an academy of learning or ascribe Sabbath observance to Abraham, is of no import to them, provided these concrete instances help them to teach or to make emotionally meaningful some significant religious idea.

It would be absurd to imagine that confusion of thought produced these anachronisms, for the minds that exhibited the fine-spun reasoning, the impeccable logic of the *Halakhah* cannot be accused of carelessness about "facts" or of sheer fuzziness of thought. When we find such apparent naïveté on the part of the Rabbis, we may be certain that it is not accidental. On the contrary, if we understand it, this type of exposition reveals to us what is unique and important in the religion of the Rabbis —their values, or better, their value-ideas: God's loving-kindness, Torah, God's Kingship, Israel, Holiness, the Sabbath, and many more. The Sabbath is so precious in their eyes, so basic to the whole universe, that God Himself rested on the Seventh Day. Surely, the Patriarchs, those fathers of great stature, can hardly be conceived to have been other than Sabbath-observers. The "facts of history" are for the moment irrelevant, for by this association of the Patriarchs with the Sabbath, the Rabbis are able to undescore the value and universality of the Sabbath.

Psalms 104 and 120 to 134 are read on Sabbath afternoon. During the summer months, it is customary to study a tractate of the Mishnah known in English as *The Ethics of the*

Fathers, but in Hebrew called *Avot,* that is *Fathers.* This tractate came to be separately available as a part of the *Siddur,* and it was then titled, *Pirkay Avot,* literally, *Chapters of the Fathers.* The word "Ethics" in the English title is, in other words, a gratuitous addition, devised by a translator.

The *Minḥah* Service closes, as usual, with *Alaynu* and the Mourners' *Kaddish.*

15

The Sabbath Departs

In Hebrew there is a name for the night the Sabbath ends. It is *Motza'ay Shabbat*—literally, the Departure of the Sabbath. Nearly as much ceremony surrounds the end of the Sabbath as its beginning. With great reluctance the Jews part from their Sabbath Queen. The evening prayer (*Ma'ariv*) is delayed until it is dark enough for three stars to be visible, in order to lengthen out the Sabbath, to "add from the workaday to the holy," as they put it.

Two Psalms, 44 and 67, preface the Evening Service on *Motza'ay Shabbat*. The service proceeds as on week nights until the fourth benediction of the *Amidah*. There, a paragraph is added to take note of the basic distinction between the Sabbath that is leaving and the work week ahead. It is made clear that this distinction is a fundamental one, for God Himself "differentiated between the holy and the ordinary, between light and darkness, between Israel and the [other] peoples, between the Seventh Day and the six days of work." But the prayer looks not only backward to the departing glory of the Sabbath. It faces squarely forward to the week ahead, and it ends on this note: "Our Father, our King, may the days coming to meet us begin in peace; may they be free of sin and cleansed of iniquity and marked by attachment to reverence for Thee." In Hebrew, this last phrase is *Beyiratekha,* with the connotations of *Yirat Shama'yim* which we discussed above.

After the *Amidah,* selections from Scripture are recited. Throughout the service on *Motza'ay Shabbat,* we feel not only the regret Jews experienced at leaving the spiritual heights to which the Sabbath had raised them but a brooding anxiety over the trials of the coming week. Life in Palestine under the Romans, and indeed wherever the Jews lived during those years, was hard and dangerous. The work of most men (and this included the Rabbis who earned their livelihood by a trade like other Jews) was physically exhausting and the wages pitifully small. Men needed encouragement and they found it in the selections from Scripture which they read as the new week was about to begin on Saturday night. The verses chosen recount numerous blessings from the Torah. There are those given by Isaac to Jacob, his son: "God give thee the dew of heaven and the fatness of the earth . . . God Almighty bless thee and make thee fruitful and multiply thee . . . ;" and the blessing Jacob gave to his son, Joseph: ". . . the Almighty, may He bless thee with the blessings of the heavens above and of the deep that crouches beneath. . . ." There are blessings chosen from those God gave Israel "because ye hearken to these ordinances and keep them . . . , He will love you and bless you and multiply you. He will bless the fruit of your body and the fruit of your land. . . . The Lord will take away from you all sickness. . . ." All these and others are quoted from the Pentateuch. But promises of God's help, of joy and peace for Israel, have been culled from the Prophets too. A note of comfort has been discovered even in Jeremiah and included here: ". . . for I [God] will turn their mourning into joy and will comfort them. . . ."

Perhaps, after all the blessings and the praise and encouragement, some caution against too much self-confidence was felt to be necessary. And so an excerpt from the Talmud on humility is appended here. "Rabbi Yohanan said, 'In every passage in which you find the greatness of the Holy One blessed be He there you will find also His humility.' "[1] Together with humility, the rest of this passage teaches the ideal of equal justice for all, and it has been suggested[2] that this Midrash, placed here just as the week of business is about to begin, is meant to be a warning and a reminder to deal with everyone in absolute fairness and to be especially tender of the interests of the weak and the helpless, for God Himself "executes justice for the fatherless and the widow, and loveth the stranger. . . ."

Psalm 128, which sings the praises of honest labor, follows. It is a fitting reminder that the hard labor of the week has a noble side to it. "When thou shalt eat of the hard labor of thy hands, happy shalt thou be and it shall be well with thee. . . . May the Lord bless thee out of Zion; mayest thou see that all is well with Jerusalem all the days of thy life and mayest thou see thy children's children. . . ."

Havdalah is said both at the synagogue as part of the service and at home. When it is part of the Evening Service at the synagogue, it is recited after Psalm 128 and begins with the benediction over wine, omitting the introductory verses, "*Hinay El Yishu'ati*, Behold, the Lord is my salvation." *Ma'ariv* closes with *Alaynu* and the Mourners' *Kaddish*.

Havdalah—THE NEW WEEK BEGINS

Havdalah is a rite that marks the formal close of the Sabbath and the beginning of the new week. The word *Havdalah* means, literally, differentiation or separation. Essentially, *Hav-*

dalah on Saturday night consists of three parts: One—an introductory prayer, said only when *Havdalah* is recited at home; Two—the benedictions over wine, over spices, and over the "lights of fire"; Three—the benediction on God Who differentiated between the Sabbath and the six work days of the week.

Exactly when *Havdalah* was first instituted and in what form is not altogether clear. According to the Talmud, it was established as part of the synagogue service for the night of Sabbath by the "Men of the Great Synagogue" (about 400 B.C.E.). In corroboration of its relatively early origin, we may note that the teachers of the Mishnah, who lived in the second century C.E., take the *Havdalah* entirely for granted as a well-established rite. The Tadmud implies that *Havdalah* was originally a synagogue prayer, later introduced into the home as well, in order to make sure that all the members of each household would hear it.

But this is not, apparently, the view of the teachers of the Mishnah who lived several centuries earlier than the Rabbis of the Talmud. In their discussions, the *Tanna'im* (teachers of the Mishnah) seem to assume that the blessings of the *Havdalah* were associated with the last meal of the Sabbath, late in the day near sundown. We can readily understand how, in this kind of setting, wine, spices, and light (or fire) came to be the means of signalizing the close of the Sabbath. Wine was part of every festive meal and the benediction on wine was pronounced when it was drunk, probably at the close of that late Sabbath meal. That would account for the wine and the benediction on wine in the *Havdalah* ceremony.

As for the spices, it was customary to bring to the table a brazier of glowing coals on which spices had been sprinkled to release their fragrance. Spices were in wide general use in those days when plumbing was unknown and hot water was rarely available. They were used for everything from perfuming one's hands and person to sweetening the odor of cooking pots. On the Sabbath, the hot coals which released the odor of the spices were naturally not permitted, and therefore the close of the Sabbath was the first occasion of the week for again introducing the spices, preceded by the appropriate blessing. And that is why the spices are sniffed and the benediction on them recited in the *Havdalah* ceremony to this day. Of course, we no longer sprinkle the spices on a bed of glowing coals. We are content to enjoy their fragrance through a lacy, filigree silver spice box.

The benediction on light, the third in the *Havdalah* service, stems obviously from the fact that on the Sabbath it was forbidden to kindle fire. Therefore kindling a fresh light marked the end of the Sabbath, and was followed by a special benediction. For this fresh light and this benediction, we use a candle. But it is a peculiar kind of candle, braided of several strands of wax so that at least two wicks, often more, are lighted at once. Many fanciful reasons have been advanced to explain the use of a multiple light. But one of them has the weight of tradition to support it.

The text of the blessing on the light is taken from the Mishnah.[3] The two leading Schools of thought and of the interpretation of the law in the time of the Mishnah were those of Hillel and Shammai who lived in the first century of the Common Era. In general, the School of Shammai was the stricter and that of Hillel, the more lenient in the application of the law, and these differences may reflect basic differences in the characters of the two leaders and of those who chose to follow one or the other of them; Hillel was the gentler, Shammai the sterner, personality. Now, the Schools of Hillel and of Shammai had proposed slightly different forms of the benediction on the lights at *Havdalah*. Usually, when the Mishnah records a difference of opinion between the Schools of Hillel and of

Shammai, the law is with Hillel. That is why the version we use today is the one proposed by Hillel. It reads: "Blessed art Thou, O Lord our God, King of the Universe, Who creates the lights of fire (*Me'oray Ha'aysh*)." Note the words, ". . . Who creates [now, in the present] the lights of fire [many lights]. . . ." On the basis of the present tense of the verb (*creates*) and the plural form, *lights*, commentators have explained the blessing in a way that may well also represent what Hillel intended when he worded the benediction as he did. Many lights, in many forms, they say, are continually being kindled, recreated by us. The wisdom to create fire and to kindle anew all kinds of lights is wisdom given us by the Holy One blessed be He. We thank Him for this gift and bless the Lord, King of the universe, for it is He Who is really the Creator of all these continually renewed, rekindled lights. This then is the reason for using the multiple light of the braided candle for *Havdalah*. The braided candle, shedding several lights at once, represents the *Me'oray Ha'aysh*, the many lights continually created afresh by man through God's gift of understanding.

Numerous explanations, mystical and poetic, have been advanced to account for each of the objects used in the *Havdalah* ceremony. The spices, particularly, have intrigued mystics since the days of the Talmud. Some said that since the additional Sabbath oversoul, the *Neshamah Yetayrah*, departs with the Sabbath, the spices are offered to help speed it on its way. Another view would have it that the fragrance of the spices is inhaled to revive the saddened soul left behind. But we have tried to confine ourselves here to the more prosaic historical background of these customs wherever it is available.

When the third benediction, on the "lights of fire," has been pronounced, we hold our fingers up to inspect them by the light of the candle in order to "use" the light for which we have just thanked God in the benediction. And for the same reason—

because we must always use or do the thing to which a blessing refers when we have recited it—we actually sniff the spices
after we have said the *Berakhah* on them.

The fourth benediction of the *Havdalah* repeats the list of
"differentiations" between the holy and the ordinary, between
light and darkness, Israel and the other peoples, and between
the Seventh Day and the six working days of the week.

"FAITH IN GOD" AS JUDAISM CONCEIVES IT

These are the four benedictions of the *Havdalah* common
to the service in the synagogue and at home. But when a man
returns from the synagogue or has said his evening prayer at
home, he gathers his family about him for the full *Havdalah*
service. He lights the plaited candle and gives it to the young-
est to hold. The spice box and the wine cup have been set out.
He lifts the cup of wine in his right hand and says: "*Hinay El
Yeshuati,* Behold, God is my Savior. I will trust [*Evtah*] and
have no fear for God, the Lord, is my strength and my song
and He will help me." These two verses from Isaiah are a
profession of faith in God, of trust in his protective care. The
anxieties and problems that await one after the Sabbath respite
is over are easier to contemplate if one is assured of God's
help in meeting them.

The word used in this Bible verse to express trust in God is
Evtah, I will trust. In rabbinic literature, we find the same
idea represented by the noun *Bitahon,* trust or faith. Both are
from the same Hebrew root, though the connection is not apparent in the English transliteration. To understand just what
the Bible and the Rabbis mean by the words *Evtah* and *Bitahon*
is to penetrate very deep into the heart of the Jewish religion.

We must be careful not to confuse the Jewish idea of *Bitahon* with the idea of faith as it is commonly understood in other religions. For faith in the sense of credence or belief in "sound doctrine" is entirely foreign to Judaism. In the Jewish religion, faith in God does not mean belief in His existence, nor is "belief in God" a Jewish dogma. In fact, there is no word or phrase in rabbinic Hebrew that expresses the idea of *belief* in God. There is another word, *Emunah,* faith, which has the same connotations as *Bitahon* in rabbinic texts, but which medieval Jewish philosophers appropriated to express their idea of religious *belief*.[4] Moore, in his monumental work, "Judaism," sums up the status of "belief" in the Jewish religion thus: "The words for faith in the literature and thought of this age [the rabbinic] are not used in the concrete sense of creed, beliefs entertained—or to be entertained—about God."[5] *Bitahon* quite clearly means confidence in God, a confidence achieved through daily, personal experience of His love and His nearness, expressed, as we have shown, in the name *Shekhinah.*

Judaism is not committed to logical consistency, for it is grounded in a variety of human experiences and not in a single system of philosophical premises. The result is that Judaism is not, like Greek philosophy, devoted to "right thinking." Plato would imprison men for five years if they do not hold the correct religious beliefs, even if they are "the natural possessors of righteous disposition . . . and ally themselves with the good."[6] If, after five years of imprisonment and instruction, they still do not accept the right beliefs, they are to be killed! This Greek philosophical dogmatism has no doubt contributed to the emphasis on creeds—that is, on faith in the right beliefs or "sound doctrine" in the Christian Church.[6] But rabbinic Judaism has no authoritative "right beliefs." In Judaism, the term *Bitahon,* faith, therefore connotes not belief at all but trust in God and reliance on Him for personal, individual security, particularly in time of trouble. That is why these verses from Isaiah, recited on Saturday night, are so relevant to the uncertainty men feel as they stand on the threshold of a new and perhaps frightening week.

It was in the Middle Ages, during the period of the Crusades, that this prayer was added as an introduction to the *Havdalah* ceremony by the pupils of Rashi, the greatest of the Talmudists, who lived in France in the eleventh century. Besides the verses from Isaiah, the prayer includes several from the Psalms, similarly chosen for their emphasis on the idea of trust in God. They, too, reflect the confidence that He will continue to be a Fortress in time of need. There is also a verse from the Book of Esther, the only one from that Book in the liturgy. It says that after their escape from the plots of Haman, "The Jews enjoyed light and happiness and joy and honor." The closing verses are from Psalms, yet the flow of thought from the previous sentence out of "Esther" is perfectly smooth: "So may it be for us. I will lift up the cup of salvation and I shall call upon the Name of the Lord."

In this triumphant and courageous mood each householder proceeds to recite the four benedictions of the *Havdalah*. He ushers in the new week on a note of *Bitahon*, of trust and confidence in God.

16

The Grace

The earth is the Lord's and the fullness thereof" (Psalm 124, 1). These are not mere words to the Jew. Everything he enjoys in this world belongs to God, and he does not expect to use God's bounties without a word of thanks for them. Yet it is not gratitude alone that he conveys by his *Berakhah* on bread, water, fruit, the fragrance of a flower, the rising of the sun at dawn, or any of the good things of life. The *Berakhah* is far more profoundly motivated. Because the Jew sees manifestations of God's love in so many of the commonplace situations and events of his life, they are able to evoke in him a religious experience and he is moved to respond to that religious experience by an act of worship, a *Berakhah*.[1] Thus, the simplest, least unusual events of life are endowed with significance and every day is lifted out of the merely routine.

Man's regular sustenance is in fact regarded as one of those *Nissim* that God does for us and "no man knoweth of them," as the Midrash puts it; for God "feeds the whole world with His goodness, grace, loving-kindness and tender mercy" (The Grace). Eating, the most ordinary act of man, is in Judaism surrounded with ceremony. Rites that are intended to stimulate in us the experience of holiness are associated with the selection, preparation and use of food, (dietary laws) and its enjoyment is the occasion for benedictions both before and after eating.

The Grace before meals is the short benediction over bread, called "*Hamotzi,* Who brings forth," from the key word used in the blessing. "Blessed art Thou, O Lord our God, King of the universe, Who brings forth [*Hamotzi*] bread from the earth." Finding his daily bread never ceases to be a *Nes* even to the farmer who toils so hard to produce the grain, for he recognizes its ultimate source to be God's loving care for all His creatures. It is God "Who brings forth [the] bread from the earth."

THE GRACE AFTER MEALS

The Grace after Meals is much longer. It is among the very few prayers, authority for which the Rabbis derive directly from the Bible. As warrant for the blessings to be pronounced after eating, the Mishnah cites [2] the verse from Deuteronomy 8, 10 which reads, "When thou hast eaten and art satisfied, thou shalt *bless* the Lord thy God. . . ."

In Hebrew, the Grace after Meals is called *Birkat Hamazon,* The Benediction on Food. We do not know when the *Birkat Hamazon* was instituted, but it probably goes back to the days of the Second Temple, for Josephus and other sources of the first century of the Common Era speak of it as an old and accepted institution.

According to the Mishnah, there are three benedictions in the Grace:

1. On food—"Blessed art Thou, O Lord, Who provides food for all [*Hazan et Hakol*]."

2. On the Land of Israel—"Blessed art Thou, O Lord, for the Land and for the food [*Al Ha'aretz Ve'al Hamazon*]."
3. On the rebuilding of the Temple in Jerusalem—"Blessed art Thou, O Lord, Who, in His compassion will rebuild Jerusalem. Amen [*Boneh . . . Yerushala'yim. Amen*]." Only this, the third benediction, ends with *Amen*, for originally it was the last one and the Grace ended here.

A fourth benediction was added later, in tragic circumstances. In the year 137 c.e., after the failure of the revolt of Bar Kochba against the Romans who had ruled Israel with such brutality, and after all the Jews in the last stronghold at Bethar had been slain, the Roman Emperor, Hadrian, refused the Jews permission to bury their dead. Though their army had been decimated, their land laid waste, and their dead lay still unburied, the Rabbis of that time nevertheless added to the Grace after every meal a fourth benediction—on God's great goodness! "Blessed art Thou, O Lord our God, King of the universe, the good King Who visits His goodness upon us. May He visit good upon us now and in the future as He has done in the past."

Thus did the Jews refuse to lose faith in God's abiding goodness. Thus did they refuse to lose courage even when it seemed as if no hope were possible. Unfortunately, this kind of desperate *Bitaḥon* (confidence that God would send succor) has often been crucially necessary in Jewish life. Many of us remember how the Jews of the Warsaw Ghetto sang, "I believe, I believe in the coming of the Messiah; yea, though he tarry, I believe, I believe."

These four benedictions constitute the "statutory" *Birkat Hamazon* according to the Talmud. But, like the *Prayer Book* itself, the Grace continued to grow because some Jews felt that the four benedictions did not fully express all their needs and hopes. From time to time, therefore, they added to the four benedictions. Among the additions was a group of their own pious wishes or requests, couched in a formula that began, "*Harahamon*,[3] May the Merciful One." Some of the nine petitions found in our *Prayer Book* (beside those for Sabbath and Festivals) are: "May the Merciful One grant us an honorable livelihood. May the Merciful One send a generous blessing upon this household and upon the table at which we have eaten. May the Merciful One bless my honored father, master of this household and my honored mother, mistress of this household." The *Harahamon* additions vary in number and in content from community to community. In fact, Abudraham, the great medieval authority on the *Siddur*, looks upon them as entirely personal and private petitions to be added as occasion demands. That is why it is considered quite proper to insert any special wish into this list. An important guest, for example, is often honored by the recitation of an appropriate *Harahamon* for him.

After these petitions, there is a paragraph beginning, "*Magdil*, May He magnify. . . ." An alternate form with nearly the same meaning, *Migdol*, is used on the Sabbath. People often ask what significance is hidden in this special Sabbath variation of the word. The mystery of the two forms is soon solved. There are two verses in the Torah, Psalm 18, verse 5, and verse 51 in the Second Book of Samuel, Chapter 22, which are identical except for the first word of each. One begins, *Magdil* and the other, *Migdol*. In spite of all the elaborate explanations that have been offered for the use of one of these on Sabbath and the other for "every day," the simple truth of the matter is that there is no important difference in the meaning of the two words nor is there any special significance in the use of *Migdol* (rather than *Magdil*) on the Sabbath. But so precious, so almost personified were the words of the Torah, that both verses were included, one for the Sabbath, the other for daily use—so as not to discriminate between them, so as not to give offense to either!

The closing verses of the *Birkat Hamazon* are from Psalms and are said silently, out of consideration for the feelings of the poor who might be guests at the table. "They that fear the Lord, know no want," says the Psalmist, and he continues, "I have been young and now I am old; yet have I not seen a righteous man forsaken, nor his seed begging for bread." Jews knew that these statements are not, alas, always true. They describe not conviction about a fact but an ideal, a hope for what may at some future time come to pass.[4] The Grace ends, as do other prayers (the *Amidah, Musaf* and *Kaddish*), with a plea to God for peace.

One of the earliest additions to the *Birkat Hamazon*—if it was not an integral part of it to begin with—is a matter we have not yet discussed. It is the interesting introductory formula for Grace when three or more persons are present. Whereas ten men constitute a quorum or *Minyan* for the usual service, only three persons are required (and in this case, it is three men *or* three women) for a group service when the Grace is said. This quorum of three is called a *Mezuman*. When there is a *Mezuman*, the leader, the head of the household or an honored guest designated by the host, calls upon those who have eaten to recite the *Birkat Hamazon*. "Gentlemen," he says, "let us say Grace [*Rabbotai, Nevaraykh*]." The others respond, "May the Name of the Lord be blessed from this time forth and forever." The call to say Grace is similar to the *Barakhu* (the Call to Prayer) at the formal beginning of the morning and the evening services; the response is very like that of the congregation at those services, and almost exactly like the Aramaic response of the *Kaddish*, "*Yehay Shemay Rabbah* . . . , May His great Name be blessed from this time forth. . . ." In each case, these responses are expressions of reverent assent to the invitation to praise the Name of God and to say a *Berakhah*.

The custom of reciting Psalm 126 (*Shir Hama'alot*) before the Grace on the Sabbath and on Festivals began in the sixteenth century. Like many other prayers, it stresses the memory of Zion. "When the Lord returned the captivity to Zion, we were like dreamers. Our mouths were filled with laughter and our tongues with joyous song. . . . He who went forth weeping, carrying his store of seed, shall come back with joy, bearing his sheaves." Again and again we hear the cry for the return to the Land of Israel.

A LEGAL SHORT FORM OF THE GRACE

All these additions have made the Grace inconveniently long for daily use after each meal. That is why we find numerous efforts to produce an acceptable shorter form. Many of these are recorded in the literature. One, for use by workmen on a job, is mentioned in the Talmud. But there is another short version which includes all the essential elements required by the Talmud for the *Birkat Hamazon*. It was written—one should really say, constructed—by Rabbi Naphtali ben David Zechariah Mendel of Venice, in 1603. So completely did his version satisfy all requirements, in spite of its brevity, that it was approved by many great Rabbis as a perfectly adequate substitute for the full Grace, whenever brevity was necessary. Later, it was included in the text of a standard commentary to the *Shulḥan Arukh*. The *Shulḥan Arukh* is the Code of Jewish law and practice prepared from authentic sources by Joseph Caro in the sixteenth century. It is still accepted as the authoritative guide in matters of Jewish law and practice by Orthodox Jewry all over the world. The Commentary which records the Shorter Grace is known as the *Ba'ayr Haytayv*. But *Ba'ayr Haytayv* is not the author's name. It is a phrase taken from verse 8 in Deuteronomy, 27, which reads, "And thou shalt write upon stone all the words of this teaching, *Ba'ayr Haytayv* [that is, plainly put or well explained]." What an ingenious name for a commentary, since everyone who would be likely to consult it knew the verse to which the name referred and knew, therefore, exactly what it meant! The author's name is Yehudah ben Simon Ashkenazi of Frankfort, and he lived in the first half of the eighteenth century. The short Grace is included in his *Ba'ayr Haytayv,* in the remarks on Paragraph 192, Sentence 1 of the Section of the *Shulḥan Arukh* called *Oraḥ Ḥayim.*

We give here a translation of the Short Form of the Grace according to the text found in the *Ba'ayr Haytayv.*

TEXT OF THE SHORT FORM

Blessed art Thou, O Lord our God, King of the universe, Who nourishes all the world in His goodness, in grace, loving-kindness and compassion. He gives bread to all flesh, for His loving-kindness extends over the whole world.[5] Through His great goodness food has never failed us; may it never fail us for His great Name's sake. For He feeds and sustains us all and provides food for all the creatures he has created. Blessed art Thou, O Lord, Who provides food for all.

We thank Thee, Lord our God, for having granted our fathers as a heritage a precious, a good and a spacious land; and for having given us the covenant, Torah and generous sustenance. Blessed art Thou, O Lord, for the Land and for the food.

Have compassion, Lord our God, on us, on Israel Thy people, on Jerusalem thy city and on the royal [6] House of David, Thy Messiah. Speedily increase the glory of the Temple, and comfort us over and over.[6] Blessed art Thou, O Lord, Who in mercy will rebuild Jerusalem. Amen.

Blessed art Thou, O Lord our God, King of the universe, God, our Father, our King, the good King Who visits His goodness upon all of us; may He cause only good to be visited upon us, now and in the future, as He has done in the past. As He has rewarded us, may He now and forever continue to reward us with grace, with loving-kindness and with compassion; and may we inherit the Days of the Messiah.

May He Who makes peace in His high places, make peace for us and for all Israel, and say ye, Amen.

THE RABBINIC USE OF BIBLE TEXTS

No abridgment of the first paragraph of the Grace has been attempted in the Short Form; it retains the full text of the magnificent first *Berakhah*. Only one idea is contained in it— the universal, all-embracing quality of God's Providence, His love.

"Blessed art Thou," it begins, "Who nourishes *all the world.* . . . He gives bread to *all flesh.* . . . He feeds us *all* and sustains us *all,* is good to *all* and provides food for *all the creatures* He has created. Blessed art Thou, O Lord, Who provides sustenance for *all.*" So intense is the effort to convey God's tender care for all living things, that in this one short paragraph, the word *Kol,* all, is reiterated six times!

Another word in this blessing, several times repeated, emphasizes the same universalistic idea. That word is *Olam*. Now, *Olam* in the Bible means forever, or a very long stretch of time either in the past or extending into the future. But in rabbinic literature, the meaning of *Olam* has been enlarged.[7] Occasionally, the Rabbis do use it in the older, Biblical sense of forever, and we find an instance of this in the blessing we are studying. It reads, ". . . may food not fail us *Le'olam Va'ed*, forever and ever." Ordinarily, however, the Rabbis use *Olam* to mean the world, the universe. In the first benediction, there are three examples of *Olam* in the sense of world or universe.

We must bear in mind that the Grace is a rabbinic prayer and that the ideas, as well as the meanings of the words, are necessarily rabbinic, and not Biblical. As we have frequently noted, the prayers of the *Siddur* make liberal use of the Bible. Sometimes they quote, occasionally they paraphrase the Bible text. In some instances, a verse is quoted only in part, with the result that it acquires a meaning not intended in the original at all. In the *Prayer Book*, for example, we read (on the Festivals, just before the Torah is removed from the Ark): "Lord, Lord God, merciful and gracious, slow to anger and abounding in loving-kindness and truth, extending mercy to the thousandth generation, forgiving iniquity and transgression and sin, and Who will acquit [*Venakay*]." But, let us see how the whole of this verse reads in the Bible, in Exodus 34, 6. There it says: "Lord, Lord God, merciful . . . forgiving iniquity . . . and Who will *by no means* acquit [*Venakay, Lo Yinakay*]." The form used here is the reiteration of the verb, an emphatic construction peculiar to Hebrew grammar, in which the negative, *Lo*, is attached to the second form of the verb. Just by cutting off the last two words (*Lo Yinakay*) from the quotation, the Rabbis effected a complete reversal in the meaning of the verse. In the *Prayer Book*, this truncated verse has become a character-

istic rabbinic prayer, emphasizing God's quality of mercy, His
Middat Rahamim, a quality so often stressed in the writings of
the Rabbis. Even when they quote the Bible, we must recognize that they are simply using it to express or to point up
their own ideas.

When a Bible verse is quoted as proof of or authority for a
rabbinic statement, it is often introduced by a formula, "As
it is written [*Kakatuv*]," or, "As it is said [*Shene'emar*]." These
phrases are abbreviations for the full forms, "As it is written in
Thy Torah," or, "As it is said in the Torah." Even in these cases
—when the Bible is directly appealed to for support—it may
happen that it is the rabbinic interpretation of the text, not its
meaning in the Bible which the *Prayer Book* actually implies.
The problem of how the Rabbis use Bible texts is a very complex one and we cannot begin to treat it adequately here. Yet
it is important to recognize that without a proper evaluation
of the way in which the *Siddur* uses Bible material, it is often
impossible to understand the prayers at all. A striking example
of this is found in the first benediction of the Grace.

It begins, "Blessed art Thou, O Lord our God, *Melekh
Ha'olam* [King of the universe], Who nourishes *Ha'olam* [the
whole world]; in His goodness. . . . He gives bread to all flesh,
for *Le'olam Hasdo* [His loving-kindness is for the whole
world]." This last sentence is, with one minor addition, a quotation from Psalm 136, verse 25. There it is the refrain, repeated
after each of the twenty-six verses of the poem. Each verse of
the Psalm gives an example of God's loving-kindness to His
creatures. These build up by repetition into an impression of
repeated deeds of love. The phenomena of nature over eons
of time and every event of Israel's long history demonstrate
over and over again God's loving care for mankind in general
and for Israel His people in particular. In Psalm 136, *Ki Le'olam
Hasdo* does refer to a long stretch of time, does mean "for His

loving-kindness endureth forever." But in the context of the first blessing of the Grace, to understand *Olam* in its Biblical sense and to read the verse, "He gives bread to all flesh for His loving-kindness *endureth forever*," is to break up the continuity of thought in that paragraph and to miss the pointed emphasis of the prayer on God's *all-embracing* love. It is not the enduring quality of God's loving-kindness that is expressed in this benediction, but the fact that it is available to the whole world, *Ki Le'olam Ḥasdo*.

It has for a long time been recognized that the word *Olam* in the Bible means time, eternity, a long time in the past or into the far future. But in rabbinic literature the word takes on a new, universalistic connotation. It becomes *the world*.[8] This enlargement of meaning in the word *Olam* to include the whole world is indicative of a general trend in rabbinic thought toward universalism and this trend is expressed in other words and in other ways as well.[8] The rabbinic prayer of Grace is only one example of the gentler, more personal, and at the same time more universalistic, religion which is the authentic Judaism of the rabbinic, Talmudic period.

17

The Marriage Service

THE *Ketubah*—THE MARRIAGE CONTRACT

L ike every Jewish institution the marriage ceremony has a long and continuous history.[1] It is entangled in ancient social forms and its rites can be understood only in terms of its past. In the modern state, and according to English common law, the state binds in marriage, and only the state can issue a decree of divorce. A Justice of the Peace, or the Judge of any court, performs the marriage ceremony. Religious functionaries—priests, ministers, or rabbis—can also officiate at a marriage, but only because they are delegated and therefore licensed by the state to perform this function.

In ancient systems of law, the Jewish among them, marriage is a voluntary agreement between a man and a woman. And because it is the man who marries the woman, it is he who gives the divorce. The voluntary agreement to marry is attested to, among the Jews, by a contract. Originally a verbal agreement, it later developed into a formal written contract called the *Ketubah*, literally, the Writ.

Normally every contract, in Jewish law as well, is made out in duplicate. Both copies are signed by each party to the agreement and one copy is retained by each of them. But a *Ketubah* is not duplicated. There is only one copy and that one is retained by the wife because the *Ketubah* is meant to protect *her*. It describes the husband's obligations and the wife's rights.

At first each *Ketubah* was individually drawn. It detailed the money transactions involved, arranged for the disposition of property in case of divorce, and provided for the wife and the unmarried daughters in case of the husband's death. Some *Ketubot* (plural of *Ketubah*) contained specific limitations to polygamy and many included the formula: ". . . and I shall serve and honor and maintain thee in the manner of Jewish husbands. . . ."

In the course of time, the form of the *Ketubah* has become relatively fixed. In it the husband promises to pay his wife two hundred *Zuzzim* (a silver coin) and other sums should the marriage be dissolved. He promises her bed, board, and raiment—in other words, adequate support. The *Ketubah* also records the names of the contracting parties (the bride and groom) and the place and date of the marriage ceremony. It is signed just before the ceremony by the bride, the groom, and two competent witnesses—adult males, not related to either the bride or the groom.

The *Ketubah,* however, is not fixed by law in every detail. Its present form is established by custom, but there is nothing in Jewish law that would preclude making additional conditions and premarital agreements part of the *Ketubah.* Records of a great variety of particular conditions which have at one time or another been written into *Ketubot* are readily available, as we have just indicated. This fluid nature of the marriage contract has made it possible to meet certain social changes in our time by varying the *Ketubah* form. The new *Ketubah* recently formulated by the authorities at the Jewish Theological Seminary is a modern instance of such adaptability.

In Jewish law every contractual agreement is validated in three ways, all of which are ordinarily required in order to legalize the agreement. The first is money (*Kesef*) which is passed from one party to the other as the "consideration." In the marriage contract, this money has been symbolized since the Middle Ages by the ring the man gives to the woman. It was expected to be plain, without engraving or stones, and of pure gold because such a ring had a constant, known value. Yet in Jewish law, no such expensive ring has always been deemed necessary. The Talmud rules (according to Hillel) that even the smallest coin, a *Peruta,* is an adequate marriage-payment symbol. The second condition to consummation of an agreement is a written contract, the *Shetar;* in marriage, the *Shetar* is represented by the *Ketubah.* And the third condition is "use," called *Bi'ah* in the marriage situation—that is, cohabitation. Since all three conditions are normally required for validation of a contract, "common law" marriage is not recognized in Judaism. In certain circumstances, however, if a man makes a verbal marriage declaration to a woman before two competent witnesses and gives her a *Peruta* or a ring, this may be considered a legal marriage, even without a written *Ketubah.*

The *Ketubah,* legal document that it is, represents a notable advance in woman's legal status, in her personal rights under the law. For before the time when a man married by giving his bride a *Ketubah,* he used to buy her. He acquired a wife for a sum paid to her father. This very ancient form of marriage is called *Kinyan,* purchase, and the term is still preserved in the Mishnah. As the institution of marriage developed among the Jews, the purchase money, instead of being turned over to the bride's father, became a fund set aside by the husband for his wife, a sum that would be hers in case of divorce or the death of the husband. Under these conditions, a clear agreement on money matters had to be made prior to marriage, to protect the wife's interests. And this agreement grew into the *Ketubah.* It is at once a wife's insurance policy and her "Bill of Rights." It is interesting to note that in the English language, the old widespread "purchase" situation is still reflected in the phrase, "the father gave the bride away." In Jewish custom, the bride is escorted to the marriage canopy by her father and her mother.

As early as the period of the Prophets, Jewish women were no longer acquired by purchase; they were already then protected in marriage by a contract known as a *Brith*,[2] a covenant. And this is the same word the Bible uses to describe the covenant between God and Israel. The Prophet Ezekiel, in one of his visions (16, 8) says: "When I passed by and looked upon thee, and behold thy time was the time of love . . . I swore unto thee and entered into a covenant [*Brith*] with thee . . . and thou wast mine." In Chapter 2, 14, Malachi speaks of "the wife of thy youth against whom thou hast dealt treacherously, though she is thy companion and thy wife by covenant." From this verse especially, we can see that not only was there a marriage contract between a man and a woman, but the relationship between them was far from that between a man and his chattel, for she was his "companion and [his] wife by a *Brith*."

Jewish marriage is obviously not to be considered merely a civil institution, a contract entered into, signed, and sealed by the two parties concerned, as if it were a business transaction. Though subject to the laws of contract, it had, by the time of the Mishnah, become "holy matrimony," *Kiddushin*, literally, Sanctification. The Mishnah had reinterpreted the ancient notion of acquisition (*Kinyan*) of a wife by purchase, and the word *Kinyan* gave way to the newer word *Kiddushin* as the usual term for marriage. When the Mishnah says, "a man sanctifies his wife [*Ha'ish Mekadaysh*],"[3] the meaning is that he marries her. This position is carefully reiterated in the Talmud. Indeed, the entire section in the Mishnah and in the

Talmud dealing with marriage is called "*Massekhet Kiddushin,* the Section of *Kiddushin.*"

It is true that one of the ancient meanings of the term *Kadosh,* holy, probably is "to set aside for the exclusive use of [the god]." But how much of this old connotation still clings to the word *Kiddushin,* as applied in the Talmud to marriage, it is hard to say. Nevertheless, it is the later idea of holiness as developed by the Rabbis which undoubtedly characterizes the relation of a husband to his wife in Judaism, and this was true as early as the prophetic period, as we have shown.

EVOLUTION OF THE JEWISH MARRIAGE CEREMONY

In the earliest days of the Bible, there was probably no formal marriage ceremony. A man purchased a woman from her father; she was brought to his home and became his wife. As the status of woman improved and she was no longer acquired by purchase, marriage was celebrated in formal ceremonies. By the period of the Mishnah, weddings had come to be celebrated in two stages: the Betrothal, called *Erusin,* and, after a lapse of time, the Nuptials or *Nisuin.*

The Betrothal was a far more serious commitment than an "engagement" as we understand it today, for divorce was required if either party wished to withdraw from the agreement. After the ceremony of Betrothal, the bride remained in her father's home, sometimes for as long as a whole year, until the Nuptials were celebrated. This division of the wedding into two stages was made necessary by the fact that, in those days, parents often arranged a match for a daughter who was a minor. In that case, the marriage could not be completed at once since in Jewish law the woman was guaranteed the right to dissent from a marriage her father had arranged for her, and a minor, of course, has no power in law to assent or to dissent.

The betrothal ceremony consisted of three parts: Benedictions, *Ketubah* (including a marriage declaration), and the Feast. Before the ceremony, the *Ketubah* was written, signed, and witnessed. The ceremony itself began with two benedictions. The first, as is usual on happy occasions, was the benediction on wine. The second was in the nature of a warning on the limitation of privilege in betrothal. The blessing reads, "Blessed art Thou, O Lord our God, . . . Who has forbidden to us the betrothed, but has sanctioned those that are wedded by the rite of the nuptial canopy [*Ḥupah*] and *Kiddushin*. Blessed art Thou, ... Who hallows His people Israel by the rite of *Ḥupah* and *Kiddushin*." After these blessings, the groom gave the *Ketubah* to his bride. The exact wording of the earliest *Ketubot* is not known. Probably they did contain (or were accompanied by another brief document containing) the stereotyped declaration of marriage: "I, So-and-So, do hereby betroth thee, So-and-So, according to the law of Moses and Israel." [4] After the formalities were completed, the joyous event was celebrated in the Feast of Betrothal. Thus, legally, the *Erusin* was tantamount to marriage, except that the marriage could not be consummated by cohabitation and that, in addition, all the property clauses of the *Ketubah* remained in abeyance until after the Nuptials.

The Nuptials or actual marriage ceremony was very brief. It is called variously *Nisuin* or *Ḥupah,* Canopy. It took place in the home of the groom under a specially constructed canopy, supported on four poles. The *Ḥupah* is probably a vestige of the marriage chamber to which, in very ancient times, the bride and groom were conducted as part of the marriage ceremony. But long ago the *Ḥupah* came to be understood as a symbol of the new home about to be established by the bride and groom.

The Nuptial ceremony at first consisted merely of the recitation of the Seven Benedictions of Marriage; somewhat later, the breaking of a glass by the groom was added. In the course of time, the Betrothal became less important and the Nuptials in turn acquired more importance as the real marriage ceremony. The history of the changes in both ceremonies and the shifting about of the various elements in them from one to the other is very complex and cannot be completely traced, it seems, even by specialists in the field. Suffice it to say here that in the early Middle Ages, the *Erusin* and *Nisuin* (Betrothal and Nuptials) were coalesced into a single event and what emerged is the wedding ceremony we know today.

THE MARRIAGE CEREMONY IN OUR TIME

The marriage ceremony today still bears some marks of its former dual nature (Betrothal–Nuptial). Just before the wedding, the *Ketubah* is signed by the bride and groom and properly witnessed. The ceremony itself can be conducted, as far as Jewish law is concerned, by any adult Jew; no Rabbi or other functionary is essential.

Both parents conduct the bride to the *Ḥupah*, where she stands to the right of the groom. First, a short selection from a medieval marriage hymn is sung as introduction. It calls upon God Who is powerful and great to bless this tiny new unit in Israel, the bridegroom and the bride: "May He Who is mighty above all, blesséd above all and great above all, may He bless the bridegroom and the bride." The first part of the ceremony is reminiscent of the *Erusin*. It begins with the recital of the benediction on wine, after which the bride and the groom each sip from the cup. Then follows the second benediction of the old *Erusin,* the warning against intimacy during the betrothal period. Since now there is no interval at all between Betrothal and the Nuptials, the repetition of this benediction of warning at the beginning of the marriage ceremony can be understood only in terms of its history. For when the two stages of the wedding were telescoped into one, nothing was omitted from either!

Following these blessings, the real *Kiddushin* (marriage) takes place. The groom declares to his bride, "*Haray At Mekudeshet Li. . .* , Behold, thou art consecrated unto me by this ring, according to the law of Moses and Israel." This formula is given, with minor variations, in several places in the Talmud and, as we have seen, was at one time probably included in the document the groom handed his bride during the betrothal ceremony. The essential phrase in the formula is, "*At Mekudeshet Li,* Thou art consecrated, or made holy, unto me." The core of the marriage is *Kiddushin,* "making holy." As he recites the marriage formula, the groom slips the ring on the index finger of the bride's right hand. This is the "ring finger" in the Jewish marriage ceremony, for it was felt that the ring should be worn on the most important finger, the one we use most. To complete the marriage, the groom used to hand the *Ketubah* to the bride. But today it is read aloud by the officiating Rabbi. At least a synopsis of the *Ketubah* is usually given in English to make sure that it will be fully and clearly understood by the bride. With this, the *Erusin* part of the service is completed.

When no fewer than a *Minyan* of men is present at the wedding, the Seven Benedictions of Marriage are then recited. Since these blessings are the beginning of the old *Nisuin,* they too begin with a benediction on wine. But according to the

Talmud, "One does not say two *Kedushot* [here, two benedictions] on one cup." That is why a fresh cup of wine is provided for this second *Berakhah* on wine. Again, history alone can explain what otherwise may seem like a needlessly complicated procedure.

Against the dark background of hardship and persecution which constituted the daily fare of Jews for generations and the disciplined control of a life regulated by the commandments of the Torah, the merriment and gaiety of their marriage celebrations stand out in brilliant relief. Every opportunity for rejoicing was ardently embraced. The singing and dancing at the Festival of *Simhat Torah* [1] (the Rejoicing in the Torah) was exuberant; on *Purim* one drank until he could not distinguish between, "Cursed be Haman" and "Blessed be Mordecai!" But the most joyous occasion of all was a wedding. In fact, a *Baraita* [5] states that one should even suspend the study of Torah in order to help celebrate a marriage. Feasting, drinking and dancing until the wee hours of the morning were not unusual.

This spirit of joy is reflected too in the Seven Marriage Benedictions which are quoted in the Talmud and which continue to be recited at Jewish weddings to this day. They are:

1. On wine.
2. On God "Who has created all things to His glory."
3. On God, "Creator of man."
4. Two related themes: man is made "in the image of His (God's) likeness," and God has "prepared for him [man] out of his very self a perpetual fabric," woman.
5. Jerusalem which is never to be forgotten even in our moments of chiefest joy, Jerusalem, too, will rejoice when her children return to her. This benediction is based upon Isaiah 62, 5: "As the bridegroom rejoices over the bride, so shall thy God rejoice over thee [Jerusalem]."

6. A prayer for a perfect love between these beloved companions, like to the relation between Adam and Eve in the Garden of Eden. "Blessed art Thou, O Lord, Who makes bridegroom and bride rejoice," is how this benediction closes.

7. The culmination of the expressions of happiness in the other six blessings. In six different words for joy and in four synonymns for love and friendship, the *Berakhah* conveys the profound faith that a life of happiness, peace, and affectionate companionship awaits the new husband and his wife. It is derived from one of the few passages of gladness found in the prophet Jeremiah. In Chapter 33, 10-11, he says, "Yet again there shall be heard . . . in the city of Judah and in the streets of Jerusalem . . . the voice of joy and the voice of gladness, the voice of the bridegroom and the voice of the bride."

After the last blessing, the bridegroom breaks a glass. Like every ancient custom, this one, too, has been explained in many ways. The anthropologists see in it a symbol of the husband's conquest of the virgin. But in the Talmud,[6] this tale is told: "When the son of Rabina was married, the father saw that the Rabbis present at the marriage feast were in an uproarious mood; so he took a costly white crystal vase worth four hundred zuzzim and broke it before them to curb their spirits." And a famous medieval commentator on the Talmud, in explanation of this passage remarks, "Hence we break a glass at weddings." The moderating effect of the breaking glass on spirits become a little too exuberant is thus the explanation offered in the Talmud. But another reason often given, and very widely held today, stresses not the excessive hilarity of the wedding guests but the obligation never to forget Jerusalem, the holy City. The breaking of the glass, in this

view, is a *Zaykher Lehurban*, a memorial to the destruction
of Jerusalem. In spite of these lugubrious associations, the
crack of the breaking glass under the bridegroom's foot has
come to seem not a mournful reminder of destruction but a
triumphant and joyous sound, heralding the beginning of a
new life. And it is always followed by happy exclamations of,
"*Mazal Tov*, Good luck, Congratulations!" on the part of all
the assembled guests.

We have tried to present a picture of the complex yet pure
form of the *Siddur*. More important than its classic beauty of
structure or its great antiquity or even its perfection of literary
style, more important than all these which are merely its ex-
ternal qualities, is the rich tapestry of religious ideas which
the *Siddur* exhibits. And these ideas, these Jewish values, when
we understand them, we find as moving today, as potentially
meaningful in our lives, as when they were created by the
Judaism of more than two thousand years ago.

Appendix

A Note on Transliteration and a Guide to Its Use in This Book

A universally accepted, accurate, easily comprehensible and consistent transliteration of Hebrew into English is not available. The use of such transliteration in books and articles on Judaism is continually increasing, but a chaotic variety of symbols and equivalents for the Hebrew has left the layman bewildered and unable to recognize a Hebrew word for what it is even when he meets it again and again. Often the same Hebrew letter or vowel is represented by several different English letters in a single book, not to speak of the variations in usage from book to book and from author to author. The differences between modern Israeli (or Sephardic) and European (or Ashkenazic) pronunciations of Hebrew have contributed to the confusion, since we often find inconsistency in the use of one or the other system.

In scholarly works, of course, these faults are absent. Their perfectly accurate rendering of each consonant and each vowel sound of the Hebrew has, however, resulted in a text that is all but unreadable by the uninitiated. These transliterations often look like a study in phonetics, which they are, or like a message in code. It is therefore decidedly impractical to try to use the scholars' system for the ordinary reader.

We have attempted to develop here a relatively simple, consistent system of transliteration from the Hebrew which will be easy to read and which at the same time will reflect the structure and the character of the Hebrew word. Each Hebrew letter or vowel, except where we quote verbatim from a source with a different system, has always been represented by the same English letter or letters. In the case of five words, *El* (pronounced *Ayl*), *Brith* (pronounced *Brit*), *Yisrael* (pronounced *Yisra'ayl*), *Levi* (pronounced *Layvi*) and *Seder* (pronounced *Sayder*), we have accepted the spelling in so general use as to have become familiar to many people.

The Hebrew alphabet has twenty-two letters, all consonants. The vowel sounds are indicated by marks placed below, above, or by the side of the consonants to aid in correct vocalization. All ancient texts, as well as modern books not especially intended for students or children, are written without vowels. The Bible and the *Siddur*, however, are today ordinarily printed with vowel signs.

Below is a list of the names of the Hebrew letters and vowels, and the English letters we have used to represent their sounds.

Names of the Letters of the Hebrew Alphabet	English Equivalent of Each Letter and Its Pronunciation
Alef	Silent
Bet	*B*
&	*ϐ*
Vet	*V*. *Bet* and *Vet* are really the same letter, pronounced differently depending upon its location in the word. *Pay* and *Fay*, *Kaf* and *Khaf* are similar pairs. *Sin* and *Shin* are also a pair, but of a different order.
Gimmel	*G*, as in *g*ood or in *g*old
Dalet	*D*
Hay	*H*, as in *h*ear or in *h*elp
Vav	*V*
Za'yin	*Z*, as in *z*ebra or in *z*oom
Ḥet	*Ḥ*, pronounced like the *Ch* in the German *Kuchen* or *Lachen;* this gutteral sound has no equivalent in English.
Tet	*T*
Yod	*Y*, as in *y*ear or in *y*es
Kaf	*K*
&	&
Khaf	*Kh*, a guttural, pronounced much like *Ḥ*. The use of a separate symbol for this sound is motivated by the desire to indicate, through the English spelling, the relation between certain words derived from the same Hebrew root. This relation would not be apparent in English transliteration unless the *Kaf* and the *Khaf* were written similarly.

Hebrew Alphabet (*cont.*)	English Equivalent (*cont.*)
Lamed	*L*
Mem	*M*
Nun	*N*
Samekh	*S*
A'yin	Silent
Pay	*P*
&	ↄ
Fay	*F*
Tzadi	*Tz*, a combination of sounds not found in English
Kuf	*K*
Raysh	*R*
Sin	*S*
&	ↄ
Shin	*Sh*, as in *sh*irt or hu*sh*
Tav	*T*, in Israeli (Sephardic) Hebrew there is no difference between a *Tav* and a *Sav;* both are pronounced *T*.

Following is a Table of the names of the Hebrew vowel signs and the English equivalents used to represent their sounds.

Hebrew Vowel	English Equivalent and Its Pronunciation
Kametz	*A*, as in f*a*ther or p*a*rdon
Patah	*A*, as above; in Israeli Hebrew, the *Kametz* and the *Patah* are pronounced alike.
Short Kametz	*O*, as in C*o*ntain or C*o*mpare
Holem	*O*, as above; related grammatically to the short *Kametz*
Tzayray	*Ay*, as in pl*ay* or s*ay*
Hirek	*I*, as in t*i*n or w*i*n
Segol	*E*, as in m*e*t or s*e*t
Kibbutz	*U*, as the second *U* in us*u*al. A better English equivalent would have been *OO*, but here we

Hebrew Vowel (*cont.*)	English Equivalent (*cont.*)
	bow to a widely accepted usage, derived originally from the pronunciation of the letter *U* in German.
Sheva	This sound, when it is vocalized at all, is nearer the *E* in the French word *Le* than it is to any English vowel; in order, however, not to complicate our transliteration unduly, we have represented it by the letter *E*, as for the Segol. The distinction in sound between them is not great.

Glossary of Hebrew Words
and Phrases

NOTE: *Each Hebrew word or phrase is followed by its literal translation; after the semicolon, we have indicated the derived meaning, the connotations, or the special usage of the term. Where it would prove helpful, we have also specified the context or prayer in which the term appears.*

Aba'ya—loose mantle, worn by desert Arabs today; Arabic, not Hebrew

Adon Olam—Master of the universe; name of a medieval hymn

Ahavat Olam—everlasting love; name of a prayer, the second benediction before the *Shema* in the evening

Ahavah Rabbah—great love; parallel benediction (to *Ahavat Olam*) in the morning

Alaynu—it is incumbent upon us; see *Alaynu Leshabay'ah*

Alaynu Leshabay'ah—it is incumbent upon us to praise; the first words of a prayer said thrice daily.

Al Ha'aretz Ve'al Hamazon—for the land and for the food; one of the benedictions of the Grace after Meals

Am Ha'aretz—the people of the soil, the peasants; in the course of time came to mean, ignoramus

Amidah—standing; a prayer of benedictions, so called because one stands while reciting it

Ani Ma'amin—I believe; the name of the Thirteen Creeds of Maimonides

Apikoros—doubter; word of Greek origin, with connotations of heretic

Aron Hakodesh—the holy Ark; the cabinet holding the Scrolls of the Torah in the synagogue

227

Arvit—of the evening; the name of the Evening Service, also called *Ma'ariv;* see there

Ashkenaz—German or European

Ashray—happy; the first word of a composite Psalm (84 and 145) recited thrice daily—twice at the morning service and once at the afternoon service

Atah Elohaynu—Thou art our God; a verse in the hymn, *Ayn Kelohaynu*

Avodah—work, service; the sacrifice or the prayer service

Avodah Shebalayv—the service of the heart; prayer, in contrast to sacrifices

Avodah Zarah—strange worship; idol-worship, paganism

Avot—fathers; refers to Abraham, Isaac and Jacob

Ayn Kelohaynu—there is none like our God; first verse and name of a hymn sung near the close of the morning service

Ayshet Ḥa'yil—a woman of strength (valor is the usual translation); from Proverbs 31; sung at home Friday evening as an ode to the wife by her husband

Ba'ayr Haytayv—well explained; name of a commentary to the *Shulḥan Arukh;* see there

Bahar—He has delighted in; past tense of *Boher;* see there

Bakashot—requests, supplications; prayers of supplication

Baraita—a collection of rabbinic lore contemporary with, but not included in the Mishnah

Barakhu—Bless (imperative); from the Call to Prayer that precedes the *Shema*

Bar Mitzvah—the son of the commandment; coming of age at thirteen, acquiring moral responsibility for the performance of *Mitzvot*

Barukh—blessed or praised; the first word of all benedictions

Barukh She'amar—blessed be He Who spoke; from a benediction preceding the Preliminary Psalms in the morning.

Bat Mitzvah—the feminine of *Bar Mitzvah;* see there

Beraḥamim—with compassion, or mercy

Berakhah—a benediction; plural, *Berakhot*

Berakhot—the name of a tractate of the Talmud

Bet Hakenesset (or, *Bet Kenesset*)—the House of Assembly, the synagogue

Bet Midrash—House of Study

Betuvo—in His goodness (in God's goodness)

Beyiratekha—in fear (or reverence) of Thee; see *Yirat Shama'yim,* from the same root

Bi'ah—cohabitation

Bimah—platform; the platform on which the Ark of the Torah stands in the synagogue

Birkat Hamazon—the benediction on food; the Grace after Meals

Birkot Hashahar—the morning benedictions.

Bitahon—trust, confidence (in God); cf. also *Evtah* and *Emunah* with the same or related meanings

Boher—He loves, takes delight in

Boneh Yerushala'yim—He will build (or, Builder of) Jerusalem; from the third benediction of the Grace

Brith (pronounced *Brit*)—an agreement, a covenant

Ehad—one; in the *Shema,* one, alone, unique

El (pronounced *Ayl*)—God

Elo'ah—a god

Elohaynu—our God

Elohim—God; though this is a plural form, the meaning remains, God

Emet Ve'emunah—true and trustworthy; the first words of a benediction after the *Shema* in the evening service

Emet Ve'yatziv—true and well-established; the first words of a benediction parallel to *Emet Ve'emunah,* in the morning service

Emunah—trust (in God); cf. *Bitahon*

Erusin—betrothal

Evtah—I will trust (in God); cf. *Bitahon*

Ezrat Avotaynu—the Help of our Fathers (God)

Gadelu Iti—Magnify with me; the Reader's call to praise God, said as the Torah is taken from the Ark

Gaon—great or illustrious one; the title of the spiritual head of Jewry in Babylon; since then applied to a few very great rabbis, as the "Gaon of Wilna"

Gemara—the body of Jewish law and lore developed after the Mishnah

Gemilut Hasadim—deeds of loving-kindness

Ger—a stranger, a sojourner (in the Bible), a convert (in rabbinic writings)

Ger Tzedek—a righteous convert; a true convert

Ge'ulah—redemption; refers to the redemption of Israel from exile

Guf, Gufah, Gufa—body

Haftarah—conclusion; the section of the Prophets read in the synagogue after the reading from the Torah

Haggadah—from a root meaning, to tell, to relate; the text of the order of service for the *Seder* on Passover evening

Halakhah—law, or a law

Ḥallah, plural *Ḥallot*—the white loaves used in the *Kiddush* on Sabbath and Festivals

Ḥakhamim—wise or learned men; refers to the Rabbis of the Talmud; see *Talmid Ḥakham*

Hakol Yodukha—all will acknowledge Thee

Hamakom—the Place; a rabbinic name for God

Hamotzi—Who brings forth (bread)—the name of the benediction over bread

Ḥanukkah—dedication (of a house); the Festival commemorating the rededication of the Temple after the Maccabean victory

Ḥanukkat Haba'yit—the dedication of the house (the Temple)

Ha'olam—the world, the universe

Haraḥamon—the Merciful One; a rabbinic name for God; the name of each of a series of petitions in the Grace beginning, "May the Merciful One . . ."

Haray At Mekudeshet Li—Behold thou art consecrated unto me; from the marriage formula

Har Haba'yit—the mountain of the house; the Temple Mount in Jerusalem

Hashkivaynu—cause us to lie down; the first word and name of a prayer in the evening service

Ḥasidim—(the) pious

Hatefillah—The Prayer; a rabbinic name for the *Amidah*

Havdalah—separation, distinction; the ceremony at the close of the Sabbath that signalizes the separation of the Sabbath from the other days of the week

Hazan Et Hakol—Who provides food for all; from a benediction in the Grace

Ḥerem—excommunication

Ḥillul Hashem—desecration of the Name (of God); obverse of *Kiddush Hashem;* see there

Hinay El Yishuati—Behold, the Lord is my salvation; part of the *Havdalah* service

Ḥovah—duty, obligation; in Jewish law, certain specific acts under specific circumstances are *Ḥovah,* obligatory

Ḥumash—the Pentateuch, the Five Books of Moses

Ḥupah—the marriage canopy

Kabbalat Shabbat—receiving or welcoming the Sabbath; the service that precedes the regular Evening Service on Friday night

Kabbalah—received or traditional lore; esoteric or mystic doctrine concerning God and the universe

Kaddish—sanctification; a prayer of praise, hallowing and proclaiming God's Name; the mourners' prayer

Kaddish Titkabal—the *Kaddish* of, "May (our praises) be accepted (by God)"; recited as a close to the major part of the service by the Reader

Kadosh—holy (adj.)

Kakatuv—as it is written (in the Torah)

Kavanah—intention, aim

Kedushah—Sanctification; a prayer of praise, hallowing God; specifically, part of the *Amidah* recited responsively with the Reader during his repetition of the *Amidah*

Kedushat Ha'yom—the holiness of the day (of Sabbath or Festival); the prayer characterizing the Day

Kehillah Kedoshah—holy congregation

Kesef—silver, money

Ketubah, plural, *Ketubot*—(marriage) Writ; the Jewish marriage contract

Kheruvim—winged ones; angels, cherubim

Kibbutz Galuyot—ingathering of the exiles; the return of the Jews to the Land of Israel

Kiddeshanu Bemitzvotav—He (God) hallows us by His commandments; part of the formula of benediction accompanying the performance of a rite

Kiddush—sanctification; the benediction over wine on Sabbaths and Festivals

Kiddush Ha'yom—sanctification of the day; refers to the Sabbath and Festival *Kiddush*

Kiddush Hashem—sanctification of the Name (of God); proclaiming God in public

Kiddushin—consecration; the marriage ceremony

Ki Le'olam Ḥasdo—for His loving-kindness is (endures) forever, or in the context of the Grace, His loving-kindness is for the whole world

Kinot—penitential prayers

Kinyan—possession by purchase

Ki Yashar Adonai—for the Lord is just; from Psalm 92, recited Friday evening

Kofer—a doubter; one who denies a dogma

Kohen, plural *Kohanim*—a priest; of the priestly family of Aaron

Kol—all, every, the whole of

Kol Nidray—all vows; the opening words and name of the opening statement of the Eve of the Day of Atonement

Layv—heart; used often to mean the "seat of the mind"

Lekhah Dodi—Come, my beloved; refrain and name of a sixteenth century hymn to the Sabbath, sung on Friday evening

Lekha Levadkha—to Thee alone; a phrase in the *Nishmat* prayer; see there

Le'olam Ḥasdo—see *Ki Le'olam Ḥasdo*

Le'olam Va'ed—forever and ever

Le'olam Yehay Adam—Let a man always . . ; from a prayer in the Morning Service

Levi—of the tribe of Levi, one of the twelve tribes of Israel, devoted to the service of the Temple

Lulav—palm branch; used in a ceremony on the Feast of Tabernacles

Ma'asim Tovim—good deeds

Ma'ariv—causes the evening to fall; name of the evening prayer; also called *Arvit*

Maftir—concluder; the last person called up to the reading of the Torah and the one who also reads the selection from the Prophets

Magdil—May He magnify; from a verse in the daily Grace; see also *Migdol*

Magen Avot—Shield of the fathers (God); first words and name of a short form of the Friday night *Amidah;* see also *Mayayn Sheva*

Mahzor Vitry—a thirteenth century code and compendium of Jewish prayers

Malakh—messenger, angel

Malkhut Shama'yim—kingship of Heaven

Malshinim—slanderers, informers

Mattan Torah—giving of Torah (by God)

Matzah—unleavened bread; eaten on Passover

Mayayn Sheva—of the nature of seven; the name of a short form of the Friday evening *Amidah;* also called *Magen Avot;* see there

Mazal Tov—Good luck! Congratulations!

Melekh Elyon—Highest King; God, most high; a name of God

Melekh Ha'olam—King of the universe; a name of God

Menuhah—rest

Me'oray Ha'aysh—the lights of fire; refers to the light of the plaited candle used in the *Havdalah* ceremony

Meturgeman—translator; originally, translator of the Bible; see *Targum*

Mezuman—more correctly, *Zimun,* appointment of a time (to eat together, so as to preface the Grace with a responsive praise of God requiring a quorum of three); the quorum of three

Mezuzah—the scroll, on which is inscribed the *Shema,* in a case attached to the right door-post of a Jewish home and of each room in the house.

Middat Rahamim—(God's) quality of compassion, love or mercy

Middot—plural of *Middah*, quality or principle; the "Thirteen *Middot* (principles)" of Bible exegesis

Midrash—nonlegal rabbinic literature, contemporary with the Mishnah and the Talmud; plural, *Midrashim*—various collections of such material or individual statements in a Midrash

Migdol—May He magnify; from a verse in the Sabbath Grace after meals; cf. *Magdil*

Mi Kelohaynu—Who is like our God? a verse in the hymn "*Ayn Kelohaynu*"

Mi Khamokha . . . Adonai—Who is like unto Thee, O Lord; from Exodus 15, quoted in the second benediction after the *Shema*

Min—kind (noun); a (different) kind of person, a sectarian or a sect

Minhah—the afternoon service

Minyan—the quorum of ten required for public worship

Mishebayrakh—He Who blessed; the first words and the name of a blessing recited for those who are called up to the Torah reading

Mishnah—the body of Jewish law and tradition committed to writing about 200 C.E.

Mishnah Zevahim—Mishnah of Sacrifices; the first tractate of *Kodashim*, one of the six "Orders" or major divisions of the Mishnah

Mitzvah, plural *Mitzvot*—commandment; a Jewish value-concept, hard to translate because of its many connotations

Modeh—thank, or acknowledge

Modim—(or, *Modim Anahnu*), We acknowledge (that Thou art our God); name of a prayer, part of the *Amidah*

Motza'ay Shabbat—the departure of the Sabbath; the night at the end of the Sabbath day

Musaf—Addition; the additional *Amidah* said on Sababths, Festivals and Holy Days

Nefesh—a person or soul, mind, will

Nefesh Mayt—a dead person, a dead body

Nes, plural *Nissim*—miracle

Neshamah—the spirit of life, soul

Neshamah Yetayrah—over-soul; the additional Sabbath-soul which leaves man at the end of the Sabbath

Nisgav Levado—(He) alone is exalted; from a verse in Psalm 148, sung as the Torah is returned to the Ark

Nishmat Kol Hai—the soul of every living thing; the first words and name of a prayer recited on Sabbath and Festival mornings, and at the *Seder* on Passover

Nisuin—nuptials, the marriage rite

Nodeh Laylohaynu—We will acknowledge our God; a verse in the hymn *"Ayn Kelohaynu"*

Nussaḥ—(the) text, or the traditional chant for each prayer and occasion

Olam—forever, an indefinite, long time (in the Bible); forever, or more frequently, the world, the universe (in rabbinic texts)

Oraḥ Ḥa'yim—the manner or order of life; name of a section of the code, "The *Shulḥan Arukh*"; see there

Ot—a sign or indication

Oz—strength; figuratively, sometimes Torah

Parashah—a section or part; the specific section of the Torah assigned for reading in the synagogue each week and on each Festival, Fast, and Holy Day

Pasuk—a verse (in the Bible)

Perutah—the smallest coin in ancient Israel

Pesukay de Zimra—verses of song (*Pesukay* is a plural form of *Pasuk*); refers to the Psalms and verses from Psalms read every morning in the preliminary part of the service

Pirkay Avot—Chapters of the Fathers; a tractate of the Mishnah usually called in English, "Ethics of the Fathers"

Piyyutim—poems; post-rabbinic liturgical poems included in various services

Purim—lots (to cast lots); the name of the holiday commemorating the escape of the Jews from the edict of destruction in Persia under King Ahasuerus, at the instigation of Haman

Rabbotai Nevaraykh—Gentlemen, let us say Grace; said by the leader when there is a quorum of three

Rosh Hashanah—the head or first of the year; New Year

Rosh Ḥodesh—the head or first of the month; First of the Month, a minor festival

Ru'aḥ Hakodesh—the Holy Spirit; a name for God; divine inspiration

Seder—order, arrangement; the ceremonial service and meal for the eve of Passover

Seder Tefillot—the order of prayers; the *Prayer Book*; see *Siddur*

Sefarad—Spain, Spanish; and by extension, pertaining to those Jews who came from Spain

Selihot—pardon, forgiveness (plural in form); Penitential Prayers

Serafim—fiery ones, angels; Seraphim

Shabbat—Sabbath

Shaharit—of the early morning, the Morning Service

Shaliah—messenger, angel

Shalom Alaykhem—Peace be unto you; the first words and title of a hymn sung at home on Friday evening

Shama'yim—Heaven; a name for God

Shavu'ot—Pentecost; fifty days after Passover, the Feast of the first (barley) harvest, associated with the giving of the Torah on Mt. Sinai

Shekhinah—dwelling (fact of dwelling); a name of God, associated with His near presence

Shekhinato—His *Shekhinah;* a reverential way of referring to God

Sheliah Tzibur—messenger or representative of the community; the Reader who leads the congregation in the conduct of the service

Shelishi—third; the third man called up to the reading of the Torah at a service

Shema—Hear! the *Shema* refers both to the single sentence, "Hear, O Israel, the Lord our God etc." and to the three paragraphs from the Torah which, in the *Prayer Book,* follow this sentence

Shemoneh Esray—eighteen; one of the names of the *Amidah* which originally consisted of eighteen benedictions; see *Amidah*

Shene'emar—as it is said (in the Torah)

Sheol—the grave, a shadowy place where the dead are

Shetar—a writ, document

Shir Hama'alot—a Song of Degrees (or Steps); first words of Psalm 126 sung before the Grace on Sababths and Festivals

Shulhan Arukh—a prepared (or set) table; name of a code of Jewish law compiled by Joseph Caro in the sixteenth century

Siddur—arrangement, order (of prayers); the *Prayer Book*

Sidrah—order, portion (of the Torah); see *Parashah* of which this is a synonym

Sifra—a rabbinic text of the second century C.E.

Simhat Torah—Rejoicing in (the) Torah; the last day of the Feast of Tabernacles when the annual cycle of reading the Pentateuch is completed and at once begun again

Sukkah—a temporary hut in which Jews dwell (or at least, eat) during the eight days of the Feast of Tabernacles

Ta'anit—a tractate of the Babylonian Talmud

Tallit—cloak; the shawl with fringes (*Tzitzit*) on it, worn at prayer

Talmid Hakham—wise student; scholar

Talmud—lit., learning, study; the body of Jewish law and tradition recorded in the Mishnah and the Gemara; also used to designate the Gemara, which see

Talmud Torah—study of Torah

Tamid—lit., always; the daily sacrifice offered in the Temple, in the name of the whole people of Israel

Tanna, plural, *Tanna'im*—the teachers and authorities quoted in the Mishnah

Targum—a translation or version; refers to Aramaic translations of the Bible

Tefillin—from a root meaning prayer; phylacteries

Tehiyat Hamaytim—the resurrection of the dead

Teshuvah—repentence

Tikanta Shabbat—Thou didst institute the Sabbath; from the Sabbath Morning Service

Tinokot—little children

Tishah Be'Av—the ninth of (the month of) Av; a Fast Day commemorating the destruction of the First Temple in 586 B.C.E. and the Second Temple on the same day, in 70 C.E.

Torah—a Jewish value-concept of many meanings: Pentateuch, Bible, Mishnah and Gemara, inspired religious teachings of the Rabbis, and more

Torah Shebe'al Peh—the oral Torah; the religious tradition handed down by word of mouth from very early days

Totafot—reminders; reminders of the commandments of the Torah, the *Tefillin*, which see.

Tzadikim—the righteous, pious or saintly

Tzedakah—charity, love (in rabbinic literature); justice (in the Bible)

Tzitzit—the knotted fringes on the *Tallit*

Tzur Mishelo—Rock from Whose (store); first words of a Sabbath table hymn

Uva Letzion Go'ayl—and a Redeemer shall come to Zion; recited at the Sabbath and Festival afternoon services and in the daily morning service

Uvayrakhta—and thou shalt bless; from the Biblical source for the Grace after Meals

Vehu Rahum—and He is merciful; from a prayer for forgiveness said as a prelude to the daily Evening Service

Venakay—and He acquits (forgives)

Venakay Lo Yinakay—and He will certainly not acquit

Vetaher Libaynu Le'ovdekha Be'emet—and purify our hearts to serve Thee in truth; from the Sabbath *Amidah*

Vihi Ratzon—May it be (Thy) will

Yah Ribon Olam—God, Master of the universe; a Sabbath table hymn

Yehay Shemay Rabba Mevorakh—May His great Name be praised; from the response of the people to the opening statement of the *Kaddish*

Yekum Purkan—May salvation arise; a prayer for the scholars, the pious and the people at large, said on Sabbath morning

Yetziat Mitzra'yim—the exodus from Egypt

Yigdal—He will be exalted; a hymn based on the Creeds of Maimonides

Yirat Shama'yim—fear of Heaven; refers to devotion to God, piety

Yishtabakh—He will be praised; from the benediction said after the recital of the Passages of Song (Psalms) in the morning

Yitgadal—May (His great Name) be magnified; the first word of the *Kaddish*

Yitgadal Veyitkadash—May (His great Name) be magnified and hallowed; opening statement of the *Kaddish*

Yom Kippur—Day of Atonement

Yotzer Or—Creator of light; name of a benediction preceding the *Shema*

Zaykher Lehurban—(in) memory of the destruction (of the Temple)

Zekhut Avot—merit of the fathers; a rabbinic value-concept expressing the moral relationship of the generations; corporate responsibility

Zemirot—songs; especially the hymns sung at the table on Sabbath

Zuzzim—(plural form) silver coins roughly equivalent in social value to our dollar

Notes

CHAPTER 1

1. Dates are given in this book according to the Gregorian calendar in common use, but Jews use B.C.E., Before the Common Era, in place of B.C., which stands for "Before Christ," and they say C.E., Common Era, instead of A.D., *Anno Domini*, which is Latin for "in the year of the Lord"—in this context, of Jesus.

2. This is a famous statement from the Talmud quoted by Joseph H. Hertz in his *Authorised Daily Prayer Book* (Rev. Ed.; New York: Bloch Publishing Co., 1948), p. 26.

3. *The Ethics of the Fathers*, Chap. II, 18.

4. *Pesikta d'Rab Kahana*, 157b. The translation is Schechter's: S. Schechter, *Aspects of Rabbinic Theology* (New York: Macmillan, 1909), p. 156.

5. *Mishneh Torah*, Hilkhot Tefillah, 4:16.

CHAPTER 2

1. The First Temple was built by Solomon in about 950 B.C.E. and destroyed in the war with Babylon which ended with the exile of the Jews from Palestine in 586 B.C.E. The Jews returned to Palestine about fifty years later and a short time after that began to rebuild the Temple on the same holy Mount in Jerusalem. This was the Second Temple, and it too was destroyed—by the Romans in 70 C.E. By a strange coincidence, both Temples were destroyed on the 9th of Av, *Tishah Be'Av*.

CHAPTER 3

1. As quoted from Saadia by Louis Ginzberg in his article, "Saadia's Siddur," *Jewish Quarterly Review*, New Series, Vol. XXXIII, 1942, p. 327.

2. *Ibid.*, p. 328.

3. *Sephardic*, from the Hebrew, *Sefarad*, Spain, means "related to the Jews who lived in Spain." Since, after their exile in 1492 they spread over all the shores of the Mediterranean, *Sephardic* has come to apply to the Jewish communities of Greece, North Africa, and Middle Eastern lands.

Ashkenazic, from the Hebrew, *Ashkenaz,* Germany, refers to Jews of Northern and Western Europe and of Russia.

4. Cited by J. D. Eisenstein in his article, "Prayer Books," in the *Jewish Encyclopedia,* Vol. X, p. 172.

5. Pp. xvii-xx of the Introduction to the *Sabbath Prayer Book* (New York: The Jewish Reconstructionist Foundation, 1953).

6. *Sabbath and Festival Prayer Book* (New York: The Rabbinical Assembly of America and The United Synagogue of America, 1954), pp. iv, vi.

7. Max Kadushin, *The Rabbinic Mind* (New York: The Jewish Theological Seminary, 1952), pp. 1-6, 77-78, where the nature of the value-concept is delineated.

8. Max Kadushin, *Organic Thinking* (New York: The Jewish Theological Seminary, 1938), pp. 25-29.

CHAPTER 5

1. Quoted by Solomon Schechter, *Studies in Judaism* (First Series; Philadelphia: Jewish Publication Society, 1919), pp. 173-74.

2. (Rev. Ed.; London: Eyre and Spottiswoode [Bible Warehouse], Ltd., 1922), pp. civ-cv.

3. Whereas a single sentence of the Bible is called a verse (*Pasuk*), a single sentence or unit of thought in the Mishnah is called a *Mishnah.*

4. For a description of his term, the value-concept, see Kadushin, *The Rabbinic Mind,* pp. 35-52 and pp. 107-11.

5. See Kadushin, *ibid.,* for a full discussion of the nature and the function of the *Berakhah,* especially pp. 167-68, 207-08, and 267-70.

6. *Ibid.,* Chap. VI, "Normal Mysticism," pp. 194 ff.

7. *Sifre on Deuteronomy* 2, 13, edited by Friedmann, p. 80a.

8. See, for example, Ruth Benedict, *Patterns of Culture,* where the social dependence of such ideas is developed.

9. From an address by John Herman Randall (Professor of Philosophy at Columbia University) before the Fourth Annual Conference on Science, Philosophy, and Religion, 1944.

10. The *Sifra* is a rabbinic text of the early Mishnaic period, about the second century of the Common Era.

11. Umberto (Moshe David) Cassuto, late Professor of Bible at the Hebrew University in Jerusalem. On the *Totafot,* see his commentary on the Book of Exodus, *Payrush Al Sayfer Shemot* (Jerusalem: Hebrew University, 1952), pp. 105-06.

12. Yehezkel Kaufmann, *Toledot Ha'emunah Ha'yisre'elite(The History of the Religion of Israel)* (Tel Aviv: Dvir Publishing Co., 1938).

13. See pp. 112 ff., where the development of the *Kaddish* into a mourner's prayer is discussed.

14. David de Sola Pool, *The Kaddish* (New York: Bloch Publishing Co., 1929). This is the most exhaustive study of the *Kaddish* in English. See especially pp. 111-12 and the references there.

15. Louis Finkelstein, "The Meaning of the Word *Paras* in the Expressions

etc.," *Jewish Quarterly Review*, Vol. XXX, No. 1, 1942, pp. 29-48. See also Pool, *op. cit.*, pp. 21 and 45-48.

16. *Seder Eliahu* (Friedmann ed.; Vienna: 1902), pp. 88, 184.

17. *Ibid.*, pp. 48, 65.

CHAPTER 6

1. Kadushin, *The Rabbinic Mind*, p. 184 and pp. 186-88.

2. Louis Ginzberg, *A Commentary on the Palestinian Talmud* (New York: Jewish Theological Seminary, 1941), English Introduction, p. xxxv.

3. Abraham J. Heschel, *Man Is Not Alone* (Philadelphia: Jewish Publication Society, 1951), pp. 111-19.

4. *Mekhilta* (Lauterbach ed.; Philadelphia: Jewish Publication Society, 1935), Vol. III, p. 199.

5. Kadushin, *Organic Thinking*, p. 110, and the references there.

CHAPTER 7

1. Max Kadushin, *The Theology of Seder Eliahu* (New York: Bloch Publishing Co., 1932), pp. 182 ff., pp. 191 ff.

2. *Seder Eliahu, op. cit.*, p. 79.

3. *Ibid.*, p. 189.

4. *Midrash Tehillim* to Psalm 106, 2, edited by Buber, p. 227a.

CHAPTER 8

1. See pp. 75-80 where the early history and background of the *Kaddish* are discussed in some detail.

2. I am indebted to Professor Shalom Spiegel of the Jewish Theological Seminary for this point and for his guidance in helping to unravel the many intertwining strands in the history of the *Kaddish*.

3. Quoted in Hebrew by Pool, *The Kaddish, op. cit.*, pp. 104-05.

4. William F. Albright, *From the Stone Age to Christianity* (Baltimore: The Johns Hopkins Press, 1940), p. 204.

5. *Ibid.*, p. 172.

CHAPTER 10

1. Kadushin, *The Rabbinic Mind*, pp. 361, 366. On this matter of rabbinic dogma, see the section on "Rabbinic Dogma," pp. 340-67.

2. Marcus Jastrow, *A Dictionary of the Targumim, The Talmud Babli and Yerushalmi, and the Midrashic Literature* (London: Valentine Co., 1927).

CHAPTER 11

1. *Mishnah Shabbat*, 2, 2; quoted by Eliezer Levi, *Yesodot Hatefillah* (Tel Aviv: Bitan Hassefer, 1946), p. 173.

2. *Midrash Tannaim*, Hoffman Edition, p. 103; quoted by Kadushin, *The*

Rabbinic Mind. Also in Kadushin, see pp. 83-84, note, on democracy and the flexible nature of such social ideas.

3. Abraham J. Heschel, *The Sabbath* (New York: Farrar, Straus, 1953), Chap. IX.

4. *Rosh Hashanah* 8 and *Yoma* 80, quoted by Levi in *Yesodot Hatefillah.*

CHAPTER 12

1. Ginzberg, *A Commentary on the Palestinian Talmud, op. cit.,* Vol. I, p. 211.

2. Kadushin, *The Rabbinic Mind,* pp. 344-45.

3. A *Baraita* is a collection of law and lore contemporary with, but not included in, the Mishnah. Its date is somewhere around the second century of the Common Era.

CHAPTER 13

1. Kadushin, *The Rabbinic Mind,* pp. 194-207, on the rabbinic idea of God.

2. *Seder Eliahu,* Friedmann Edition, p. 30.

3. *Ibid.,* p. 139.

4. In the poem *Yigdal* (see p. 52), Moses is glorified above all men, but this is a medieval, not a rabbinic, poem.

5. See the explanation of this status of the Decalogue, p. 115.

6. Kadushin, *The Theology of Seder Eliahu,* pp. 50 ff., on terms for God; also see Kadushin, *The Rabbinic Mind,* Chap. VI, Section III, "Revelation of Shekinah [God]," pp. 222-61.

7. *Seder Eliahu,* Friedmann Edition, p. 89.

8. *Sanhedrin,* 22a.

9. From a *Midrash* quoted by Kadushin, *The Rabbinic Mind,* p. 352.

10. See p. 127 on the lighting of candles on Friday night.

11. From the Talmud, *Berakhot,* 16b.

12. George Foote Moore, *Judaism in the First Centuries of the Christian Era* (Cambridge: Harvard University Press, 1927), Vol. II, pp. 96-101.

13. *Seder Eliahu,* Friedmann Edition, p. 132.

14. Quoted by Moore, *op. cit.,* from the Talmud, *Sotah,* 31a.

CHAPTER 14

1. *Otzar Hageonim,* Shabbat, 43 and 314, quoted by Levi in *Yesodot Hatefillah,* p. 184.

2. Jacob Mann, "Changes in the Divine Service of the Synagogue Due to Religious Persecutions," *Hebrew Union College Annual,* Vol. IV (1927), pp. 241-310.

3. Jastrow, *A Dictionary of the Targumim, op. cit.*

4. This Samuel is, of course, not the Samuel of the Bible, but a scholar of the rabbinic period. The quotation is from *Sanhedrin,* 99a.

5. According to Louis Finkelstein, *Mabo le-Massektot Abot ve-Abot d'Rabbi Natan* (New York: Jewish Theological Seminary of America, 1950), pp. 220 ff.

CHAPTER 15

1. *Megillah*, 31a.
2. Seligman Baer, *Seder Avodat Yisrael* (Berlin: Schocken Press, 1936), p. 309.
3. *Mishnah, Berakhot*, 8, 5, and 6.
4. Kadushin, *The Rabbinic Mind*, pp. 42 ff.
5. Moore, *Judaism in the First Centuries of the Christian Era, op. cit.*, Vol. I, p. 238.
6. Quoted by John Baillie, "The Idea of Orthodoxy," *Hibbert Journal*, 1925 to 1926, Vol. XXIV, pp. 232-49.

CHAPTER 16

1. Kadushin, *The Rabbinic Mind*, pp. 167-68.
2. *Mishnah, Berakhot*, 3, 4.
3. A rabbinic name of God. See pp. 149-51, on the various names for God in rabbinic literature.
4. This interpretation was suggested by Professor Shalom Spiegel of the Jewish Theological Seminary.
5. This phrase, *Ki Le'olam Ḥasdo*, in the Hebrew, is usually translated, "for His mercy endureth forever." Our translation is explained in some detail at the end of the text of the Short Grace.
6. I am indebted for these two translations to Dr. Judah Goldin, Dean of the Teachers' Institute of the Jewish Theological Seminary.
7. Kadushin, *The Rabbinic Mind*, pp. 293-95.
8. *Ibid.*, Chap. VII, Section II, "Organismic Development," pp. 288-98; see especially pp. 293-95.

CHAPTER 17

1. On Jewish marriage, see the two excellent books by Louis M. Epstein, *The Jewish Marriage Contract* (New York: Jewish Theological Seminary of America, 1927); *Marriage Laws in the Bible and the Talmud* (Cambridge: Harvard University Press, 1942).
2. *The Mishnah*, a New Edition with Introduction and Notes by Ch. Albeck (in Hebrew) (Jerusalem: Bialyk Institute, 1955), "Introduction to *Kiddushin*," pp. 307-09.
3. *Mishnah, Kiddushin*, 2, 1.
4. Epstein, *The Jewish Marriage Contract, op. cit.*, p. 5.
5. A literature contemporary with, but not included in, the Mishnah.
6. *Berakhot*, 30b, quoted by Israel Abrahams in *A Companion to the Authorised Daily Prayer Book*, p. ccxvii.

Index

245